Praise for

THE CIA

'The CIA is often portrayed as a quintessentially American institution, but Hugh Wilford shows it is also a product of European imperial history. By delving into the life stories of key officers, he sheds new light on a complex and sometimes terrifying story. Placing the CIA in its global context allows us to understand this shadow world in a completely new way'

Stephen Kinzer, author of *Poisoner in Chief*

'Wilford's new history of the CIA is a spectacular achievement: learned, thoughtful, frequently surprising, often wryly funny, always gloriously readable. It is a serious work of scholarship, casting new light on dramatic episodes from the Iranian coup in 1953 to the assassination of JFK. But it is also a brilliant portrait of the men who lived in the shadows, from their gilded New England schooldays to the sweltering streets of war-torn Saigon. It's the best book yet from a supremely accomplished historian—and I loved it'

Dominic Sandbrook, cohost of *The Rest Is History* podcast and author of *Mad as Hell*

'*The CIA* is a pleasure to read, an excellent example of erudition lightly worn. Wilford shows that when CIA leaders found anti-imperial ideas did not fit their requirements, they found a new vocabulary in the very language of imperialism that their nation so often rejected. His interpretation goes far beyond the crude and opportunist assertion that British tuition facilitated the creation of the CIA'

Rhodri Jeffreys-Jones, author of *A Question of Standing*

'This elegantly written history places the CIA within the context of American empire, and, in the process, reshapes our understanding of US intelligence history. With lively prose and memorable characters, Wilford has crafted a narrative that will appeal to scholars and to general readers alike. It's simply superb'

Kathryn Olmsted, author of *Real Enemies*

'Wilford has again exposed another layer of the CIA's shrouded history by tying it to the history of the US empire. This innovative and rigorously researched merger internationalizes the agency's history even as it enhances understanding of its behavior and image. Wilford excavates the foreign and the domestic, people and places. The result is a different kind of survey that reveals a different kind of CIA'

Richard H. Immerman, former assistant deputy director of national intelligence and author of *The Hidden Hand*

'This is an ambitious and original book. It is not only richly informative but also provocative and insightful. Filled with fascinating and brilliantly researched detail, it shows how the rise of the CIA is intertwined with America's winding path to globalism'

Richard J. Aldrich, author of *GCHQ*

'The history of the CIA can seem like an exceptionally American story. But by placing it in the context of the intelligence services of European empires, Wilford reveals surprising continuities and gives us a new way of thinking about US power on the global stage. Through a series of compelling portraits, this book captures the emotions, the attachments, and the thinking of the men who sought to shape global politics. An essential contribution to the history of American intelligence and to debates about American empire'

Patrick Iber, University of Wisconsin, Madison

'In this fast-paced, absorbing, and insightful narrative, Wilford offers a bracing new interpretation of the Central Intelligence Agency. By focusing on the backgrounds, biographies, and career trajectories of some of the agency's most legendary, and controversial, figures, Wilford shows how the motives, methods, and organizational ethos of the CIA were shaped profoundly by the European experience of empire. Whether engaging in intelligence gathering, covert action, or counterinsurgency, the CIA, Wilford argues, too often followed a colonial-era script, with fateful consequences for the peoples of Asia, Africa, and Latin America, and major implications for the United States itself. A story packed with intrigue, rivalry, and scandal, this is history at its bold and provocative best'

Simon Hall, author of Ten Days in Harlem

'*The CIA* is one of those rare and irresistible publications which transform how you think about its subject matter. Wilford, author of several critically acclaimed books about the secret world of intelligence, blends persuasion with provocation to make the case that the CIA is—and always has been—a servant of American empire, albeit with little self-awareness that it performs this role. The cast of characters is a rogue's gallery of swashbuckling spies and saboteurs inspired by the imperial tales of novelist Rudyard Kipling and the real-life exploits of Lawrence of Arabia. In charting how this band of imperial adventurers looked to covertly redraw the map of the world, especially in the global south, this magnificent book will change our understanding of the history of the CIA and American foreign relations'

Christopher Moran, author of Company Confessions

'Wilford's new book places the CIA in its imperial setting—a covert empire but one deeply, subtly, and violently felt, especially in the Global South after 1945. But it does more by bringing the CIA's history up to the present, looking at its roles in the global war on terror and the hyper-rivalries between the USA, Russia, and China in an increasingly fractured world system. The past lives but it needs to be brought to life—and Wilford has shown once again that he is a master of that particular art'

Inderjeet Parmar, author of *Foundations of the American Century*

THE
CIA

ALSO BY HUGH WILFORD

The New York Intellectuals: From Vanguard to Institution

The CIA, the British Left, and the Cold War: Calling the Tune?

The Mighty Wurlitzer: How the CIA Played America

*America's Great Game: The CIA's Secret Arabists
and the Shaping of the Modern Middle East*

THE CIA

AN IMPERIAL HISTORY

HUGH WILFORD

BASIC
BOOKS

LONDON

First published in Great Britain in 2024 by Basic Books UK
An imprint of John Murray Press

1

Text design by Sheryl Kober

A CIP catalogue record for this title is available from the British Library

Hardback ISBN 9781399816847
Trade Paperback ISBN 9781399816854
ebook ISBN 9781399816878

Typeset in Minion Pro

Printed and bound in Great Britain by Clays Ltd, Elcograf S.p.A.

John Murray Press policy is to use papers that are natural, renewable and recycla-
ble products and made from wood grown in sustainable forests. The logging and
manufacturing processes are expected to conform to the environmental regula-
tions of the country of origin.

Carmelite House
50 Victoria Embankment
London EC4Y 0DZ

www.basicbooks.uk

John Murray Press, part of Hodder & Stoughton Limited
An Hachette UK company

For my colleagues and students, near and far

CONTENTS

ABBREVIATIONS

AAA	American Anthropological Association
AFL	American Federation of Labor
AFME	American Friends of the Middle East
AFV	American Friends of Vietnam
AHA	American Historical Association
AIOC	Anglo-Iranian Oil Company
AMSAC	American Society of African Culture
ARAMCO	Arabian American Oil Company
ARIO	Association of Retired Intelligence Officers
ASC	American Security Council
AVC	American Veterans Committee
CAZAB	Canada, Australia, New Zealand, America, and Britain
CENIS	Center for International Studies (MIT)
CIS	Counter-Intelligence Staff
COIN	counterinsurgency
DCI	Director of Central Intelligence
DCIA	Director of the Central Intelligence Agency
EDCOR	Economic Development Corps
EIT	enhanced interrogation technique
FBI	Federal Bureau of Investigation

FPCC	Fair Play for Cuba Committee
GWOT	Global War on Terror
HSCA	House Select Committee on Assassinations
IO	International Organizations division
MI5	Security Service (UK)
MI6	Secret Intelligence Service (UK)
MIT	Massachusetts Institute of Technology
MSU	Michigan State University
NCL	Non-Communist Left
NSC	National Security Council
ONE	Office of National Estimates
OPC	Office of Policy Coordination
OPS	Office of Public Safety
OSS	Office of Strategic Services
PFIAB	President's Foreign Intelligence Advisory Board
RAF	Royal Air Force
RDI	Rendition, Detention, and Interrogation program
S/LPD	Office of Public Diplomacy for Latin America and the Caribbean
SDS	Students for a Democratic Society
SMM	Saigon Military Mission
SOG	Special Operations Group
TRIM	Training Relations and Instruction Mission
USIA	United States Information Agency
WMD	weapons of mass destruction

LIST OF CENTRAL INTELLIGENCE
AGENCY DIRECTORS

Roscoe H. Hillenkoetter (1947–1950)

Walter Bedell Smith (1950–1953)

Allen W. Dulles (1953–1961)

John A. McCone (1961–1965)

William F. Raborn Jr. (1965–1966)

Richard M. Helms (1966–1973)

James R. Schlesinger (1973)

William E. Colby (1973–1976)

George H. W. Bush (1976–1977)

Stansfield Turner (1977–1981)

William J. Casey (1981–1987)

William H. Webster (1987–1991)

Robert M. Gates (1991–1993)

R. James Woolsey (1993–1995)

John M. Deutch (1995–1996)

George J. Tenet (1997–2004)

Porter J. Goss (2004–2006)

Michael V. Hayden (2006–2009)

Leon E. Panetta (2009–2011)

David Petraeus (2011–2012)

John Brennan (2013–2017)

Mike Pompeo (2017–2018)

Gina Haspel (2018–2021)

William J. Burns (2021–)

INTRODUCTION

The history of American intelligence has an established narrative, and it goes something like this. With their nation naturally defended on both sides by vast oceans and, for the most part, lacking foreign enemies, US citizens have never much felt the need for espionage or covert action, practices that smack of Old World intrigue and despotism anyway. Americans were prepared to put their scruples aside in times of war, when national survival demanded it, and use subterfuge to uncover and frustrate the plans of the enemy. During the American Revolution, George Washington sent spies into the British camp and employed clandestine methods to root out enemy agents in his own (an early example of "counterintelligence"). After independence was won, however, the young Republic, fearing the potential for unchecked, despotic government, shied away from creating a permanent secret service. The same pattern—of the nation creating clandestine organizations in times of war, then disbanding them afterward—carried on down through later emergencies: the Civil War, World War I, and World War II. It was not until 1947, when it embarked on a different kind of war with the Soviet Union, a cold one that did not involve direct military engagement with the enemy, that the United States created a peacetime spy service, the Central Intelligence Agency. After the Cold War ended just over four decades later with the Soviet collapse of the late 1980s and early 1990s, the CIA seemed to lose its raison d'être—but then rediscovered it after 2001, when the nation entered into a new kind of unconventional war, the Global War on Terror.

This narrative has, of course, a great deal of truth to it. No one could seriously deny that war has played a huge part in the history of US intelligence generally and the CIA in particular. Created just after World War II, the Agency employed many of the same people and methods as its wartime predecessor, the Office of Strategic Services (OSS). Histories of the CIA tend to start with the OSS and its chief, William J. "Wild Bill" Donovan, for good reason; Donovan deserves his reputation as the Agency's great trailblazer. Similarly, in recent years, the CIA has played a leading role in the war on terror, carrying out such crucial secret missions as the hunt for Osama bin Laden. Above all, the Agency is still defined in the popular imagination by the Cold War: spy battles against the Soviet KGB featuring double agents and moles—the superpower conflict at its coldest.

But step back a little in both time and geography—to before World War II and beyond American shores—and a less obvious narrative reveals itself. Although the United States lacked a foreign intelligence agency prior to the Cold War, other Western nations did not. During the late nineteenth and early twentieth centuries, the European imperial powers had created a host of new secret services, such as Britain's MI5 and MI6. While rooted partly in traditional inter-European rivalries, these institutions were also designed to meet the challenges of governing and defending great empires in the age of the "New Imperialism," the scramble for colonies under way in Asia and Africa. Britain and France, in particular, controlled vast new territories yet lacked the conventional military forces to occupy them—rather a problem given the competition they faced from other imperial powers and the fact that many of their new colonial subjects did not much want to be ruled by them. Their solution was secret intelligence: using espionage to find out the intentions of rival imperialists and taking covert measures to suppress potential insurgencies or strengthen client regimes in the colonies themselves.[1]

Although the first battles of the Cold War occurred mainly in Europe, from the early years onward much of the new superpower conflict took place in precisely those regions of the world that the Europeans had competed for during the age of the New Imperialism. In fact, viewed from the perspective of those regions, the Cold War looked a lot like a traditional imperial rivalry, just bigger and with different protagonists. It was perhaps only to be expected, therefore, that the tactics adopted by Americans in the contest for what they called (using a French coinage) the "Third World," such as covertly working to overthrow governments deemed hostile to US interests or using counterinsurgency to defend others regarded as friendly, resembled and sometimes even borrowed directly from those of the European colonial powers. Similarly, it should not have come as much of a surprise that Americans' experience in the post–World War II era should have echoed those of earlier imperialists in another important respect: overseas interventions, they discovered, had a way of boomeranging home, affecting domestic US life in a myriad of unexpected ways. Nor were such dynamics confined to the Cold War: the Global War on Terror, too, was largely fought in what had once been the colonial world and carried echoes of earlier imperial wars, not least in its boomerang effects on the home front.[2]

This is not to claim that US interventions in the Third World—or "Global South," to use today's terminology—merely replicated those of prior imperial powers. For one thing, the post–World War II period was the era of decolonization, the collapse of the old colonial empires in the face of worldwide resistance movements, so the new superpowers were compelled to avoid doing anything that smacked of overt imperialism. For another, US citizens themselves did not accept the label "imperial," reserving it for the old European powers. Empires not only subjugated foreign peoples, so Americans believed, but also created imperial establishments that threatened the liberty of their own inhabitants. So strong was this anti-imperial mindset that it even influenced the early CIA. Many of the Agency's first recruits had served in World War II alongside nationalist resistance fighters and developed sympathies for their anti-colonial struggles; some had grown up overseas as the children of international businessmen or missionaries and had felt such sympathies since childhood.

But anti-imperialism was not the only ideological influence on the new intelligence agency. Despite its history of empire denial, the United States had its own imperial past, arguably dating back to the nation's very beginning, with European migrants to North America practicing a form of "settler colonialism," and certainly to 1898, when the United States defeated Spain in the Spanish-American War and, over anti-imperialist objections, annexed several Spanish island colonies in the Caribbean and Pacific. The American resort to overseas colonialism around the turn of the twentieth century was minimal compared with what the Europeans were up to in Asia and Africa, but it helped cement in positions of power within American society a distinct imperial class of citizenry that consciously borrowed its values from the British Empire: an elite of white Anglo-Saxon Protestant men inculcated with the ideals of imperial manhood at a select group of eastern seaboard schools. It was from this class that the CIA would recruit many of its early leaders, ensuring that, alongside missionary-style anti-colonialism, the young Agency would also demonstrate an appetite for imperial adventure reminiscent of the era of the New Imperialism.

Moreover, whatever their personal beliefs, CIA officers operating in the Global South constantly found themselves in, so to speak, imperial situations. It was not just that successive postwar US presidents wanted to use the covert powers of the Agency to do imperial-like things such as getting rid of some foreign governments while strengthening others (not, by the way, the CIA's original purpose—its founders had envisioned it merely as an intelligence unit). It was also that young American intelligence officers ended up leading imperial-like daily lives, residing in white enclaves, for example, and socializing in colonial-era hotels and bars. Given all these continuities from the imperial past, it was no wonder that many citizens of the postcolonial world came to view even the best-intentioned of Americans as carrying on where the European colonials had left off and acted accordingly, resisting the new US presence in their midst, sometimes violently. This, in turn, was why Americans ended up fighting neocolonial wars in former European colonies, often with behind-the-scenes European support. Ironically, the twin factors of decolonization and US anti-imperialism only served to strengthen these imperial tendencies, as they incentivized American leaders to resort to covert operations to hide their interventions in the Global South, not only from anti-colonial foreigners but also from anti-imperial US citizens.

In short, war is not the only key to understanding American intelligence history and the CIA; so, too, is empire.

There are already many excellent books about the history of both the CIA and American empire. Few, though, combine the two: that is, barely any of the large literature about the CIA engages with the wider field of imperial history, while the by now voluminous scholarship known as "America in the world," including even a deservedly celebrated 2019 volume entitled *How to Hide an Empire*, has surprisingly little to say about the covert dimensions of US state power. My aim here is to bring the two subjects together in ways intended to advance understanding of both. More specifically, I place the CIA in the context of modern imperial history, comparing, contrasting, and connecting it with prior colonial intelligence services. In doing so, I hope not only to show the CIA in a different and revealing light but also to say something new about America in the world as a form of covert empire.[3]

Like other single-volume histories of the CIA, this one is broadly chronological. In the Prologue, I survey the history of Western imperial intelligence in the period leading up to the CIA's 1947 founding. In the main body of the book, I focus on the Cold War era, tracing three distinct phases in the Agency's development: first, its emergence during the 1950s and 1960s as Americans' go-to weapon in their imperial contest with the Soviet Union for dominance in the Global South; second, its decline in the 1970s against a backdrop of superpower détente and an anti-imperial backlash against its power at home; and, third, its revival in the last years of the Cold War, the 1980s, when the administration of President Ronald Reagan wielded its power for unapologetically imperial purposes. Finally, in a substantial Epilogue, I examine the CIA's contribution to the US Global War on Terror in the opening years of the twenty-first century before concluding with the implications of the recent resurgence of Cold War–like tensions with Russia and China for the Agency's role going forward.

But my approach is not just chronological. In contrast with other histories of the CIA, I have also tried to identify distinct themes in the events that make up the Agency's past and arrange my narrative around them. In Part One, consecutive chapters deal with the main types of CIA operation in the Cold War–era Third World: the Agency's original function of intelligence gathering and analysis, then the two main kinds of covert action that gradually overtook intelligence as CIA missions in the years that followed, regime change (including that most characteristic of covert US interventions, the CIA-instigated coup) and regime maintenance or counterinsurgency. In the book's second part, I follow the imperial boomerang home to Cold War–era America, analyzing CIA counterintelligence and domestic surveillance programs, efforts to propagandize a US citizenry historically suspicious of foreign entanglement, and, in the final chapter, the multiple unintended repercussions of Agency overseas operations on the home front.

In each of these chapters, I have selected an individual officer to represent the type of operation concerned, with just one exception, Chapter 6, in which the whole cast of characters makes a curtain-call appearance. In most cases, my choice of representative figure was straightforward: few would dispute Sherman Kent's position as the founder of CIA intelligence analysis, or James Angleton's primacy in the field of counterintelligence. Cord Meyer was also an easy selection for the chapter on domestic publicity due to his lengthy command of Agency "front" operations during the early Cold War. Candidates for the chapters on regime change and maintenance were more plentiful, but in the end I opted for two other "legendary" members of the CIA's founding generation, Kermit "Kim" Roosevelt and Edward Lansdale, respectively. These picks were guided in part by both men's leadership of particular operations that set the template for subsequent covert action in the category concerned and probably proved to be the most historically consequential of the

CIA's many interventions in the postcolonial world: the 1953 Iranian coup in Roosevelt's case, and, in Lansdale's, efforts to strengthen client regimes in Southeast Asia (successful in the Philippines, unsuccessful in South Vietnam).

In part, I chose to highlight these individuals simply because I wanted to give a human face to the historical developments I am describing. But I also did so to make a point: the human factor mattered. CIA officers were not insensate tools of US foreign policy; they were human beings shaped by personal histories of culture, identity, and emotion. For some, their primary motivation appears to have been a yen for manly imperial adventure; others were impelled just as much by a missionary-style desire to do good in the world. Sometimes the impersonal forces and the human motives were in sync; at other times they conflicted. With the exception of James Angleton, none of my main characters—Kent, Roosevelt, Meyer, and, especially, Lansdale—wanted to repeat the imperial past; yet, for historical reasons somewhat beyond their control, that is just what they all ended up doing.

While I have striven to be as fair-minded in my portrayals of these individual CIA officers as possible, I appreciate that some readers still might not be able to get past my depiction of the United States as a form of covert empire and the Agency as an imperial intelligence service. I do not necessarily expect to persuade such readers of my larger thesis, but I do hope that they might at least find some value in the book's comparative approach to particular matters of interest to them—for example, my suggestion in Chapter 1 that a comparison between the intelligence failures of the CIA and those of earlier Western imperial powers such as the British in India might yield some insight into the causes of the former. Such failures have, after all, had catastrophic consequences for US citizens, and preventing similar ones in the future is an urgent enough task that those charged with it should be open to diverse historical perspectives.

Equally, other readers might wonder why I have chosen to focus on the lives of CIA officers rather than those of the citizens of the postcolonial nations in which they were operating. The reason is that, as my title suggests, this is an imperial rather than colonial history of the Agency; that is, it is concerned as much with the domestic origins and consequences of the US covert empire as with its neocolonial manifestations on the ground in the Global South. That said, it is, of course, neither desirable nor possible to write an imperial history of the CIA sans postcolonial actors. Some served as local agents of the United States, and without them the Agency would have been unable to perform even its most basic operations. Others resisted or otherwise frustrated the plans of their would-be CIA controllers, making operational failures and unintended consequences, both characteristic experiences of earlier would-be empire-builders, major themes in the history of the Agency as well. For that matter, postcolonial agency even impacted the CIA's domestic fortunes: the example of Third World nationalism inspired and emboldened American anti-imperialists, fueling the US backlash against the Agency that took place in the 1970s.[4]

Finally, I am painfully conscious that this is a very male story. Quite simply, the great majority of CIA officers were men, a fact not changed by the recent appointment of women to senior positions in the Agency (about which more in the Epilogue). Still, rather than just assuming this male preponderance as a given and moving on, I try to think through its implications. Masculinity, I argue, has been an important motivating force in the CIA's history, whether in the form of the call to imperial adventure felt by many Agency officers or in the shape of the intimate male friendships they often forged with their agents in the Third World.

Such intimacies were sometimes shared with Agency men's wives and children (contrary to the picture presented in most spy novels, many intelligence officers undertook overseas postings with their families in tow), and these people appear in the pages that follow, for the first time in a single-volume history of the Agency, as a significant presence in their own right.

In other words, I try to capture intimate aspects of CIA officers' lived experience that have not featured in previous histories of the Agency while, at the same time, telling the larger story of America's covert empire. Although this might sound contradictory, it is not. Empires have always worked at multiple levels, combining grand historical forces with the personal and private. For proof of this, one has to look no further than the history of imperial intelligence prior to the CIA's founding.

PROLOGUE

Imperial Precursors

Boosters of the CIA like to talk up its American ancestry, pointing out that spies helped win the Republic's founding struggle against the British Empire as well as all its subsequent victories in major wars. Less often trumpeted but also part of this homegrown intelligence tradition was the role of scouts and spies in US continental expansion: the nineteenth-century US conquest of "Indian Country" and later skirmishes in the nation's continental borderlands, including the 1916 "Punitive Expedition" that crossed the Texas border in pursuit of the Mexican revolutionary Pancho Villa. It is telling that William Donovan, widely seen as the CIA's greatest American trailblazer, not only served (heroically) in France during World War I but also led a cavalry troop to join General John J. Pershing's hunt for Villa in Mexico. US incursions south of the border, into "America's backyard"—Central America and the Caribbean—were also part of the CIA's American prehistory.[1]

British imperial agent T. E. Lawrence in a photograph taken by American journalist Lowell Thomas in 1918. Thomas would go on to launch the "Lawrence of Arabia" legend that beguiled later generations of intelligence officers.
World Digital Library

But this is not the whole story. The CIA was, after all, a *foreign* intelligence agency, so it makes sense that its genealogy would feature other, non-American branches, including a line descending from the New Imperialism. In part, this strand in the Agency's DNA was a result of cross-fertilization—trans-imperial connections with other empires, the British especially. The CIA's early leadership would prove highly susceptible to such influences because it was drawn over-whelmingly from a social class that already shared British imperial values. But even Agency officers who were not so enthusiastic about empire, including some who were consciously anti-imperial, would find themselves unable to climb out from under the weight of the recent imperial past when they began moving into the decolonizing world during the Cold War.

If Bill Donovan was the CIA's principal American trailblazer, who were the Agency's main precursors from the age of the New Imperi-alism? Among several candidates for this honor, four stand out: two Britons, a Frenchman, and an American who participated in the most significant overseas US imperial venture of the era, the colonization of the Philippines. Between them, these individuals influenced or at least anticipated elements of all the CIA's main types of operation: the gathering and analysis of intelligence, counterintelligence, and covert action, the last particularly in the realm of counterinsurgency. More negatively, they also foreshadowed many of the challenges and problems that would later confront CIA officers: intelligence fail-ures, unintended operational outcomes, and the tendency of overseas interventions to boomerang home, whether in the form of publicity campaigns designed to whip up imperial sentiment or surveillance programs targeting anti-imperial dissenters.

Together, these four men's lives tell the story of imperial intelligence in the years before the 1947 creation of the CIA—a necessary prologue to the history of the Agency, and a past that has haunted it down to the present day.

Among the CIA's imperial precursors, one was especially important in shaping a crucial but often overlooked part of the Agency's institutional identity: its *imagination*.

Rudyard Kipling was born to British parents in colonial Bombay (now Mumbai) in 1865. After a childhood spent largely in England, including a dismal stint in a grim South Coast boardinghouse, he gladly returned to India at age sixteen to launch his literary career. Young Ruddy loved the subcontinent, its "heat and . . . puffs of temple incense . . . and, above all, things wonderful and fascinating innumerable" (as he told his editor). Yet, despite this fascination, expressed most famously in his adventure stories *The Jungle Books* and his 1901 masterpiece *Kim*, Kipling was an ardent imperialist, utterly convinced that "Orientals" benefited from British rule. The imperial mission was, Kipling sincerely believed, a form of heroic self-sacrifice—the "White Man's Burden," as he entitled a hugely influential 1899 poem that secured his reputation as, to quote a recent biography, "the Laureate of the Empire."[2]

Look a little closer, however, and Kipling's imperialism does not appear quite so confident. Recent histories of Britain's colonial rule of India, the Raj, have dwelt less on its surface splendor than on its underlying insecurity. The British were spread very thin in India. In all, a mere 1,200 colonial officials administered a nation of some 280 million. Although British Victorians shared their American cousins' dislike of spying—the word *espionage* was French, after all—the precariousness of this position placed a tremendous premium on intelligence. The Raj employed networks of local agents—secretaries, newsmen, and "running-spies"—to eavesdrop on Indian society. This strategy was effective, but only up to a point. The loyalty of the native informants was never entirely certain and, as Kipling himself admitted, the attitude of the majority of Indians toward colonial rule was "sullen" at best. The result was a constant, nagging sense of anxiety about possible intrigues by "inscrutable" yet "wily" Orientals, punctuated by occasional information panics about imagined plots and conspiracies. Yet the British failed almost entirely to detect signals of the impending Indian "Mutiny" of 1857, a massive colonial rebellion that nearly swept them from the subcontinent.[3]

Compounding this sense of internal insecurity was an additional worry: the threat of invasion by a rival great power. Initially, the focus of such fears was France, but after the defeat of Napoleon it shifted to czarist Russia, transforming India's mountainous North-West Frontier into the setting for an Anglo-Russian espionage contest, the "Great Game," that prefigured the later Cold War between the United States and the Soviet Union. There was some basis to these invasion fears: Russia was jealous of Britain's control of India, the "jewel in the crown" of Queen Victoria's empire, and was sending probes beyond its southern flanks in a manner that also alarmed the Ottomans and Chinese. Nevertheless, there was a strong hint of paranoia in the behavior of both sides, with the British committing themselves to a series of ill-advised incursions into Afghanistan that again foreshadowed later Western misadventures in that tragic country. In 1842, for example, Britain suffered one of its worst-ever military disasters when Afghan tribesmen wiped out a garrison beating a chaotic retreat from an uprising in Kabul.[4]

All these elements would come together in *Kim*, Kipling's 1901 novel about an Anglo-Indian orphan, Kimball O'Hara, who spies on behalf of the British while crossing northern India on a spiritual quest. On the one hand, *Kim* is a picaresque romp, bathed in nostalgia for the author's country of birth (Kipling had left India in 1889 to travel the world): its space, color, and scope for adventure. At the same time, the novel is a classic statement of imperial anxiety. Kipling was writing against the backdrop of the Boer War of 1899–1902, a botched British counterinsurgency campaign against rebel Afrikaans farmers in South Africa that fueled a growing sense among metropolitan Britons of imperial fragility. While Kipling's vivid depiction of his Indian characters tends toward condescension, his treatment of certain British colonial types, *sahibs* with "dull fat eyes," is downright hostile. The implication is that ignorant, complacent Britons posed as great a danger to the empire as did unruly colonial subjects or imperial rivals. In *Kim*, the only thing standing between the Raj and the Russians is an orphan boy and a handful of loyal native accomplices.[5]

Among its many claims to distinction—critics have lauded it variously as a masterpiece of Indian, imperial, and children's literature—*Kim* is remarkable as the first great spy novel. Intelligence historians have debated the verisimilitude of its portrayal of the Great Game, some claiming Kipling entirely made up his story, others pointing out that Indian agents or *pandits* disguised as Buddhist pilgrims really did roam the North-West Frontier. But *Kim* did not merely reflect the real spy world; it also helped shape it. In the years after its publication, Kipling became increasingly outspoken in his criticism of imperial security, complaining not only about India's vulnerability to Russia but also about the growing threat posed by imperial Germany to Britain itself. Other, lesser writers joined in the chorus, coming up with invasion-scare stories that featured plucky gentlemen spies foiling dastardly German plots to conquer England. (The best of these, Erskine Childers's *Riddle of the Sands*, still bears reading; others, such as the works of William Le Queux, have aged less well.) With British public opinion gripped by a veritable spy mania, in 1909 the Committee of Imperial Defence created the Secret

Service Bureau, Britain's first independent, professional intelligence agency, and the direct organizational forerunner of both the foreign Secret Intelligence Service, MI6, and the domestic Security Service, MI5. Two years later, in 1911, the government rushed through the extraordinarily sweeping Official Secrets Act, effectively hiding the new intelligence apparatus from the British public. Kipling, by helping invent a new literary genre, the spy thriller, had also contributed to the creation of the actual British secret services.[6]

Nor was Kipling's real-world influence confined to Britain. He was immensely popular in the United States as well, which perhaps was not surprising given that he lived there for four years during the 1890s, married an American woman (Caroline "Carrie" Balestier), and, despite some reservations about "uncouth" American manners, regarded the United States, an "Anglo-Saxon" power, as sharing the same imperial destiny as Great Britain. In 1898, when the Americans defeated imperial Spain and won control of, among several other Spanish colonies, the Philippines, Kipling urged them to follow in British footsteps and annex the islands as a colony. Indeed, the 1899 poem in which he exhorted his readers to take up "The White Man's Burden" was subtitled "The United States and the Philippines."[7]

Not all Americans welcomed this intervention. Many, including such famous names as Mark Twain and Andrew Carnegie, protested that the proposed Philippine annexation flew in the face of American republican ideals of self-government and non-intervention. Some anti-imperialists parodied Kipling in verses with titles like "The Black Man's Burden." Others insisted that the original poem made the task of colonial administration sound so thankless that Kipling surely must have intended it ironically. The majority of Americans, though, their patriotism fanned by the jingoistic "yellow press," followed Kipling's friend Theodore Roosevelt, Spanish-American War hero and future US president, in supporting annexation. The publication of "The White Man's Burden" in February 1899 was accompanied by a "Kipling boom" in the United States—and the US Senate voting to annex the Philippines.[8]

Kipling would never again wield the extraordinary public influence he had enjoyed at the turn of the twentieth century, when the British Empire was at its zenith. In the decades that followed, growing anti-colonial unrest in the colonies and an accompanying rise in anti-imperial sentiment in Britain transformed him from imperial laureate to cantankerous prophet of national decline. He died in 1936, anticipating the empire's imminent collapse. However, his literary spirit would live on, not only in Britain but also in the United States, where his romantic tales of imperial adventure would beguile later generations of readers, among them many of the young men who would staff the infant Central Intelligence Agency during the first years of a new iteration of the Great Game: the Cold War.

The era of the New Imperialism did not just produce writers. Also shaping the collective imagination of imperial societies like Britain and France were men of action, heroes famous for exploring, subduing, and governing Europe's new colonies. At first sight, these men seem unlikely precursors of the CIA. They were, after all, public figures, celebrities even, venerated by their fellow citizens as living embodiments of the imperial mission—not spies serving a nation that denied it was an empire. Yet, on closer inspection, it turns out that these imperial heroes prefigured key aspects of the US intelligence experience in the postcolonial world.

Take, for example, the French empire-builder Marshal Louis Hubert Gonzalve Lyautey. Born into an aristocratic, military family in 1854, Hubert Lyautey grew up a conservative, intensely patriotic youth. But there was also a bookish, romantic side to the young Frenchman, a legacy perhaps of a grievous early childhood fall that had left him bedridden for several years. After spells at the elite military academy Saint-Cyr and in the French cavalry, Lyautey accepted a posting to colonial Algeria. There he developed a Kiplingesque fascination with Arab Northwest Africa, known as the Maghreb, and a passion for colonial service. This might have had something to do with his sexuality: several scholars have speculated that Lyautey was homosexual, one even identifying him as the inspiration for a gay character in Marcel Proust's *À la recherche du temps perdu*, the Baron de Charlus. It certainly seems that he preferred the homosocial life of the colonial military to what he perceived as the restrictive, enervating influence of domestic life in metropolitan France. Indeed, Lyautey came to hold an almost mystical notion of the colonies as a potential site of national rejuvenation for a country still traumatized by its defeat in the Franco-Prussian War (1870–1871) and the Paris Commune (1871). Conveniently, this vision imputed to Lyautey a better sense of what was in the national interest than politicians and civil servants in Paris had. Both these impulses—the masculine flight from domesticity and the temptation to improvise policy on the ground in the postcolonial world—would also be observable in the CIA.[9]

During subsequent assignments in distant imperial outposts, Lyautey developed a strategy to go with his vision. In 1894, partly to escape pressures to marry, he traveled to French Indochina. There, amid the colonial villas and gracious boulevards of Hanoi, he fell under the influence of his commander, Joseph Gallieni, another soldier with big political ideas. Lyautey helped Gallieni develop and apply his concept of a "progressive occupation," a method of colonial pacification in which the occupying army built roads, telegraph lines, and even medical clinics as it moved through conquered territory, steadily extending the benefits of Western civilization to new populations in a process Lyautey likened to the spreading of an oil drop, *une tâche d'huile*, in water. The idea of "peaceful conquest," which Lyautey assiduously promoted through a barrage of articles, lectures, and letters, played extremely well in metropolitan France. Here, it seemed, was a military doctrine that complemented the nation's self-proclaimed *mission civilisatrice*. Similar notions of "population-centric" counterinsurgency would exercise a comparable appeal in Cold War Washington, DC.[10]

The trouble was that, on the ground in the colonies, *la méthode Lyautey* was not always peaceful. Just as in British India, many inhabitants of France's new colonies resented their subjugation by European invaders, and resisted it. In their next posting, to colonial Madagascar, Gallieni and Lyautey responded to such resistance with "brisk action"—a "bloody campaign," as one historian describes it, "complete with the assassination and exile of indigenous rulers." They also stepped up French surveillance of Malagasy society, importing the latest social scientific and policing breakthroughs from home—the Bertillon method of fingerprinting, for example—for the purpose. Faced with this regime, some inhabitants of France's African and Indochinese colonies began to compare their lives with those of inmates in a giant prison.[11]

A similar pattern prevailed when Lyautey, now a general himself, returned to his beloved Maghreb, first to Algeria, then Morocco, which France declared a "protectorate" in 1912, with him as its *résident-général*. Aspiring to make the country into the jewel in France's colonial crown,

Lyautey set about building railroads, schools, and hospitals with his usual gusto. In keeping with his "progressive" and "peaceful" methods, he also worked to avoid the appearance of direct colonial rule, publicly deferring to the authority of the sultan. ("Rule with the mandarin, and not against him," Lyautey explained. "Once the mandarins are our friends, . . . the country will be pacified.") The French public responded delightedly, hailing Lyautey (Marshal Lyautey after 1921) as a great imperial "proconsul" and indulging in what one historian has called a "Morocco mania." Moroccans themselves, though, were less persuaded. Many regarded the sultan as a French puppet and rebelled against his rule. The mountainous Rif proved particularly hard to subdue, compelling Lyautey to try starving out the restive Berber tribes living there. Eventually, Paris placed the protectorate under direct administration, effectively forcing the marshal's resignation in 1925.[12]

Lyautey spent the remainder of his life—he died in 1934—in his birthplace, Lorraine, like Kipling unhappy about what he saw as the decline of the empire he had spent his life serving. Still, he had enough energy to perform one last imperial mission, this time on the home front. In 1928, he was recalled to Paris to organize a great exhibition celebrating France's colonial empire. Opening in 1931 on the capital's outskirts, the Exposition Coloniale Internationale featured, among other attractions, replicas of villages in Madagascar and the Maghreb and, as its Indochinese centerpiece, a vast plaster reproduction of the great Cambodian temple Angkor Wat. Some anti-imperialists denounced the show, and a group of surrealist artists staged a rival exhibit with the manifesto "Ne visitez pas l'Exposition Coloniale." But French citizens attended in the millions, many coming back multiple times. Lyautey, for one, believed that his project had succeeded in its aim of "making the French . . . proud of being a citizen of 'la plus grande France.'"[13]

A few decades later, the US government would launch a similar effort to grow domestic support for its interventions in the postcolonial world, including in Lyautey's old stamping grounds of Africa and Indochina. But whereas the French government overtly sponsored Lyautey's campaign, in the American case the job went to a covert agency, the CIA.

Hubert Lyautey's career offered a preview of later CIA counterinsurgency operations overseas and publicity work at home, but his name was not on the lips of American intelligence officers, who tended rather to distance themselves from the legacy of French colonialism. The same was not true of another imperial hero, this one British—his name would feature plenty, in American spy memoirs and field manuals alike.

T. E. Lawrence was born the illegitimate son of an Anglo-Irish nobleman in 1888. A brilliant young scholar, he wrote a thesis at Oxford on Crusader castles before joining a British Museum excavation at Carchemish in Syria, still then a province of the Ottoman Empire. During his three years at Carchemish (1911–1914), Lawrence developed a strong admiration for the Arabs he encountered there along with a sympathy for their anti-colonial struggle against the Ottomans. In 1914, the dig was interrupted by the outbreak of war with Germany and, soon after, the ratification of a German-Ottoman alliance. The following year, Lawrence joined British military intelligence in Cairo, then, in 1916, traveled to Arabia with orders to liaise with Arab forces who had just launched an insurgency against Ottoman rule.[14]

Lawrence had met his imperial destiny. Embedding himself with the Arab rebels, and donning Bedouin clothes suited to desert warfare, he led a series of dazzlingly effective guerrilla attacks on Turkish and

German targets. Meanwhile, British forces in Palestine and Syria won a series of decisive victories, culminating in their capture of Damascus in 1918. The Arabs' revolt had triumphed—but it did not result in the political independence for which they and Lawrence had hoped. Earlier in the war, British officials had struck a secret deal with the French—the Sykes-Picot Agreement of 1916—to carve up the Ottoman territories between them if they emerged victorious. Attending the 1919 Versailles peace conference, Lawrence tried, unsuccessfully, to prevent Syria from falling into French hands. Later, while serving as an advisor to Colonial Secretary Winston Churchill in 1921–1922, he did manage to secure the new kingdoms of Iraq and Transjordan for the Hashemite princes alongside whom he had fought during the war—but, under the mandate system, even these were to function as de facto British colonies.

Historians have disagreed, sometimes bitterly, about the military value of Lawrence's wartime exploits, some questioning the Arab revolt's effect on the outcome of the wider war and others accusing Lawrence himself of exaggerating his contribution after the event. Among intelligence experts, however, there is near-universal agreement that the desert campaign was extraordinarily important. In addition to pioneering intelligence-gathering technologies such as aerial photography, Lawrence helped invent a new kind of "irregular warfare" based on the concept of small, nomadic military units operating like the desert Bedouin. He was also a pioneer of psychological warfare and deception operations, fabricating disinformation to lure Ottoman forces away from the real battlefield. Above all, Lawrence personified the principle of deep area knowledge—"knowing the country," as the British put it. His example would exert a powerful hold on later generations of Western spies, even those who espoused less intuitive, more scientific methods of intelligence gathering and analysis.[15]

But the main reason for Lawrence's wider fame was not intelligence tradecraft—it was imperial romance. Even before World War I ended, the British government sensed the propaganda value in the story of a fair-haired young Briton leading the Arab revolt. Here was an inspiring, perhaps redemptive tale of individual heroism to distract attention from the mechanized slaughter taking place on the Western Front. The chief of wartime propaganda, John Buchan, himself the author of imperial adventure novels featuring a spy hero, Richard Hannay, arranged for the American journalist Lowell Thomas to visit Lawrence in his desert tent. Immediately after the war, Thomas gave a series of illustrated lectures about the Arab revolt that launched Lawrence on a new career as an international celebrity.

Meanwhile, the British government carried on its domestic propaganda campaign. The nation's new imperial responsibilities in the Middle East were costly and hard to manage without resort to some distasteful expedients: a continuing reliance on secret intelligence to avert the threat of new Arab revolts, and an extension into peacetime of the World War I regime of aerial surveillance and occasional bombing of ground targets. (Prior to World War II, the Royal Air Force's main experience of bombing was in Iraq.) Not surprisingly, a sizable element of public opinion objected to the expense, secrecy, and brutality involved. Fears that "Oriental" despotism was infecting the British state itself gave rise to a rash of conspiracy theories about secretive aristocratic cabals taking over government policy, some featuring imperial spies such as Lawrence in central roles.[16]

Officials responded by quietly encouraging a range of interested parties to defend Britain's Middle East mandate. Imperial agents charged with proconsular duties in the region, Lawrence's fellow Arabist Gertrude Bell, for example, wrote newspaper articles portraying their mission in Kiplingesque terms: they were developing and modernizing the Arab world, not exploiting it. "It's the sort of thing that happens under the British flag," explained Bell. "Don't ask us why." It helped that the 1917 Russian Revolution had revived British fears of Muscovite meddling in the region, only this time in the more insidious form of Bolshevism, enabling officials and their private allies to paint Arab resistance as part of a sinister communist plot. The aim was basically the same as Lyautey's in France: strengthening the domestic foundations of overseas empire.[17]

On the surface, Lawrence seemed to resent the fame his wartime adventures had won him. After resigning from the Colonial Office in 1922, he enlisted in the RAF under a new name to escape further press attention. But Lawrence was a complicated man, deeply insecure about his illegitimate birth and short stature (he stood only five feet five inches tall), and he was unable to resist feeding the legend of "Lawrence of Arabia." In 1926, he published an epic account of the desert campaign, *The Seven Pillars of Wisdom*; the following year, an abridged version, *Revolt in the Desert*, became an international best-seller. As the journalists who pursued Lawrence liked to say, he had a talent for "backing into the limelight."[18]

Then there was the question of Lawrence's professed support for Arab nationalism. Detractors claim that Lawrence had known about the Sykes-Picot Agreement all along, yet, as a loyal imperial agent, let the Arabs under his command carry on fighting in the belief they would gain their independence. Some have even denounced Lawrence's famous wartime habit of dressing in Bedouin robes as fundamentally imperialist and "Orientalist," that is, reflecting imperial Western stereotypes about the colonized peoples of "the East." Several Victorian explorers and soldiers had tried to "pass" as natives before Lawrence, as had Kipling's fictional boy-hero Kim. As if confirming the association with *Kim*, shortly after the publication of *Revolt in the Desert*, Lawrence accepted a transfer to an RAF base in Waziristan on India's North-West Frontier. The British newspapers frothed with excitement, reporting that the assignment was cover for a "Secret Mission" that had Lawrence disguised as a Muslim holy man while "Countering Red Activities in the Punjab."[19]

Yet there was more to Lawrence than the publicity-hungry imperial spy. His lobbying on behalf of the Hashemites after the war would be hard to explain if he did not have some real attachment to the Arab cause. Several of his public utterances in this period sounded distinctly anti-imperialist, as when he claimed in the *Sunday Times* that the British government was misleading the public about the true situation in Iraq with "a steady withholding of information." Indeed, there were clear signs that the stress of reconciling his roles as Arabist and imperial agent, combined with the aftereffects of various wartime traumas (including, possibly, being raped while a Turkish prisoner in 1917), took a terrible psychic toll on Lawrence, causing him bouts of depression and self-degrading masochism. His pro-Arab pronouncements also, not surprisingly, earned him the mistrust of military and political superiors already disapproving of his rebellious streak. Perhaps he had spent too much time in the desert, they grumbled; he was more "Arab than the Arabs." After his return home from Waziristan in 1929, Lawrence was threatened with dismissal from the RAF and ordered not to travel. When he died after a motorcycle accident in 1935 at the tragically early age of forty-six, rumors circulated that he had been assassinated.[20]

In addition to his pioneering tradecraft, Lawrence had offered a glimpse of the darker side of modern intelligence work: divided loyalties, unwanted publicity, and conspiracy theory. There was even a hint about Lawrence of the national security whistleblower, a figure who would later dominate headlines about the CIA.

Compared with the British and French, the Americans appear barely to have featured in the history of the New Imperialism. True, they did take some island colonies during the 1890s, but viewed next to the vast swaths of territory controlled by the European colonial powers, these did not amount to much: 1 percent of the world's total land surface, as compared with the 23 percent covered by the British Empire. Moreover, the US colonial empire, such as it was, was self-liquidating. Within a few years of annexing the Philippines, the Americans began preparing their inhabitants for self-rule. The first US civilian governor, future president William Howard Taft, even created a public school system for the purpose, staffing it with "Thomasites," American teachers named for the army transport ship in which they sailed, to inculcate the necessary republican ideals in young Filipinos. The experiment appeared to work. The United States granted the Philippines commonwealth status in 1935 and then, after liberating the islands from Japanese occupation in 1945, complete independence on July 4, 1946. At a time when the Europeans were fighting desperately to cling to their empires in the face of growing anti-colonial resistance, America became the first great power to divest itself of a colony willingly.[21]

But for all these contrasts, there were also several underlying similarities and connections between the Americans and Europeans in the New Imperial era. To begin with, many of the forces driving them to expand overseas were the same: a quest for new resources and markets, strategic calculations such as, in the US case, a desire for island naval bases, and a racialized sense of national destiny—like Rudyard Kipling, white Americans tended to believe that the Anglo-Saxon race was ordained to rule the world. There were also various trans-imperial overlaps and entanglements on the ground in the colonies themselves. The US authorities in the Philippines built their administration on institutions inherited directly from the Spanish: the colony's census, police, and prisons. Other models they imported from the British Empire. Colonial architects in the Philippines, for example, imitated European "hill stations" such as Shimla, the summer capital of the Raj. Americans in the Philippines were not Orientalists in the nineteenth-century European sense of the word: specially trained experts on colonial cultures and societies. But they did exhibit Orientalist prejudices about alleged Asian character flaws, accusing Filipinos of indolence and trickiness.[22]

Above all, Americans in the Philippines resembled European colonials in that they too confronted an anti-colonial rebellion. In 1899, Filipino nationalists, dismayed that they appeared to have exchanged one imperial oppressor for another, launched a bloody guerrilla war against their American occupiers. US military forces responded with a counterinsurgency campaign that, while in some respects replicating the "Indian Wars" that had just taken place in the American West, also bore comparison with the brutal tactics then being employed by the European powers in their wars of colonial pacification. US troops indiscriminately killed some civilians, herded others into relocation camps, and practiced a torturous form of interrogation, the "water cure," that foreshadowed a technique used by CIA officers in the Global War on Terror: waterboarding. Later, in part because American public opinion had begun to turn against the occupation, US authorities resorted to less egregious forms of repression that were also reminiscent of techniques used by the British in India and the French in Madagascar: the enlistment of local elites to crush remaining pockets of nationalist resistance, and the importation of modern policing methods and surveillance technologies from the metropole. As one American officer in the new Philippines Constabulary put it, "We began to live Kipling for ourselves."[23]

If any one individual embodied the American colonial regime in the Philippines, it was a young US military officer by the name of Ralph H. Van Deman. True, Van Deman was far from the imperial hero type exemplified by Lyautey or Lawrence. Gawkily tall with a long, lugubrious face, he shunned the limelight and gladly pursued his calling in bureaucratic obscurity. But as an intelligence officer, he was a genius. Born in Ohio the same year as Rudyard Kipling (1865), Van Deman graduated from Harvard before studying law, then switched to medicine, joining the Army as a surgeon. The 1890s was a decade of intense industrial unrest in the United States, and it seems that Van Deman's participation in the military suppression of a violent miners' strike was a formative experience, one that left him with an enduring suspicion of labor protest and radicalism. After arriving in the Philippines in 1899, he took over the Bureau of Insurgent Records, which he soon helped transform into the Military Information Division of the Philippines—the US Army's first field intelligence unit. Drawing on a network of Army personnel, Manila police, and civilian informants, Van Deman methodically compiled a vast file-card index of Filipinos resisting the US occupation. He also oversaw improvements to the islands' telegraph system designed to speed up the transmission of tactical intelligence to US combat units pursuing insurgents across the Philippine countryside. By the time Van Deman returned to the United States in late 1902, he had laid the foundations of a colonial surveillance state.[24]

But this was only half of his contribution. After his return to the United States, Van Deman began lobbying his superiors for the creation of a stand-alone, centralized intelligence and counterintelligence system like the one he had built in the Philippines. At first, the Army high command, displaying the usual Anglo-Saxon suspicion of secret state power, resisted his urgings, but in 1917, against a backdrop of US entry into World War I, Van Deman eventually got what he wanted: a new Military Intelligence Section under his command. In organizing the division, Van Deman (now a colonel) borrowed heavily from the recently created British intelligence services, setting up separate branches designated with the initials MI followed by a number and even using British spellings. His methods, though, were much the same as in the colonial workshop of the Philippines: maintaining a vast file-card database consisting of intelligence gathered from a public-private network of sources, including in this instance a small army of patriotic citizen vigilantes, the American Protective League. Now, rather than Filipino insurgents, his targets were US dissenters with anti-war or other "subversive" tendencies: pacifists and anarchists, German and Irish immigrants, East Indian nationalists, and, a particular bugbear of his, African Americans. Indeed, it was as though the colonial intelligence expert was treating minority groups in American society like colonies *within* the United States. Meanwhile, the October Revolution in Russia stirred up Van Deman's old suspicion of working-class activism. In Paris in 1919 to run counterintelligence for the Versailles peace conference, he met with British intelligence officials and discussed the need to track Soviet operations "in all parts of the world."[25]

In 1929, Van Deman left the Army with the rank of major general, retiring to a modest bungalow overlooking San Diego Bay. From there, he carried on his colonial-style surveillance operation as a private citizen. Aided by his loyal wife, Cherry, and with discreet administrative support from the Army, Van Deman built up his archive of American subversives with data gleaned from the same sort of public-private sources as before: government officials, law enforcement officers, and sympathetic civilians. By the time he died in 1952, Van Deman had collected intelligence on some 250,000 individuals—information he reputedly shared with Federal Bureau of Investigation director J. Edgar Hoover and a young California Republican, Richard M. Nixon. It was also during his retirement that he handed on the counterintelligence baton to successor organizations. In 1940, Van Deman attended a meeting with Hoover and the chief of Army intelligence where it was agreed that the FBI would run counterintelligence in the Americas and the military would do so in the rest of the world. During World War II, the Office of Strategic Services would largely take over the latter function, which, after the war, would in turn be inherited by the OSS's peacetime legatee, the Central Intelligence Agency. In other words, it is possible to trace a thread of organizational descent from the US colonial occupation of the Philippines to CIA counterintelligence. By coincidence, control of the latter would also fall into the hands of a gaunt obsessive who conducted his business in the bureaucratic shadows.[26]

Of course, Kipling, Lyautey, Lawrence, and Van Deman are not the only candidates for the honor roll of CIA trailblazers. More obvious American names belong there too—Bill Donovan's, for example, and that of Allen W. Dulles, Donovan's OSS European deputy.

But to focus only on the usual OSS suspects is to miss other possible CIA genealogies, imperial ones included. Among other things, Kipling bequeathed the first generation of Agency officers a love of romantic overseas adventure combined with a whiff of imperial paranoia. Lawrence's legacy was similarly ambiguous: a real-life Kim, he blazed the trail of intelligence tradecraft in the colonial world while exemplifying the tendency of imperial influences to return home in unanticipated ways. The same was true of two other, lesser-known Agency precursors from the New Imperial era: Hubert Lyautey, with his efforts to galvanize French support for the colonial campaigns he was waging abroad, and Ralph Van Deman, importing new surveillance techniques from the colonial laboratory of the Philippines to the American homeland. The Frenchman and the American also anticipated key features of two major CIA disciplines. Like Lyautey, later US counterinsurgency experts would try to employ peaceful methods of pacifying occupied countries until continuing local resistance caused them eventually to resort to violence. Similarly, CIA counterintelligence would follow Van Deman's example in borrowing extensively from the imperial British and targeting American dissidents and minorities for state surveillance.

Individual CIA officers were not necessarily aware of these imperial parallels and influences; if anything, they tended to be anti-imperialist in their conscious intentions. But the shadow of empire spread over everything they did—including the Agency's core founding mission, intelligence analysis.

PART ONE

OVERSEAS

CHAPTER 1

Intelligence

When he retired in 1967 after fifteen years directing the Office of National Estimates (ONE), the unit that sat atop the CIA's machinery for analyzing intelligence, Sherman Kent received more than his share of plaudits. He was, so his colleagues agreed, an Agency "legend." No one had done more to establish US intelligence on a professional footing and define it as a discipline with its own unique standards and methods. He was also a CIA "character," known for his mix of personal decency and rough-and-ready manners, the latter a legacy perhaps of his western upbringing (prior to attending Yale and training as an academic historian, Kent had, unusually for a first-generation CIA man, grown up in California). Stories abounded about "Sherm": his tobacco-chewing, his bright red suspenders, and his notoriously "salty" vocabulary. One anecdote in particular made the rounds. Kent had been on the warpath about what he saw as the sloppiness of the language used in the National Intelligence Estimates, the predictive reports issued to government consumers by ONE. What, exactly, he wanted to know, did a word like "probable" mean in the context of an intelligence estimate—a 75 percent likelihood of an event occurring? When a less mathematically minded deputy objected that his use of terms such as "50-50 odds" threatened to turn the CIA "into the biggest bookie shop in town," Kent retorted, "I'd rather be a bookie than a [blank-blank] poet."[1]

This story is telling not just about Sherman Kent's personality but also for what it says about his approach to intelligence. In his day-to-day management of ONE and his several, highly influential publications on the subject, Kent constantly touted a proposition that amounted almost to an article of faith for him. Rather than being an art (as the imperial British, with their talk of plumbing the "native mind," had tended to think), intelligence was a *science*. Intuition or presupposition had no place in his profession, Kent insisted; intelligence officers must conduct their business much like practitioners of the natural or social sciences, "through research guided by a systematic method." It was only by using such an approach that intelligence officers could accurately analyze the world and thereby predict the likely course of future events—assuming that the language they used was precise enough to capture the right degree of "estimative probability." In other words, the riposte to his complaining deputy was not just a throwaway line: Kent really did not want poets for colleagues, preferring mathematicians.[2]

If this all sounds rather conceptually naive to the postmodern, twenty-first-century ear, it is only fair to acknowledge that Kent was not alone in his beliefs. The social sciences and their increasingly quantitative research methods commanded extraordinary prestige in post–World War II American intellectual life, and many other members of the US intelligence community shared the ONE director's confidence in their ability to predict the future. Indeed, Cold War–era scientism has never really gone away as an influence on American intelligence. The CIA's School for Intelligence Analysis was named for Sherman Kent in 2000, and his mathematical principles are still taught in the Agency's Career Analyst Program today.

Nor, it should be noted, was Kent entirely unquestioning in his devotion to the scientific method. He did realize that what he and others called the "Intelligence Cycle"—the whole process of foreign intelligence production, from the tasking of field officers through the collection of data to its analysis at headquarters and the preparation and dissemination of estimates—contained some potential pitfalls. Individual analysts might display "confirmation bias," unconsciously selecting from the raw intelligence data only those facts that conformed with their preexisting beliefs, or they might unwittingly let political considerations creep into their estimates, tailoring them to support predetermined policies. This was why Kent strongly encouraged vigorous debate within ONE, as a means of ensuring that its estimates would express an institutional consensus, supposedly uncontaminated by personal or political bias.

Unfortunately, Kent was less attuned to another possible problem in the Intelligence Cycle: that the raw intelligence data itself might be imperfect. The CIA officers tasked with gathering secret intelligence abroad were, after all, human beings, each with their own distinctive social identity and personal history. Typically, they had no experience of the foreign country to which they had been assigned, yet they were expected to penetrate it so intimately as to be able to learn its best-protected secrets. And, as they gathered intelligence, they were usually interacting with other human beings, local sources or "agents," who possessed their own motivations, agendas, and, sometimes, prior experience of dealing with spies from other Western intelligence services.

The aim of this chapter is to tell the story of CIA intelligence with the human element included, following the arc of the Intelligence Cycle, from tasking to finished product, but also factoring in an important stage missing in the official model: the backgrounds of Agency officers prior to their assignment to the field. What this approach reveals is that science was not the decisive factor operating at the intelligence grassroots. More important were the personal histories and emotional lives of the people involved—and the long shadow of the imperial past.

Although Sherman Kent's western American upbringing was unusual, his background was in most other ways typical for a CIA leader of his generation. Born in 1903, young Sherm enjoyed a privileged, even aristocratic childhood. His parents were a three-term US congressman from California, William Kent, and Elizabeth Thacher Kent, a prominent women's rights campaigner and descendant of US Founding Father Roger Sherman. After attending an elite California boarding school founded by an uncle, Kent crossed the country to enroll at Yale, where his maternal grandfather had taught. Initially, he too appeared bound for an academic career, staying on in New Haven to complete a PhD in nineteenth-century French history and subsequently joining the Yale History Department as faculty. In 1941, however, he received a call summoning him to Washington, DC, where World War I hero and Wall Street lawyer William Donovan was organizing what would become the wartime US intelligence agency, the Office of Strategic Services. Along with hundreds of other scholars, Kent joined the OSS's Research and

Analysis branch (the "Bad Eyes Brigade" or "Chairborne Division," as Washington wags rather unfairly nicknamed it), rapidly rising, by dint of his manifest analytical and managerial talents, to chief of R&A's Europe-Africa division. The fierce purposefulness and excitement of wartime secret service left a deep impression on Kent and, even after the OSS was disbanded in 1945 and he had returned to Yale, he kept a foot in the intelligence world, teaching at the National War College and publishing a 1949 book that would soon become a classic text on the subject, *Strategic Intelligence for American World Policy*. Hence, when in late 1950 he received a second summons from Washington, this time to help reboot the new CIA's analytic effort following an unsteady start, he answered it gladly. By 1952, he was in charge of ONE, a position he would occupy for the remainder of his CIA career.[3]

Kent's personal origins were reflected in the intelligence bureaucracy he helped create. "Frankly elitist in its conception" (as one Agency historian puts it), ONE was made up of only twenty-five to thirty staff members, almost all of them young men drawn from the graduate schools and junior faculty of Ivy League universities. The Board of National Estimates, the even smaller unit within ONE responsible for preparing the National Intelligence Estimates before they went out the door to consumers, was more exclusive still. It consisted mainly of senior Ivy League academics, several of them former Yale colleagues of Kent's, with (in the words of the same CIA historian) "a leavening of members from the military and the ranks of the professional intelligence officers." This homogeneity made for a collegial, productive working environment, presided over by the hard-driving Kent. "ONE was not Camelot, but Sherm did run a fine show," one staff member remembered fondly. Still, some outsiders wondered if the common-room-like atmosphere was not breeding a slightly blinkered view of world events.[4]

The elitist tone was not confined to the analytical staff of ONE and the CIA's Directorate of Intelligence. It also prevailed in the division responsible for overseas espionage as well as other forms of covert action (known in Kent's time as the Directorate of Plans and later as the Directorate of Operations or clandestine service). Indeed, the whole Agency had a distinctly patrician feel to it, dominated as it was by young WASP men with East Coast origins and Ivy League educations. Males from other backgrounds, including even white "ethnics," were comparatively scarce. There were some white women officers, among them a handful who went on to compile distinguished intelligence careers, but the majority of female CIA employees were clerks or secretaries. Combined with measures to exclude homosexual recruits due to perceptions that they were vulnerable to blackmail and therefore unacceptable security risks, these gender dynamics made for a working environment of aggressive male heterosexuality in which women had to endure routine harassment ranging from innuendo to outright assault. Despite the CIA's location in Washington, DC, a city with a large African American population, Black people who worked at the Agency were largely confined to the roles of security guards and janitors.[5]

The WASP ascendancy at the young CIA was not accidental. Agency officers systematically tasked friendly Ivy League professors—the "P Source"—with recruiting their most promising students. Such "laying on of hands," as historian Robin W. Winks described the practice, was particularly common at Sherman Kent's Yale, occurring as it did "in the college and in the classroom, at the master's tea and in the seminar, over a cup at Mory's and during a break in crew practice." As for the new recruits themselves, they were doubtless gratified by the social exclusiveness of the infant spy agency, the sense of being elected to a secret society. But their reasons for joining the CIA were not confined to simple snobbery. More important as a motivating factor was a distinctive set of values they had acquired in childhood.[6]

Many of the Ivy League graduates who gravitated to the CIA in its first years of existence had attended one or another of a tiny group of East Coast prep schools. Foremost among these was Groton School, founded in rural Massachusetts by the Reverend Endicott Peabody in 1884. The scion of an eminent New England family, Peabody had received his education in Britain, at the boarding school Cheltenham College, then at Cambridge. Thanks to its founder's time in England, Groton was thoroughly imbued with the ideals of imperial British manhood, such as muscular Christianity and patriotic service. The "Groton ethic," as the economist John Kenneth Galbraith later called it, resonated strongly with East Coast WASP elites, especially those who believed that the United States should follow Britain in taking up an imperial role in world affairs. Theodore Roosevelt sent all four of his sons to the school, and personally attended Sunday chapel there to urge the boys to "render service to the State." Three of TR's grandsons—Kermit, Archie, and Cornelius, Groton graduates all—later joined the fledgling CIA.[7]

If answering a call to public service was one important motive for the Anglophile young men who flocked to the Agency, another was a hunger for manly adventure. Many had grown up reading the British imperial spy thrillers of the early 1900s and imagined themselves emulating the antics of fictional spies such as Rudyard Kipling's Kim. Rufus Phillips, later an undercover Agency operative in Vietnam, spent much of his childhood in rural Virginia reading Kipling and dreaming about "faraway, mysterious places." Another CIA Asia hand, the paramilitary operations expert Anthony Poshepny (known as "Tony Poe"), later described *Kim* "as one of the Agency's training manuals." Then there was that real-life role model of British imperial heroism, T. E. Lawrence. After devouring Lawrence's *Seven Pillars of Wisdom*, future Director of Central Intelligence (DCI) William E. Colby fantasized about "becoming, if not exactly a Lawrence of Arabia, then at least Colby of a French Department." For career CIA officer Duane R. "Dewey" Clarridge, later a central figure in the foreign policy adventures (and misadventures) of the Reagan-era 1980s, Lawrence was, simply, "my hero." British imperial romance bred in these men a notion of foreign lands as a refuge from smothering domestic routine, a place for masculine self-realization.[8]

This fascination with British imperial agents was not entirely spontaneous; it was consciously fostered by the British themselves. This process had begun during World War I, when London dispatched representatives of its recently created intelligence services to the United States to nudge the neutral Americans into entering the conflict. The Grotonian Franklin Delano Roosevelt, then assistant secretary of the US Navy, was a particular focus of attention, with the director of British naval intelligence, William Reginald "Blinker" Hall, deliberately encouraging his youthful, Kiplingesque interest in espionage. FDR would carry on this hobby after the war, avidly consuming reports from the "Room," a secret society of New York socialites founded by his friend Vincent Astor to conduct amateur intelligence missions abroad, often aboard Astor's yacht.[9]

A similar dynamic occurred in World War II. In 1940, Roosevelt, now president, sent Bill Donovan on a fact-finding expedition to London. After meeting British spy chiefs and Prime Minister Winston Churchill—another imperial adventurer with a particular interest in intelligence—Donovan returned to Washington advising not only that the United States back the British against Nazi Germany but also that Roosevelt set up a permanent foreign intelligence agency like MI6. Britons visiting America during the war echoed Donovan's message. A young naval intelligence officer, Ian Fleming, future creator of the James Bond series—imperial British spy fiction for the Cold War era—even claimed to have proposed the central intelligence model that would inspire the creation of the OSS and, a few years later, the CIA.[10]

Fleming was a notorious embellisher and was probably exaggerating his influence over the Americans, as were other Britons who later would claim parentage of the CIA. As we have already seen, the United States had its own intelligence history that dated back to the Revolution, including a colonial strand from the US occupation of the Philippines. Still, there was some truth to such claims. The British influence on the OSS was manifold. It included training in a range of espionage, covert action, and counterintelligence techniques—and even, as Sherman Kent himself acknowledged, the writing of intelligence estimates (according to Kent, William H. Jackson, later deputy director of the CIA, undertook "some very special investigative work with British intelligence" at the war's end, making a particular study of "how the British had gone about writing national estimates and how the U.S. should follow that model"). The war years also bred a powerful and intimate sense of Anglo-American camaraderie thanks to joint covert operations such as the Jedburghs, commando teams who bravely parachuted behind German lines in occupied Europe. Emblematic of this budding intelligence "special relationship" was the signing in 1946 of the UKUSA signals intelligence-sharing agreement (an arrangement that still exists today in the shape of the expanded "Five Eyes" intelligence alliance).[11]

In sum, World War II witnessed the culmination of a long-standing interest in British intelligence among elite American men that was part natural and part manufactured. This ensured that when the OSS was resurrected as the CIA in 1947, the new agency would bear a strong resemblance to the British secret services—which, lest it be forgotten, had been largely created in the first place to defend the British Empire.

All this said, it would be a mistake to portray the founding generation of the CIA as a complete social monolith. In addition to the Ivy League WASPs or "Bold Easterners," as journalist Stewart Alsop called them, there were some recruits from blue-collar backgrounds who had come to the Agency via routes such as J. Edgar Hoover's Federal Bureau of Investigation or the Army's Counter Intelligence Corps. Similarly, not everyone was Protestant: Catholics were sufficiently well represented (Donovan, for example, was born one) that the CIA would later acquire the nickname "Catholic Intelligence Agency." Mormons also were attractive hires due to their supposedly morally blameless personal lives, which made them low security risks, and to the foreign language skills required for their mission work.[12]

For that matter, not all the CIA's Protestants were of the Bold Easterner type. An influential minority were offspring of the mainline Protestant missionaries who had been evangelizing in Asia, Africa, and the Middle East since the 1800s. In the absence of much US government involvement in these regions, the "mish kids," many of whom had grown up overseas, were exceptional sources of foreign knowledge and experience. Combined with their inherited motivation to do good in the world, this made them highly attractive candidates for CIA employment. Indeed, two Middle East specialists of missionary descent, Stephen B. L. Penrose Jr. and William A. Eddy, played leading roles in the founding of the Agency in 1947.

This is not to say that missionary work and spying were an entirely natural fit. Some mish kids struggled to reconcile their Christian consciences with the morally dubious acts they were expected to perform as spies. "It is still an open question whether an operator in OSS or in CIA can ever again become a wholly honorable man," William Eddy confided to his memoir. "We deserve to go to hell when we die." Another issue was that the mish kids' overseas upbringings tended to produce a deep sympathy with foreign peoples that often expressed itself in opposition to European colonialism, especially French but in some cases extending to the British, too. This impulse, strengthened in some cases by the experience of wartime service alongside nationalist resistance groups—in Vietnam, for example, the OSS had supported Viet Minh guerrillas against Japanese occupation forces—would create a powerful undercurrent of anti-colonialism in the early CIA. The presence of Catholics of Irish descent in the Agency's ranks only served to strengthen this tendency.[13]

Overall, though, it was the Bold Easterners—a group with, as journalist Tad Szulc put it, "something almost British about them"—who set the social and cultural tone of the young CIA. Rather than fading, this elitist coloration if anything increased as the Agency grew in size over the next few years, especially after Allen Dulles took over as chief of the Directorate of Plans in 1951, then as DCI in 1953. Another Wall Street lawyer who had served in the OSS, Dulles was a Kipling devotee (he had a copy of *Kim* on his bedside table when he died), a personal acquaintance of T. E. Lawrence, whom he had met at the Paris peace conference, and an admirer of British intelligence. He was a bit of a snob as well, interested not only in the universities CIA recruits had attended but also in the undergraduate clubs to which they had belonged. Under his direction, the Agency became strongly identified with the so-called Georgetown Set, a clique of Washington insiders noted for their Cold War activism and tony lifestyles. In Dulles's Agency, intelligence officers who did not conform to this type found it hard gaining promotion to leadership positions, consolidating the organizational dominance of what one historian has called the "imperial brotherhood." Of course, managers in all large organizations have a tendency to promote people who look like themselves—but this effect is, arguably, unusually strong in secret government departments, where workers feel a particular need to trust their colleagues and often socialize exclusively together after hours.[14]

In other words, a variety of social and cultural influences shaped the early CIA—but the imperial impulse was the dominant one. Ironically, it would grow stronger still as the power of the European empires themselves faded in the first years of the Cold War, ushering in the era of decolonization.

The National Security Act, the 1947 legislation that established the Central Intelligence Agency and much of the United States' modern national security apparatus besides, did not mention the Soviet Union. However, its timing alone made it clear that the CIA was a by-product of growing US-Soviet tension. It came in the same year that Franklin Roosevelt's successor as president, Harry S. Truman, effectively declared cold war by proclaiming the Truman Doctrine, committing the United States to the defense of "free people" everywhere from takeover "by armed minorities or by outside pressures"—in other words, by communists. With both sides terrified by the prospect of another world war, this one likely featuring thermonuclear weapons, the US-Soviet conflict proved in large part a covert one, waged by rival intelligence services. The classic battleground of the covert Cold War, as depicted in numerous spy novels and movies, was the divided city of Berlin, and the tactics used espionage, surveillance, and psychological warfare.

Europe, though, was not the only theater of the superpower confrontation, nor was the Cold War the sole event taking place in mid-twentieth-century global politics. World War II spelled the collapse of the old European imperial order. Throughout the colonial world, nationalist leaders, ironically often emerging out of the local elites that the imperial powers had employed to impose their rule, seized on the war and its aftermath as an opportunity to declare their people's independence. Decolonization proceeded unevenly and often bloodily; the final European withdrawals from Africa did not occur until the 1970s. But the overall picture was clear. The second half of the twentieth century was to be the postcolonial era.

Inevitably, these massive, world-historical events—the Cold War and decolonization—became enmeshed. Indeed, the first post–World War II crisis in US-Soviet relations occurred not in Europe but in what Americans were soon calling the Third World. In 1946, Soviet premier Joseph Stalin violated wartime agreements among the Allied powers by refusing to withdraw Red Army troops occupying northern Iran. Within a few years, Cold War tensions were spreading to other countries in the Middle East, Southeast Asia, and, eventually, sub-Saharan Africa. Both Americans and Russians coveted the regions emerging from under European dominion for the same reasons that great powers had always sought new territory: competition, prestige, and wealth. But the Cold War superpowers also had ideological reasons for wanting influence in the postcolonial world. Each saw itself as the rightful heir to European modernity and looked upon the "new nations" as platforms for demonstrating the superiority of its civilization. They were going to modernize the postcolonial world—whether the postcolonial world wanted to be modernized or not.[15]

As in Europe, intelligence was central to the Cold War in the Global South. Not only did the superpowers need tactical information about the moves of their opponent; they also wanted knowledge about the societies they were trying to mold in their image. In the case of the United States, this meant that the CIA underwent an extraordinary burst of growth within a few years of its founding. In 1949, the Agency unit then responsible for covert action, the Office of Policy Coordination, had seven overseas bases, most housed in US embassies or consulates; by 1952, it had forty-seven. The CIA officers staffing these new stations did so under false professional identities or "cover." For most, this meant pretending to be an overt US government official, an embassy political secretary, say (an arrangement that did not always please genuine Foreign Service officers). A few operated under "non-official cover," disguised as businessmen, perhaps, or journalists. With their cover stories in place, these CIA "case officers" set about recruiting "agents," locals with access to secret information and knowledge.[16]

But CIA field operatives were more than just their official missions and cover stories: they were also people. Some had foreign experience, either having spent their childhood abroad as mish kids or having served overseas during World War II. Most, however, lacked firsthand knowledge of the specific country to which they were posted. A surprising number were married and at some point in their foreign tours were joined by their families, although some wives and children chose to remain at home. All were motivated by a desire for adventure and patriotic service, which in the context of the Cold War meant fighting communism. In many cases, these urges were mixed with a strong element of idealism, a desire to uplift the less fortunate of the world, a legacy of the missionary impulse in US foreign relations generally and the CIA in particular. For several, this meant not only saving the Third World from communism but also freeing it from the last vestiges of European colonialism.

The trouble was that the peculiar circumstances of the Cold War moment kept landing CIA officers in neocolonial roles. Although formal European empire was ending, the old imperial powers typically maintained a strong informal presence in their former colonies, including sizable contingents of spies—an "imperialism of decolonization," as British imperial historians have described it. Some CIA officers, adrift in unfamiliar environments, found themselves leaning on the local knowledge and contacts of their European colleagues. Inevitably, there were tensions in such relationships. The new US arrivals regretted their dependence on these unreconstructed colonials, while the Europeans resented the appearance in their midst of young, inexperienced, and moralistic Americans (readers of *The Quiet American*, the Vietnam-set 1955 novel by British author Graham Greene, will be familiar with these dynamics). But there was also fraternization between spies of different nationalities, especially the Americans and British, that harked back to the joint intelligence operations of the war years. One example of this is provided in the now-infamous story of MI6 officer H. A. R. "Kim" Philby's sojourn in Lebanon from 1956 to 1963, when he revealed himself as a Soviet mole by fleeing to Moscow. Despite already being under a cloud of suspicion, Philby (whose nickname, "Kim," came, of course, from the Kipling story) mixed extensively in US intelligence and journalistic circles in Beirut right up to his defection. He even married Eleanor Brewer, the former wife of an American reporter and CIA source, Sam Pope Brewer.[17]

In addition to mixing with colonial types, CIA officers found themselves leading imperial lifestyles. If American schooling was unavailable, they sent their children to European schools. They ate and drank at hotels and clubs left over from the colonial era: the Gezira Sporting Club in Cairo, the Hotel St. George in Beirut, the Hôtel Continental in Saigon. Some even took up colonial sports: Dewey Clarridge was famous for his love of polo, a relic of a 1960s posting in India, where he also developed a fondness for curry dinners washed down with copious quantities of beer. Above all, CIA officers lived in colonial villas, complete with large staffs of local servants. Some of these young American men, especially those from humbler origins, were amazed by their good fortune. Robert Baer (later played by George Clooney in the movie *Syriana*) turned up in Madras (now Chennai) on his first overseas tour expecting a hardship assignment. Instead, he found palatial accommodations and seven uniformed servants, who greeted him with a glass of mango juice on a silver tray. This was the moment Baer realized "India wasn't going to be half bad after all." Given these carryovers from the imperial past, it was perhaps predictable that locals often lumped the American newcomers together with their European predecessors, as when Congo station chief Larry Devlin heard himself addressed as *flamand*, the term used by the Congolese to refer to Belgian colonials.[18]

CIA wives had an even more imperial-like experience than their menfolk. As per the gender expectations of the era, it fell to them to manage the household staffs that came with the colonial villas. Those whose husbands operated under official cover—the majority—were also expected to play the part of diplomatic wives, attending embassy functions, where "white gloves, hats, and straight stocking seams" were still the norm (as Lorraine Copeland, the wife of a CIA Middle East operative, recalled), and entertaining lavishly in their own homes. Other domestic duties were delegated to the household staff, which typically included cooks, maids, and nannies for the children. This left plenty of time for socializing with other embassy wives, adding to the feeling of what was, according to Copeland, a "cocooned, privileged existence."[19]

Many wives enjoyed this lifestyle, whether because they were glad simply not to have to perform domestic chores or because the free time allowed them to develop other interests. Lorraine Copeland took up archaeology, eventually becoming an academic authority on the subject. Others, however, hated it. The management of local domestic staff was a complex business, requiring the ability to keep a certain distance while also involving peculiar kinds of physical and emotional intimacy—what historian of Dutch colonialism Ann Laura Stoler has described as "tense and tender ties." This is to say nothing of the inevitable stresses and strains faced by the wives of professional spies: the social demands of the embassy cocktail circuit; the secrecy surrounding their husbands' work, the nature of which CIA officers were supposed to conceal even from their families (although, in practice, wives were often expected to play supporting operational roles in addition to their other duties); and the constant disruptions to family life caused by rotations between headquarters and foreign assignments. Small wonder that some wives fled home to the United States while others battled depression and alcoholism.[20]

Although CIA wives often found themselves living in close quarters with household staff, it was the children of Agency officers who experienced the greatest intimacy with locals. Numerous sons and daughters of CIA parents formed loving relationships with native servants. Some nannies even accompanied families on new assignments to different countries. When Dewey Clarridge was transferred from Nepal to India, his daughter's Nepalese ayah went, too. CIA parents appear not to have shared the fear of earlier colonial generations that their children might somehow be racially contaminated by household servants. But many did express another old colonial concern: that doting nannies were spoiling their charges. One long-serving officer, David Atlee Phillips, later recalled an incident from a 1950s foreign tour. His three-year-old daughter Atlee was in her crib and wanted attention. "'Mommy!' she shouted. No answer. 'Daddy?' Again, no answer. Finally, Atlee screamed 'Maids!'"[21]

As adults, CIA children tended to recall their overseas upbringings with fondness bordering on reverence. They had learned their host nation's languages, played its sports, and explored its landscapes. Rather like the mish kids, Agency children often developed sympathies with Third World nationalist movements. In time, this might lead to their becoming disillusioned with the Cold War policies espoused by their parents' generation. After having spent several years of his childhood in Vietnam while his father, future CIA director William Colby, served as chief of the Agency's Saigon station, Carl Colby was dismayed by the damage to the country wrought by US bombs in the late 1960s. "The Vietnam that I knew was being destroyed," he lamented. In some families, such misgivings combined with a nagging sense of unease felt by many CIA children about the clandestine nature of their fathers' work to produce a perfect storm of generational conflict.[22]

This is not to say that CIA officers themselves did not also develop intimate relationships in the countries where they worked. "Sex was one of management's biggest headaches," according to Robert Baer. "It boiled down to the fact that the CIA did not want its employees indiscriminately cavorting with the enemy." James Bond notwithstanding, dalliances with beautiful Russian spies were rare. But it was a different story where native inhabitants of the Global South were concerned. Like earlier generations of European men in "the colonies," some CIA officers viewed the postcolonial world as a sexual playground. In Saigon, where a flourishing sex industry had once catered to French colonials, unmarried Agency men partook of, in the words of one officer who served there, "a carnival atmosphere." Another described "a glut-tony of sensual pleasures" and recalled a typical tableau of the period: a young CIA man lounging in a lawn chair as he read the morning's cables, clasping a beer in one hand and offering the other to a Viet-namese "dolly" for a manicure. Not even married officers were immune from the charms of "Orientals"—no memoir by a CIA veteran who served in Southeast Asia is complete without a reference to the beauty of the women of the region. Again, there are echoes here of earlier Euro-pean Orientalism and its portrayal of "the East" as a place of unfettered sexual license.[23]

That said, liaisons between CIA officers and Third World women were not limited to sex. A surprising number of Agency men mar-ried their local partners—sometimes divorcing American wives to do so. To some extent, this practice was simply reprising older Euro-pean arrangements. French and Dutch authorities in the "Indies" had encouraged single male colonial officers to marry local women to save them the expense of importing European women and, at the same time, gain valuable new sources of intimate intelligence. But other fac-tors were at work as well. Often, it was the most idealistic CIA officers who got married, and not just because they had old-fashioned attitudes about such matters. Rather, their missionary-style urge to uplift Third World countries became entwined with their personal relationships. In marrying local women, these men were also marrying the nations they wanted to save and protect. Graham Greene captured this phe-nomenon brilliantly in *The Quiet American*. At the center of the novel is a love triangle between a callow, painfully earnest CIA officer, Alden Pyle, an older, jaded British journalist, Thomas Fowler, and a young Vietnamese hostess, Phuong Hei. Pyle, intent on rescuing Phuong from a life of exploitation, proposes marriage to her, despite the fact she is already living with Fowler. She eventually accepts—although, in an ending that reflected Greene's anti-Americanism, Fowler wins her back by conniving in Pyle's murder.[24]

CIA officers, then, did not just spy on foreigners: they and their families interacted with them daily in the most intimate ways imaginable. Some of these encounters looked a lot like earlier relations between European imperialists and colonial peoples, others less so. This was true wherever American power rushed to fill the vacuum left by the demise of the old imperial order: the Middle East, Far East, and Africa. Central and, increasingly during the Cold War era, South America was a somewhat different case in that it was historically a US rather than European zone of influence. But even there, CIA officers found themselves leading neocolonial lives, dwelling in grand houses, managing servants, engaging in sexual liaisons—and using local agents to collect secret information about the host society.

The relationship between the CIA officer and his agent was at the heart of the Agency's intelligence mission in the Global South. Elsewhere, in the hard-to-penetrate communist bloc, technological means of intelligence gathering (TECHINT)—U-2 spy planes photographing Soviet missile installations, for example—were more important than human-source intelligence (HUMINT). But in the decolonizing "periphery," where technology was less advanced and targets more easily accessible, HUMINT reigned. Here, what really counted, according to Robert Baer, was "people on the ground, agents, . . . a network of traitors, and a case officer willing and able to work it."[25]

Where, though, to find the "traitors"? In keeping with its love of science, the CIA had a system for this process: an agent acquisition "cycle" with several distinct steps that the new intelligence officer learned in training. First, the officer "spotted" a local with access to valuable secret information—a junior government minister, perhaps, or army officer. Next, the CIA operative and Agency headquarters independently "assessed" the potential agent: Were they likely to yield valuable—and reliable—intelligence? Third came the most sensitive step, "recruitment," when the officer pitched the prospective agent, offering money or some other inducement in return for information. If the pitch was successful, the officer would "test" the new recruit, comparing their statements with already known facts, then, assuming verification, "train" them in the espionage tradecraft needed to keep their dealings secret. This might include the use of spy gear such as miniature cameras, covert communication through the non-simultaneous transfer of documents (dead drops) or apparently accidental contact in public (brush passes), and techniques for evading surveillance. Then came the sixth stage, "handling," when the espionage relationship was fully functioning and information flowing regularly, ideally over the course of several years. Finally, after the officer or agent judged the relationship had served its usefulness, came "termination," hopefully on mutually agreeable terms.[26]

But why would an agent want to pass secrets—that is, commit treason—in the first place? Again, the CIA had a theory about agent motivation, summed up by a handy mnemonic device: MICE (money, ideology, coercion/compromise, excitement/ego). The most common motive, especially in the poorer parts of the Third World, was a simple desire for money: an official on a low salary needed extra funds to send their children to school, perhaps, or finance an expensive habit. Other agents, however, were motivated less by money than by ideology, usually a hatred of communism. (Not surprisingly, CIA officers tended to prefer this type of agent.) Then came a third category, this one liable to coercion or compromise: an intelligence service had some embarrassing information about a person, often of a sexual nature, and compelled their cooperation by threatening to reveal it. Finally, there was excitement or ego—an individual looking for ways to enliven a humdrum existence or get back at a system that had somehow failed to recognize and reward their worth. Under the MICE framework, almost all agent motives were vulnerabilities of one sort or another. The challenge facing the CIA officer was to identify the vulnerability, then work out how to exploit it in order to control the agent.[27]

So much for the theory. In practice, officer-agent relationships rarely worked as smoothly as the notion of a "cycle" implied. Despite their training, many officers never developed the knack of befriending and recruiting agents, while others made dozens of successful pitches. In other words, the ability to recruit seemed to be intuitive rather than the product of training, more an art than a science. Whatever the reason, a minority of officers—20 percent or 10 percent, in some estimates—were responsible for the great majority of recruitments, as much as 80 percent or 90 percent. With CIA management encouraging competition to "score" new recruits, the men who fell into this category prided themselves on their talent, contrasting it with what they perceived as the more mundane business of handling existing agents. There was something thrilling about the intimacy of recruitment. "The process has a lot in common with seduction," reckoned Larry Devlin. Dewey Clarridge was even more explicit: "successfully making a difficult recruitment," he reflected, is like "the sensations of a sexual orgasm." After having his way, Clarridge liked to turn his conquests over to other officers for handling.[28]

Still, not all officers were in it for the thrill of recruitment. Others took pride in the long-term relationships they developed with agents, based on understanding and empathy—rather like, as one of them put it later, a lasting marriage. This was not just a matter of good espionage practice, although advocates of such an approach emphasized that it would ultimately yield better intelligence. In many cases, the officer-agent relationship developed into surprisingly strong, even sentimental male friendships, marked by moments of intense emotional intimacy.

In countries with unfriendly regimes, where citizens spying for the United States risked arrest and worse, agents often aroused the masculine admiration and compassion of their CIA handlers. "Noble spies like him helped win the Cold War," said case officer Henry A. Crumpton about one of his African recruits. The memory of another moved Crumpton to declare, "He was more than one of my best agents. He was my teacher . . . a friend and an inspiration." But even in countries where the personal stakes were not as high because the government was pro-American, officer-agent friendships bloomed. This was particularly true in Latin America among CIA officers and locals involved in joint operations against leftist opposition movements. In Ecuador during the early 1960s, the future CIA whistleblower Philip Agee bonded with a recently recruited male agent by carousing wildly with him in the "sleazy dives" of his hometown. Agee's station chief in Quito, former college football star James B. Noland, likewise built his local relationships around shared interests in drinking, soccer, and even bullfighting.[29]

CIA trainers explicitly warned new officers against "falling in love" with their agents. Doing so might lead to "clientitis," putting the interests of the host country before those of one's own (rather as T. E. Lawrence was suspected of doing by some of his military superiors). Many officers were aware of this temptation and strove to avoid it. "Emotions," Hank Crumpton reminded himself, "can undermine and destroy human relationships, especially in the espionage world." Still, this did not stop some officers from caring about particular agents so much that they protested to headquarters when instructed to terminate them or took extraordinary measures to ensure their welfare after they were terminated. In 1975, when the CIA was evacuating Laos following the victory of the communist Pathet Lao, a junior case officer, Gil Kindelan, personally transported agents to the airport and hid others in his home until they too had a chance to escape. Another young officer based in South Vietnam at the same time, Frank Snepp, became so upset about the Agency's failure to save its local assets when it was emptying out of Saigon that he subsequently turned into a CIA whistleblower.[30]

In some cases, especially among officers with strong religious faith, such solicitude probably reflected feelings of moral guilt. Several CIA officers followed the World War II missionary-spy William Eddy in admitting to deep qualms about their treatment of agents. ("When I dream of men like Carlos," Eddy had confessed, referring to a Spanish Republican the OSS had used, then discarded, "I wake in a sweat.") After President Ngo Dinh Diem of South Vietnam was murdered in a November 1963 palace coup (with, many suspected, Agency approval), the Catholic William Colby and his wife, Barbara, prayed for his soul.[31]

Other officers were just as worried about their own souls. For every noble agent of the sort described by Hank Crumpton, there were many more scoundrels, ready to betray their country for a few pieces of silver. In the sexual imagery that surrounded agent recruitment, dealing with such characters was more akin to prostitution than to seduction. In the words of one officer, it left him feeling dirty, like he needed "a hot shower." This, by the way, was another reason, in addition to its veneration of science, why the CIA tended to prefer TECHINT to HUMINT. Remote, mechanical methods of gathering intelligence were less morally compromising than the messy intimacy of human espionage.[32]

If the case officer's handling of his agents was influenced as much by emotion as by scientific method—another Cold War case of colonial-style "tense and tender ties"—agents' behavior was arguably more complex still. It is hard to say for sure exactly what motivated agents to commit treason; for obvious reasons, they did not tend to commit their feelings to paper. But enough evidence exists to suggest that the MICE framework of vulnerabilities favored by the CIA did not cover the full spectrum of motives, and that, as a consequence, the intelligence that agents provided was not always as reliable as the Agency supposed.

The threat was not limited to "dangles" (provocations by hostile intelligence services) or "paper mills" (intelligence fabricated for profit by opportunistic locals). No less insidious was the agent in good standing who slanted the intelligence they were providing for some purpose of their own: the right-wing Latin American official, for example, who exaggerated the communist connections of anti-government groups in his country in a bid to obtain CIA support for a government purge of the opposition. This would not be the first time in history such an effect had occurred: in imperial India, local informants had fed British officials census data that subtly served the interests of some elements (banking groups) over others (the land-controlling castes). In other words, the case officer was not necessarily in control of the espionage relationship, exploiting the vulnerabilities of the agent; sometimes it was the other way around. The agent had agency.[33]

Although the CIA thought it represented a new departure from the tradition of the European imperial secret services—rejecting their colonialism and intuitive, cultural approach to intelligence in favor of a noncolonial, scientific one—the Agency's actual practice of espionage in the decolonizing world was constantly influenced by the imperial past, not least in the realm of intimate human relations between CIA officers and the postcolonial peoples they encountered.

What did all this mean for the final stage of the intelligence cycle, the one presided over by Sherman Kent in Washington: the intelligence estimate?

In September 1962, Sherman Kent made the biggest error of his career. His Board of National Estimates declared it highly unlikely that the Soviet Union would emplace offensive nuclear weapons on Cuba. Fortunately, Allen Dulles's successor as Director of Central Intelligence, John A. McCone, developed a hunch that the Soviets were hiding something on the island and insisted that the Agency launch U-2 flights over it. To Kent's dismay, photographs taken by the spy planes in October revealed that McCone was right: the Soviets had already deployed medium-range ballistic missiles capable of carrying nuclear warheads 1,300 miles—as far as Washington, DC.

The CIA partially redeemed itself during the next thirteen days, providing President John F. Kennedy and his advisors with effective daily briefings that helped them bring a peaceful conclusion to the Cuban Missile Crisis. After a year he later described as "really hideous," Kent saw his personal standing recover as well. In 1964, he published an article in the CIA's in-house journal, *Studies in Intelligence*, reflecting on the causes of ONE's error over Cuba, but standing by his original estimate that Soviet premier Nikita Khrushchev's action was unlikely given that it was plainly reckless—"dramatically wrong"—and therefore hard to predict by rational, scientific standards of political behavior. Privately, he put McCone's intervention down to "some wild Irish intuition."[34]

Estimative failures such as Cuba should not entirely color assessments of the CIA's intelligence record during the Cold War. The Agency got many things right. In Vietnam, for example, it was a source of some good battlefield tactical intelligence and sensible strategic estimates of the long-term prospects for US involvement. It was politicians who got the war wrong. Also, as defenders of the Agency like to point out, the secrecy of the intelligence business makes it impossible to tell how many times good tradecraft has prevented crises from occurring. Intelligence failures are obvious; successes are, by definition, non-events.

Still, it is hard to deny that there were intelligence failures, some of them disastrous. At the beginning of the Cold War, the CIA failed to provide actionable warnings of, in rapid order, the Soviet acquisition of the atomic bomb, the fall of China to communism, and the advent of the Korean War. Later, toward the end of the superpower conflict, the Agency was caught out by the Soviet invasion of Afghanistan in 1979, the Iranian Revolution of the same year, and the rapidity of the Soviet Union's dissolution in 1991. This is to say nothing of the catastrophic intelligence failures that have occurred since the end of the Cold War.

Much ink has been spilled on the causes of these failures, and various culprits identified: "mirror-imaging," or the projection of one's own worldview onto that of opponents (as happened in Cuba); excessive background "noise" drowning out clear intelligence signals; bureaucratic turf wars; politicians either ignoring good intelligence or "cherry-picking" it for their own political purposes. Few analyses, though, have dwelt on the sort of issues raised here: the identities and emotions of intelligence officers and their agents. And, so far, there has been next to no attempt to compare or connect US intelligence failures with those of earlier empires, despite information deficits about rising threats and panics about nonexistent ones having been a recurring theme in imperial history.[35]

Taking this longer historical view has the potential to reveal US intelligence failure in a new light. Consider perhaps the most persistent and consequential American analytical error of the Cold War period: overestimating the influence of the Soviet Union (and communist China, Cuba, and North Vietnam as well) on anti-colonial struggles in the Global South. This mistake, which occurred throughout the era, precipitated numerous US interventions (typically also carried out by the CIA), some aimed at overthrowing nationalist governments perceived as being under the control of the communist powers, others at saving neocolonial regimes that also happened to be anti-communist. Many of these interventions had harmful consequences not only for the countries concerned but also for the United States itself.

Of course, the notion that communist powers were controlling Third World nationalists did have some foundation in fact. The Soviets and the others were constantly seeking influence beyond their borders, and many postcolonial leaders were doctrinal Marxists who actively courted the patronage of Moscow or Beijing. But the image that haunted American minds during the Cold War—of a monolithic international conspiracy seeking world domination—was overdrawn. The foreign ambitions of the communist powers ebbed and flowed. By the late 1950s, the Soviet Union and China saw themselves as competitors in world affairs, and neither entirely welcomed the rise of Third World communist states Cuba and North Vietnam to international prominence during the 1960s. Most importantly, local nationalists, even the Marxist ones, were not necessarily inclined to follow the Soviet or Chinese line. Anti-colonial revolutionaries had not spent lifetimes fighting one form of external domination only then to volunteer for another.[36]

To be fair, many CIA officers were aware of these complexities. During the late 1950s, analysts in the Agency's Sino-Soviet Studies Group called attention to the growing tension between Moscow and Beijing; a 1960 National Intelligence Estimate issued by ONE reflected their findings. Similarly, many field officers were aware of the strength and spontaneity of local nationalist impulses, having become so during overseas postings. In some cases, such awareness produced a readiness to challenge US government policies that conflated nationalism with communism, even if that meant inviting allegations of Lawrence-like clientitis. To cite one example, CIA officers based in Egypt during the 1950s became almost mutinous after Secretary of State John Foster Dulles (Allen's brother) reversed an earlier US policy of support for the country's nationalist leader, Gamal Abdel Nasser, on the grounds that he was allying himself with the Soviets. In a remarkable—and prophetic—statement of dissent, Cairo station chief James N. Eichelberger declared that it would be a huge error for the United States to engage "in direct combat with Arab nationalism," as such a course of action would surely lead to "the defeat of Western interests" in the region.[37]

However, such statements were rare. For the most part, CIA intelligence conformed with the conventional Cold War wisdom that Third World nationalism served the interests of communist enemies. Why? An imperial historian might answer that empires have always labored under misapprehensions about the foreign lands over which they hold sway. Despite their military and technological superiority, colonial authorities are typically overstretched, anxious, and reliant on agents whose veracity is questionable at best. This was why the British in 1800s India worried to the point of obsession about the Thuggees, gangs of robbers and murderers supposedly terrorizing the country's highways, yet failed to detect the approach of the massive 1857 Indian Rebellion, which nearly ended their rule of the subcontinent. As one local civil officer admitted, "The native is always better competent to gain information in India than the best-informed European."[38]

Beyond this general condition, several specific continuities connected the post–World War II US experience with the imperial past. The British too had tended to blame nationalist unrest in the areas under their dominion on outside conspiracies. During the 1800s, the era of the Great Game, it was the Russian czar who was to blame; in World War I, the Germans and Ottomans; then, after 1917, the Bolsheviks. Of course, there were some real conspiracies: the Communist International or Comintern, founded in 1919, did try to undermine British India by dispatching agents into Iran and Afghanistan. But London habitually exaggerated the influence of such interference and underestimated colonial nationalism. Indeed, during the 1930s the British intelligence services failed to give adequate heed to the rise of Nazism, so preoccupied were they with the threat of "Eastern unrest" orchestrated from Moscow. Behind this fixation was the Orientalist notion that "Asiatics" were peculiarly susceptible to external manipulation.[39]

Orientalist stereotypes bled into CIA intelligence about the Cold War–era Global South. In Southeast Asia, colonial French perceptions of "Orientals" as primitive, servile, and untrustworthy resurfaced in US analysis of nationalist movements such as the Viet Minh, fueling the tendency to view them as puppets controlled by distant communist masters. Similar Orientalist ideas inherited from the British colored American attitudes toward the peoples of the Middle East: the Arabs, for example, were backward, apathetic, and (ironically enough, given the sentimental nature of many officer-agent relationships) overly emotional. Some of the American prejudices of the era were no doubt homegrown, reflecting domestic histories of racism toward minority groups within US society or on its borders: a perception of Black Africans as uncivilized, for instance, or of Latin Americans as excitable. But all had the same effect in terms of the Cold War, casting Third World peoples as so many pawns in the superpower contest.[40]

In part, the recycling of Orientalist stereotypes in the Cold War era reflected a deliberate strategy on the part of the imperial European powers. Just as in the earlier part of the century, when the British had tried to guide the development of US intelligence, so now Old World spies sought to educate the American ingenues about their new international "responsibilities." To overcome the idealistic anti-colonialism many CIA officers exhibited, Europeans intentionally emphasized the alleged character flaws of "Orientals" and their vulnerability to communist machinations. So, in the Middle East, British intelligence officers exaggerated Nasser's links to communism while also pointing out the strength of the Egyptian leader's emotional appeal to other Arabs. Less to be expected, this message was repeated by some locals. Members of indigenous colonial elites still trying to cling to power—in the Arab world, client kings left over from the mandate era—told the Americans that their fellow countrymen needed authoritarian leadership to save them from communist influence and demagogues like Nasser. At the same time, they tended to overstate their own ability to suppress communism and nationalism in a conscious bid for US support to replace that of the retreating Europeans. In both cases, the aim was the same: to harness American power in service of preserving as much of the old colonial order as possible—another case of the "imperialism of decolonization."[41]

To be sure, these echoes of empire were not the only causes of American intelligence errors in the Cold War. But, combined with the

The founder of CIA intelligence analysis, Sherman Kent, in his later years, sporting a pair of his trademark suspenders.
Sherman Kent Papers, Yale University Library

effects of other factors, such as the elitist character of the CIA's workforce and the peculiar kinds of human relationships its officers formed when operating overseas, they undoubtedly contributed. Those seeking to prevent future intelligence failures of the sort that have dogged the CIA would do well to consider the lessons of imperial history.

Sherman Kent retired from government service in 1967, shortly before a new president, Richard Nixon, arrived in the White House. With Kent gone, criticism of the "rarified" Office of National Estimates increased. Nixon disliked the Ivy League atmosphere of the CIA generally, while his national security advisor, Henry Kissinger, found the National Intelligence Estimates "Talmudic." In 1973, ONE was, in the words of an Agency historian, "reorganized out of existence." Like many other retired intelligence officers, Kent filled his remaining years—he passed in 1986—entertaining friends and family with tales of his career and writing for publication. His retirement books included a historical monograph based on his doctoral research about early 1800s French politics, a series of children's stories, and an autobiography, *Reminiscences of a Varied Life.*[42]

The personality revealed in this last work is, one senses, closer to Kent's real self than the scientific voice of his previous works on intelligence: voluble, opinionated, and sentimental. Particularly revealing is a chapter in which Kent recalled leaving his post in Washington to make several brief overseas forays during the 1950s. Touring the Middle East in 1954, he was overcome with boyish excitement about a region he had first encountered in childhood tales of Oriental mystery. During a diplomatic dinner in Cairo, he listened "breathlessly" as the Egyptian leader Nasser related the events of "that famous evening," the 1952 Egyptian Revolution. The following morning, while visiting the Valley of the Kings, the CIA man encountered a comically roguish snake charmer who (according to Kent's later account) greeted him with the words "Meester, we in luck. I smell snake." In Japan five years later, Kent experienced a confusing mix of erotic excitement and physical disgust while attending a formal dinner. The geishas who hosted him were, he reckoned, "the most beautiful creatures [he] had ever seen, and the injunction of hands off was a hard one to observe." His enjoyment of the festivities was spoiled, though, by another diner, a drunk Japanese man with "evil-smelling breath," who boasted about his friendship with Kent's boss, "'Mr. Arran Durres.'"[43]

The point here is not calling out Kent for racism and sexism: his attitudes were regrettably typical of a man of his generation, class, and race (and, whatever his feelings about geishas, he was, by all accounts, a devoted family man). Rather, it lies in the contradiction between his scientific strictures about intelligence and his lived personal experience. For all his pushing of clinical objectivity and linguistic precision, Kent himself viewed foreign societies through a perceptual fog of visceral emotion and Orientalist prejudice. Intelligence as a predictive science was a noble dream, but humanity and the imperial past kept getting in the way.

Nor was Kent's discipline the only branch of CIA operation affected by such factors. If anything, the activity that gradually took over from intelligence as the Agency's chief mission in the Cold War—covert action—was to prove even more susceptible to imperial influences.

CHAPTER 2

Regime Change

E arly in the afternoon of August 26, 1953, a thirty-seven-year-old CIA officer, Kermit "Kim" Roosevelt, was ushered quietly into a drawing room in Number 10 Downing Street. There he found the prime minister of the United Kingdom, Winston Churchill, lying in bed. The veteran PM had recently suffered a stroke and was, Roosevelt subsequently reported to Washington, "in extremely bad shape." Nonetheless, the aristocratic young American—a grandson of President Theodore Roosevelt and a Grotonian—was greeted warmly and instructed to pull a chair up to the bed. For the next two hours, Churchill slipped in and out of a doze as he listened to Roosevelt telling a story. When the CIA officer had finished, Sir Winston sat up and addressed him. "Young man," he declared, "if I had been but a few years younger, I would have loved nothing better than to have served under your command in this great venture."[1]

The story Kim Roosevelt told that afternoon—of his recent partic-ipation in a coup d'état that had deposed the nationalist prime minis-ter of Iran, Mohammed Mosaddeq, and empowered the Iranian shah, Mohammed Reza Pahlavi—was indeed a thrilling one. Roosevelt had slipped into Iran on July 19, 1953, and hidden away in hills just outside Tehran. From there he had directed local American and British agents as they fomented disturbances on the streets of the Iranian capital. He also persuaded the initially hesitant shah to sign royal decrees replacing Mosaddeq with a pro-Western general, Fazlollah Zahedi. But the prime minister had uncovered the scheme on August 15 and the shah had fled the country, leaving Zahedi hiding in a Tehran basement. Undaunted, Roosevelt carried on with the plot, rallying Zahedi's supporters in the Iranian military and orchestrating a new wave of street protests. Eventually, on the morning of the nineteenth, violent demonstrations and an army mutiny combined to force Mosaddeq from office. Zahedi emerged from hiding and an emotional shah returned to his palace. There, at a secret midnight meeting, he raised a glass to Roosevelt, tell-ing him, "I owe my throne to God, my people, my army—and you!"[2]

Small wonder that Winston Churchill was enthralled.

Roosevelt received a similar reception when he returned home to the United States. During a recitation of his report on the coup to a group of senior officials in Washington, he noticed that Secretary of State John Foster Dulles was "purring like a giant cat." US leaders were delighted with what they perceived as a stunning victory in the Cold War. By the following year, 1954, when a similar operation culminated in the overthrow of the nationalist president of Guatemala, Jacobo Árbenz Guzmán, the CIA-instigated coup was firmly established in the official American mind as the preferred method of dealing with unde-sirable foreign leaders. Not only was it cheaper than overt, military means of regime change, it also enabled US officials to preserve "plausible deniability," that is, the ability to disclaim involvement in any given foreign intervention at a time when the combined circumstances of the Cold War and decolonization made it vitally important to avoid the appearance of imperialism. Working in league with local allies and surrogates, the CIA enabled successive American presidents to conceal their engagement in overseas regime change from communist rivals, postcolonial populations, and anti-imperial US citizens alike.[3]

Or such, anyway, was the theory. In practice, of course, American involvement rarely stayed a secret, not least in Iran, where memories of August 19, 1953 (28 Mordad in the Iranian calendar), remained a cause of powerful resentment against the United States for years afterward. In the minds of many Iranians, Mosaddeq was a national hero for having dared to defy Western imperialism, and his downfall was a tragedy, not a cause for celebration. Had they witnessed Kim Roosevelt's meeting with Winston Churchill, these Iranians might have interpreted it not, as Roosevelt remembered it, as "a most touching occasion," but rather as the moment when an old imperial adventurer passed the mantle of empire to a young pretender.[4]

Why, despite their history of anti-imperialism, did Americans engage in covert regime change in Third World countries such as Iran? How did CIA operations like the one commanded by Kim Roosevelt work, and why did his succeed when, as we will see, other, later ones failed? And what were the consequences of covert regime change not just for Iranians but also for other inhabitants of the Global South, the United States, and, finally, the CIA itself?

As the intimate scene in the Downing Street drawing room suggests, the answer to these questions lies not only in the immediate context of the Cold War but also in the longer arc of imperial history.

Few had foreseen the CIA's future as a scourge of Third World nationalists when it was founded in 1947. Most officials involved in the Agency's creation interpreted its functions as strictly limited to intelligence—observing the world, not trying to change it. Several had even objected to the notion of the US government engaging in covert action at all. Sherman Kent, for example, warned that the conduct of "black" operations "not only runs directly counter to the principles upon which our country was founded but also those for which we recently fought a war."[5]

But the rapid post–World War II deterioration of US-Soviet relations soon put paid to this self-restraint. A combination of anti-communist government officers led by the State Department Russia hand George F. Kennan and influential OSS veterans such as Allen Dulles urged the launch of offensive "political warfare" against the Soviet enemy. Invoking a vague clause in the 1947 National Security Act, which authorized the CIA to perform "other functions and duties related to intelligence affecting the national security," officials redefined the Agency's mission to include covert action and granted it new access to secret government funds.[6]

By 1948, the CIA was intervening extensively in Western Europe to thwart possible Soviet gains there, most dramatically in Italy, where "influence" operations were credited with securing the defeat of communist candidates in crucial spring elections. There were also missions—most, it has to be said, disastrous failures—to infiltrate émigré agents behind the Iron Curtain with the aim of sabotaging the governments there and "rolling back" the Soviet empire. The outbreak of war on the Korean peninsula in 1950 heralded the spread of CIA rollback operations into Asia, with communist China and North Korea now the targets. As in Western Europe, the Agency also ran election influence operations in post-occupation Japan, working with graduates of the imperial intelligence academy, the Nakano School.[7]

For all these interventions in the Cold War heartlands of Europe and Asia, the US government at first proved surprisingly reluctant to employ its new covert capabilities on the geostrategic periphery, in regions historically dominated by the European colonial powers. President Harry Truman was naturally suspicious of secret government power and disinclined to authorize new covert operations (years later, he confided to an interviewer that he had come to think of his creation of the CIA as a "mistake"). There was also a widespread view in the Washington foreign policy establishment, including within the CIA itself, that the United States should avoid doing anything that smelled of Old World colonialism. Indeed, some officials thought America ought to be backing nationalist movements *against* the European powers, if only because colonialism bred poverty and instability, conditions on which communism thrived. Hence, when in 1952 UK representatives first proposed a scheme for overthrowing Mohammed Mosaddeq after he had nationalized Iranian oil fields previously under British control, the Truman administration demurred. America was a friend, not a foe, of Iranian nationalism.[8]

The most obvious reason the United States ended up siding with the British in Iran—the first of many such CIA interventions in the decolonizing world—was the 1952 election of Dwight D. Eisenhower as president. Unlike Truman, Ike was a fan of covert action. As Supreme Allied Commander, he had seen it work during World War II, and now looked to it as a way of averting open warfare with the Soviet Union (a nuclear power since 1949). Top members of Eisenhower's national security team shared this preference: Ike's pick as Director of Central Intelligence, Allen Dulles, and the new secretary of state, John Foster Dulles. A corporate lawyer like his brother, and an even more devout anti-communist, Foster Dulles detested Third World leaders who resisted Western political and economic control. Their reluctance to line up with the West in the Cold War made them, in his binary world-view, the moral equivalent of communists. For Dulles, the CIA's covert powers were a conveniently flexible and disavowable means of dealing with such leaders, much more effective than the traditional diplomatic methods of his own State Department.[9]

But the US government's new willingness to intervene in the post-colonial world was not just down to anti-communism. Also in play was a factor one historian has termed the "Empire Trap": American corpora-tions pressuring elected officials into overthrowing Third World leaders who threatened their access to valuable local resources. The most obvious example of this effect was the 1954 coup in Guatemala. Jacobo Árbenz's land reform program threatened the hugely profitable banana-trading operations of the United Fruit Company, which hired Madison Ave-nue public relations experts to lobby the White House for his removal (although, in truth, they did not have to push that hard, as several mem-bers of the Eisenhower administration, including both Dulles brothers, already had business ties to the company). The threat to US corporate interests in Iran was less obvious than in Guatemala, but even there American oilmen disliked the example that Mosaddeq's nationalization of British-controlled oil fields was setting in the wider Middle East and petitioned the State Department to intervene against him.[10]

This is not to say that US corporations were behind every such move. There were interventions in Third World countries where there were few American economic interests at stake, and there were not interventions in others where local nationalists had already expropri-ated US holdings. Even in the cases just mentioned, in Iran and Guate-mala, there was little evidence of a *direct* relationship between business lobbying and official actions. Indeed, during the early 1950s, United

Fruit executives grumbled that the White House was cutting them out of decision-making about Guatemala. One member of Árbenz's cabinet reckoned that, as he put it later, "they would have overthrown us even if we had grown no bananas."[11]

Still, even when direct corporate lobbying, the Empire Trap, was not an immediate factor, wider economic considerations were. To return to the case of Iran, Mohammed Mosaddeq's nationalization of Iranian oil reserves in 1951 might not have endangered US industrial operations directly, but it was nonetheless concerning to interested American observers on several levels, both economic and strategic. By depriving Britain of a major source of cheap oil, Mosaddeq's actions weakened the economy of the United States' most important ally in the Cold War. The resulting British embargo on the Iranian oil industry in turn undermined the stability of Mosaddeq's government, thereby opening the country and its hugely valuable petroleum reserves up to possible annexation by its northern neighbor, the Soviet Union. More generally, Third World economic nationalism of the sort exemplified by Mosaddeq simply did not fit with US visions of the post–World War II global order. Americans saw US leadership of the "Free World" as involving a global commitment to defending free market exchange. According to this view of the world, the emergence of closed trading blocs such as the communist powers—and now, possibly, the postcolonial nations too—posed a strategic threat not only to US interests but to world peace as well. In a way, then, the 1953 US intervention in Iran was economic imperialism—but in a grander, more geostrategic sense than is implied in the scenario of the CIA leaping into action at the bidding of a particular corporation.[12]

This combination of motives reflected the particular geopolitical moment of the early Cold War era, but it was not without historical precedent. Earlier empires had behaved similarly, Britain especially. In the nineteenth century, exponents of the doctrine of "free trade" had argued that the British Empire existed in part to promote and protect international commerce. "It is the business of Government to open and secure the roads for the merchant," stated the arch-imperialist prime minister Lord Palmerston, a formulation that might just as easily have been uttered by a US politician in the 1950s. For that matter, the British had felt much the same set of fears as the Americans about "Persia," as they knew Iran, since the 1800s. The Russians, so they too believed, coveted both the country's oil and access to a warm-water port in the Persian Gulf so that they could realize their wider imperial ambitions. The Iran crisis of the 1950s was in this regard a direct continuation of the Anglo-Russian Great Game.[13]

If the United States' motives in the Cold War bear comparison with those of earlier empires, so too do US methods. Granted, the emphasis on covert action was somewhat novel. The British and the others had not faced the same constraints that bound the Americans after 1945: new international norms against interventionism, the fear of triggering a nuclear world war, and the rise of decolonization. It had therefore been less costly for them in reputational terms to carry out overt interventions—what Palmerston had called "gunboat diplomacy." Also, the United States had its own history of engaging in covert regime change, having occasionally resorted to the tactic in its traditional sphere of influence, Latin America, when overt military measures seemed inadvisable. For that matter, the brief surge of US overseas imperialism that took place around the turn of the twentieth century had begun with a coup: the 1893 overthrow of the Hawai'ian monarchy following plotting by local American businessmen and the US minister John L. Stevens.[14]

But covert regime change was far from being a uniquely American phenomenon. The British too had secretly plotted with local allies to get rid of undesirable foreign leaders on several occasions, some of them critical moments in British imperial history. In eighteenth-century India, Robert Clive of the East India Company (the prototype of the politically domineering corporation) laid the foundations of the British Raj by scheming with native bankers to depose the nawab of Bengal. The nawab's defeat at the Battle of Plassey in 1757, an event celebrated in Britain as a heroic imperial victory, was in essence a "palace coup." Similarly, in 1839, in an opening gambit of the Great Game, the British had intrigued to replace the uncooperative emir of Afghanistan, Dost Mohammed, with the more biddable Shah Shujah Durrani (a move that ended in the disastrous British retreat from Kabul in 1842).[15]

Nor were the Americans alone among Western nations in using such tactics in the Cold War–era Third World. The old European powers, seeking to maintain their imperial influence and grandeur even as they shed their colonies, resorted to coups constantly. The French sanctioned over a dozen military takeovers in Francophone Africa from the 1960s to the 1980s. Charles de Gaulle even established a special office in the Elysée Palace under the powerful presidential advisor Jacques Foccart to manage French-African affairs. Meanwhile, the British maintained their imperial influence in the Arab states of the Persian Gulf via a series of palace coups. The Cold War generation of Americans might have been distinctive in its attachment to covert regime change as a method of foreign intervention, but it was by no means exceptional. The technique had a prior and concurrent European imperial history. It was part of the imperial repertoire.[16]

Finally, in addition to these comparisons, there was a direct connection between the US turn to covert action during the Eisenhower era and an old imperial power—a point best made by reintroducing the young CIA officer who secretly visited Number 10 Downing Street in 1953.

There is a puzzle about Kim Roosevelt's involvement in the 1953 Anglo-American coup operation against Mohammed Mosaddeq. During World War II, while serving in the Office of Strategic Services, Roosevelt had worked in Cairo alongside several local mish kids, descendants of the large missionary community Americans had established in the Middle East during the previous century. In the process, he had absorbed some of the key values that together made up a distinctive sort of American "Arabism": respect for Arab culture, skepticism about European colonialism, and opposition to the founding of a Jewish state in Palestine. Returning home after the war, Roosevelt set about promoting these principles to a domestic American audience, trading skillfully on the cachet of his family name. He lectured widely, helped organize a series of pro-Arab, anti-Zionist advocacy groups, and in 1949, the same year he joined the CIA as chief of the Near East division in the Agency's covert operation wing, the Office of Policy Coordination (OPC), published a book outlining the Arabist case, *Arabs, Oil, and History*. In it, he argued that the United States, still a relative newcomer in a region previously dominated by Europeans, should ally itself not with the old colonial powers, nor with the new state of Israel, but rather with the democratic Arab nationalist movement. Any other approach risked squandering the considerable goodwill toward the United States that the missionaries had built up in the Middle East and creating a strain of virulent anti-Americanism in a strategically vital part of the world. "The danger of Russia versus the United States . . . is the seen danger,"

Roosevelt wrote, in an eerily prophetic passage. "The danger of Orient versus Occident seems as yet unseen; it could be ruinous; we may succumb to it from not seeing."[17]

In short, Roosevelt was a supporter of Arab nationalism and critic of European colonialism. What, then, was he doing in 1953 working with the British to overthrow the Iranian nationalist Mosaddeq?

The answer lies, in part at least, in the circumstances of Roosevelt's life prior to his wartime service in Cairo. Born in 1917, Kim Roosevelt grew up in Oyster Bay, New York, almost literally in the shadow of the home of his grandfather, Theodore Roosevelt. TR was a good friend of Rudyard Kipling, whose novel *Kim* inspired the nickname that would stay with the young Kermit into adult life. Indeed, Kim Roosevelt identified so completely with Kipling's boy spy hero that he once pretended to an elderly tutor that he actually *was* Kim, describing scenes from a "(wholly imaginary) childhood in India" while occasionally "throw[ing] in a phrase in Hindustani."[18]

If his grandfather was one imperial influence on the imagination of the young Kim Roosevelt, his father, also named Kermit, was another. A renowned hunter, explorer, and amateur spy (he was a member of the Room, the society espionage ring run by Vincent Astor), the elder Kermit resembled nothing so much as the hero of a John Buchan story. Kim Roosevelt was, as he recalled later, "brought up" on his father's stories of his "fabulous, adventurous trips," including a famous father-son expedition Kermit and TR had undertaken up the Amazonian "River of Doubt" in 1913–1914. In search of further adventure during World War I, Kermit joined up with the British to fight the Ottomans in Mesopotamia (Iraq). Returning via Cairo, he befriended T. E. Lawrence, and the two men carried on a correspondence after the war (like Lawrence, Kermit published a memoir of his Middle Eastern experiences, *War in*

Kermit "Kim" Roosevelt, CIA Arabist and latter-day imperial adventurer.
Library of Congress

the Garden of Eden). At the same time, Kermit was also corresponding with his father's friend Kipling.[19]

Even Kim's mother, Belle Wyatt Willard, boasted familial links to the imperial past. Her father, Colonel Joseph E. Willard, had fought in the Spanish-American War, commanding a company of troops from the family estate in Fairfax County, Virginia (which was the site of an OSS training camp during World War II). Later, her sister married George Herbert, Fifth Earl of Carnarvon, the English peer who excavated Tutankhamun's tomb in the Valley of the Kings and died shortly after, supposedly from the "Curse of King Tut." For young Kim, there was practically no escaping British imperial and Orientalist influences—or

"The Lure of the East," as he entitled a poem he contributed to a boys' magazine at age fifteen.[20]

It was perhaps inevitable, therefore, that after completing his education at Groton and Harvard, Kim Roosevelt should himself have gone off in search of overseas adventure, joining first the OSS and then, after a few years spent writing and publicizing the Arabist cause, the CIA. In appearance, he did not look especially dashing—of middling build and balding, he was described by another "Kim," the Soviet mole Kim Philby, as "pleasant and unassuming" in manner, "the last person you would expect to be up to the neck in dirty tricks"—but, if anything, this seems only to have increased his appetite for strenuous travel and physical danger. So too, possibly, did the rather suffocating domesticity of American family life in the post–World War II era: Kim Roosevelt had a wife, Mary Lowe "Polly" Gaddis Roosevelt, and four young children at home, whom he regularly left behind as he went on CIA missions abroad.[21]

This is not to say that Roosevelt abandoned his Arabist values altogether after joining the CIA in 1949, trading them for imperial exploits like the Iran coup. Indeed, there are tantalizing hints that his Near East division had advance knowledge of and possibly even gave some logistical support to two *nationalist* coup plots in Arab countries: in Syria in 1949, and in Egypt in 1952. Moreover, after the 1952 Egyptian Revolution, Roosevelt pushed for a US policy of supporting the "Free Officers" who had deposed the British client king Farouk, and in particular their emergent leader and rising star of the Arab nationalist movement region-wide, Gamal Abdel Nasser. In the summer of 1953, ironically enough, at almost exactly the same moment he was carrying out the Iran coup, Roosevelt sent an undercover CIA team to Cairo to "coup-proof" the new Egyptian government. In addition to training and equipping the Free Officers' security forces, the Agency team educated Nasser and his colleagues in the latest US public relations techniques (James Eichelberger, the head of the CIA Cairo station, was a former advertising executive). Reflecting their boss's Arabism, the CIA men also developed intimate, soldierly friendships with their Egyptian partners.[22]

But Iran was not an Arab country. Whatever his sympathies for the nationalist struggles of the Arabs, Kim Roosevelt seems to have viewed Iranians through an imperial lens inherited from the British. His impressions of Mohammed Mosaddeq, for example, were classically Orientalist. The "wily" prime minister "was like an ill-tempered, erratic old peasant, . . . judging all problems from his emotional standpoint," Roosevelt wrote later, ignoring the fact that Mosaddeq was an Iranian aristocrat who had received an elite education in Europe. "His great strength lay in his ability to mesmerize crowds," Roosevelt continued. "His wild exaggerations . . . led his listeners into almost insane hysteria." Like Orientals everywhere, Iranians were irrational, unmanly, and slavish—traits that made them, in Roosevelt's analysis, susceptible not just to demagogues like Mosaddeq but also to external manipulation by the Russians.[23]

It was views such as this that made Iran into an ideal environment for Kim Roosevelt to indulge his inherited love of imperial adventure—a playing field for another round of the Great Game, but this time with the Americans replacing the British as the principal Western players.

In 2017, after many years of delay, the US government released to the public a cache of previously classified records documenting the CIA's involvement in the 1953 Iranian coup. Among other things, the newly available documents revealed that Kim Roosevelt's negative assessment of conditions in Iran was not universally shared within the Agency. To-gether with some field officers on the ground in Tehran, analysts in the Directorate of Intelligence thought it unlikely that the country would succumb either to a Soviet invasion or to a takeover by the Iranian communist party, the Tudeh. (This estimate is, incidentally, borne out by recent findings in Russian archives, which suggest that Soviet leaders in fact regarded Mosaddeq as a bourgeois American puppet and the Tudeh as too weak to threaten his premiership.)[24]

The same CIA records, however, also reveal not only how deeply wedded Kim Roosevelt was to his more alarmist interpretation of conditions in Iran, but also how important his personal influence was as a driving force in US planning for the 1953 intervention. As early as March 1951, for instance, when the Truman administration was still trying to maintain a neutral position in the Anglo-Iranian oil dispute, Roosevelt could be found advising Allen Dulles (then the CIA's covert action chief, the deputy director for plans) on the need for "vigorous action" in the face of a possible "total collapse of the present government." Dulles, a Roosevelt family friend, fellow lover of Kiplingesque adventure, and founding member of the Cold War imperial brotherhood, did not need much persuading. On May 9, mere days after the shah had appointed Mosaddeq prime minister, the veteran spy told a CIA director's meeting that "only one thing could save the situation in Iran, namely to have the shah throw out Mossadeq [*sic*]."[25]

Soon after Kim Roosevelt issued his dire warning in March 1951, the Office of Policy Coordination's Near East division was running TPBEDAMN, a multipronged covert operation designed to counter the perceived communist threat to Iran. Again, US government documents released in 2017 tell the story. Local BEDAMN agents organized violent anti-communist demonstrations and counterdemonstrations, the latter staged to look like they had been planned by the Tudeh so as to discredit it. They also interfered in 1952 elections to the Majlis, the Iranian parliament, and cajoled populist religious leaders such as Ayatollah Abolqasem Kashani to declare themselves against the Tudeh.[26]

Although Roosevelt reckoned BEDAMN a "conspicuous operational success," he still feared that such measures might not avert Iran's fall to communism. Starting in August 1951, the Office of Policy Coordination ran a second, contingency operation: the creation of a "stay-behind" network capable of carrying out a guerrilla resistance campaign against a future Soviet-backed regime in Tehran. By March 1953, the powerful Qashqai tribe in southern Iran had committed to providing 20,000 fighters to this force, and the CIA had stockpiled sufficient matériel to provision a guerrilla army of 14,000 men for half a year.[27]

The BEDAMN and stay-behind operations were targeted directly at the communists. Increasingly, though, Roosevelt and Dulles focused their attention on the man whose behavior seemed to them to be opening Iran's door to communism: Mohammed Mosaddeq. The new documents show that the CIA was actively considering plans for regime change in Tehran as early as August 1952. That month, oil industry executive Max W. Thornburg—an old business associate of Dulles's whom the CIA deputy director consulted frequently in this period, ahead of the Agency's own analysts—came forward with a proposal for a military coup led by the shah. Responding to Thornburg's plan in September, the head of the OPC's Iran desk, John H. Leavitt, affirmed the notion of an army plot, to be carried out, if necessary, without the shah's approval.[28]

The problem with such proposals at this stage was twofold. First, the Truman administration was still hopeful of a diplomatic solution to the Anglo-Iranian oil dispute and therefore unlikely to support a direct move against Mosaddeq. Second, even if given the green light, the CIA was short of local allies to pull off such an operation. As several Agency reports regretfully noted, the BEDAMN agent network and the Qashqai tribe were willing to fight the communists but were either too anti-British or too pro-Mosaddeq to switch targets.

Both these obstacles were removed, almost simultaneously, in November 1952. First, the election of Dwight Eisenhower raised the prospect of a new administration more favorable to covert action against unwanted Third World leaders. Then, in the same month, UK officials appeared in Washington, bringing with them a proposal for a joint anti-Mosaddeq operation (code-named, not very subtly, BOOT) that would utilize Britain's extensive Iranian intelligence assets. The British, it turned out, had been plotting to remove Mosaddeq ever since his appointment in 1951 but, with all UK citizens having been expelled from Iran the previous month for anti-government activities, now needed US support to carry out their plans. Later, the MI6 Tehran station chief Christopher "Monty" Woodhouse admitted that he had carefully avoided any suggestion in these talks that the United States was "being used to rescue Britain's oil interest," emphasizing instead "the anti-Communist element in our plans," a stratagem the British would use with increasing frequency in the coming years when dealing with their American allies.[29]

Kim Roosevelt was in London around the time of the Washington meeting, returning home from a trip to Tehran, but MI6 made sure to rope him into the discussions. "Roosevelt was quickly seen as an important ally in our plans," Woodhouse explained later. "Like his grandfather, and also his father, he had a natural inclination for bold and imaginative action, and also a friendly sympathy with the British." Although Woodhouse did not note it, this "sympathy" had an intimate, familial quality. During visits to London, Roosevelt would stay at the Chester Square home of the Herberts, the aristocratic family into which his maternal aunt had married. When he later referred to MI6 officers as "our cousins," he meant it almost literally.[30]

Although many State Department officials and, indeed, several CIA officers remained opposed to the idea, the basic elements of the 1953 Anglo-American coup plot were now in place: the CIA's BEDAMN and stay-behind operations, and MI6's anti-Mosaddeq agent network. Following a confrontation between the Iranian prime minister and the shah in February 1953, and further pessimistic briefings by Allen Dulles (now Director of Central Intelligence), in March President Eisenhower indicated his approval. By this point, the coup plotters had agreed on a replacement for Mosaddeq—Fazlollah Zahedi—and nominated Kim Roosevelt as the operation's field commander. During meetings in Washington, London, Beirut, and Cyprus, where MI6 had set up an Iranian base in exile, US and UK officials hashed out details of the coup plan, now code-named TPAJAX. After both Winston Churchill and Dwight Eisenhower granted formal authorization in July 1953, Kim Roosevelt traveled to Lebanon and prepared to enter Iran.

Reading Roosevelt's later account of what followed next, a memoir entitled *Countercoup*, it is difficult to avoid the impression that the young CIA officer regarded the Iran coup as basically a romantic imperial adventure in the Kipling and Roosevelt family tradition, with him as its hero. As he got ready to leave Lebanon, he recalled what his father, Kermit, had written of a joint hunting expedition with his own father, TR: "It was a great adventure, and all the world was young!" He entered Iran without bothering to disguise his identity, showing his passport to an immigration official who erroneously transcribed as his name one of Roosevelt's notable features (an appropriately heroic one): "Mr. Scar on

Right Forehead." Other Iranians reminded Roosevelt of characters in *Kim*: some bearded, wandering tribesmen, for example, conjured up the Afghan horse-trader and British agent Mahbub Ali. The Kiplingesque connotations of the Great Game were echoed by the actual games, especially card games, that Roosevelt played in his hillside hideaway outside Tehran as he orchestrated AJAX. Even the operation's "theme song," a tune that he played constantly in the run-up to the coup, was about gambling: "Luck Be a Lady Tonight," from the musical *Guys and Dolls*.[31]

If anything, the game-playing increased after August 15, when the first coup plot was exposed. The response to this setback in both Washington and London was to declare the operation a failure and withdraw. Sherman Kent's Office of National Estimates described recent developments as a "crippling blow," and the State Department declared its unwillingness "to become associated with the reckless backing of a hopeless cause." Kim Roosevelt, though, had other ideas. True, a military coup as originally planned was no longer feasible—but the plotters still had an ace up their sleeves, the decrees signed by the shah dismissing Mosaddeq and appointing Zahedi. These meant that by continuing in office Mosaddeq was acting unconstitutionally. Supported by the British from their base on Cyprus, Roosevelt now turned what had been a military plot into a political warfare operation, publicizing the decrees, rallying his agents, and stimulating public unrest in an effort to force a constitutional crisis between the shah and his prime minister.[32]

By this point, Roosevelt had also ceased reporting to Washington. Although he claimed later that this was because he was so busy, another explanation is that he was deliberately avoiding communications with headquarters in case they contained orders calling him home. A recently declassified CIA message from the Tehran station to Washington of August 17 reveals the extraordinary degree to which

Agency officers in the field were now dictating US Iranian policy. "Dept. of State policy can only end in loss of Iran," it reads. "Recommend in strongest terms CIA express firm belief in constitution policy of opposition. In long run that policy will be vindicated or all lost." If Roosevelt's earlier actions had recalled T. E. Lawrence's struggle trying to reconcile his sympathy for Arab nationalism with his function as an imperial agent, now the American was acting more like the Frenchman Hubert Lyautey, taking advantage of his distance from the metropole to make up colonial policy on the spot.[33]

When the order to stand down eventually did arrive on August 18—the British base on Cyprus reputedly having held it up to allow the Americans in Tehran time to improvise—Roosevelt simply ignored it. A colleague later remembered him reading the cable, then saying, "No—we're not done here." The second stab at regime change came early the following day, 28 Mordad. Its astounding success meant that when Roosevelt returned home to a hero's welcome, he did not have to answer for what could have been interpreted as an act of gross insubordination. Instead, he joked about it. "Gentlemen," he told the September meeting where Foster Dulles purred like a cat, "I made a point of not letting you know what was happening." According to an internal CIA historical study, this statement met with "general applause."[34]

Kim Roosevelt's behavior in Iran was, admittedly, a rather extreme case of CIA game-playing. Other officers displayed less appetite for imperial intrigue. Roger Goiran, for example, chief of station in Tehran, quit his post just before the 1953 coup because he regarded the plot against Mosaddeq as, according to an anonymous CIA colleague, "putting U.S. support behind Anglo-French colonialism."[35]

Ultimately, though, it would be Roosevelt's adventurist impulse that won out. The irony was that only four years earlier, in his book

Arabs, Oil, and History, Roosevelt himself had distinguished between two Western approaches to the Middle East: an "imperial relationship" of the sort practiced by the European powers, based on "political domination and economic exploitation," and "another relationship," modeled on private American citizens' prior engagement with the region, "based on common interests, to be advanced without unfair advantage to either side." If there was a particular moment when the United States abandoned the second approach in favor of the first, it was August 1953.[36]

Three years after Iran, in 1956, the Anglo-American alliance that had propelled the operation against Mosaddeq suffered a shocking setback. Responding to another Middle Eastern nationalization, this time of the Suez Canal by Gamal Abdel Nasser, the British hatched a plot with the French and Israelis to attack Egypt, seize back control of the canal (Britain's "lifeline of empire"), and depose Nasser. Launched in late October, this brazenly imperial action took place against a background of Cold War tension caused by the brutal Soviet suppression of a popular revolt in Hungary and on the eve of a US presidential election. The Americans were understandably furious with their allies' disregard for the new international presumption against overt intervention. "What the hell is going on?" Dwight Eisenhower asked Prime Minister Anthony Eden during a telephone call on November 4. Faced with the threat of US economic sanctions, the British and French withdrew and Eden resigned in disgrace. The days of imperial European meddling in the Middle East and beyond were over at last.[37]

Or so it seemed. Despite a brief post-Suez burst of popularity in the Third World, America had not in fact thrown in its lot with the forces of anti-colonialism. The previous year, in April 1955, a conference of nationalist leaders at Bandung, Indonesia, had signaled the emergence of a "non-aligned" movement of postcolonial nations intent on preserving their independence from the Cold War superpowers. A few months later, in September 1955, one of the conference's most visible attendees, Gamal Nasser, signed an Egyptian arms deal with Soviet-controlled Czechoslovakia, enraging John Foster Dulles and bringing an end to the Eisenhower White House's flirtation with Arab nationalism. (The CIA coup-proofing mission in Cairo was already faltering due to the mixed messages Washington was sending the Egyptians and a growing suspicion on Nasser's part that Kim Roosevelt was secretly plotting against him the way he had against Mohammed Mosaddeq.) Then, in February 1956, in the same speech in which he famously denounced his predecessor Stalin, Soviet leader Nikita Khrushchev proclaimed a new communist determination to compete with the United States for leadership of the decolonizing world.

Confronted with these challenges, the Eisenhower administration doubled down on its earlier policy of covert cooperation with the European colonial powers. Unsurprisingly, this rapprochement took place through clandestine channels. Washington and London established secret "working groups" of senior officials charged with devising common approaches to pressing security issues, with spies such as Kim Roosevelt featuring prominently. As in Iran, British leaders were not above massaging American fears of communism or sentimental appeals to the "special relationship" to secure US support for UK colonial interests. Harold Macmillan, the new British prime minister, and the son of an American mother, prided himself on his clever handling of Britain's transatlantic "cousins."[38]

The result was a surge of US covert action in the Global South, starting in 1957 with a regime change operation aimed at the leftist government of Syria. The former French colony had witnessed a series of coups since acquiring independence in 1946, including a 1956 Anglo-American plot called off at the last moment because of the Suez crisis. This latest operation, run by a veteran of AJAX, Howard "Rocky" Stone, involved a cabal of exiled conservative politicians and junior army officers. The following year, 1958, the action shifted from the Middle to the Far East and the site of the 1955 Bandung conference, Indonesia. The country's charismatic president Sukarno, a hero of the successful Indonesian struggle against Dutch colonialism, had antago- nized John Foster Dulles with his "neutralist" position in the Cold War. In the largest such operation to date, the CIA assembled a small navy, air force, and rebel army of some 10,000 troops to topple him. By the end of the decade, the Cold War was spreading to another new region, the rapidly decolonizing continent of Africa. In 1960, the CIA set out to remove Patrice Lumumba, the young nationalist leader of the newly independent Belgian Congo. The vast, mineral-rich central African state appeared in danger of collapse, and the Agency actively consid- ered assassination as a means of eliminating Lumumba. In all of these operations, the Americans received extensive logistical and other sup- port from the old European colonial powers, especially the British.[39]

This time, however, none of the schemes worked as planned. In August 1957, Syria's security service exposed the "American plot"— one of Howard Stone's collaborators in the Syrian army turned out to be a government informer—and expelled Stone along with several US diplomats. In Indonesia, the hoped-for mutiny in the military failed to materialize and Sukarno actually benefited from psychological warfare measures intended to discredit him. In one notorious instance, the CIA had sponsored the production of a pornographic movie featuring an actor made up to look like the president. Rumor had it that the movie backfired because Indonesians were so impressed by the virility of the Sukarno look-alike. In the Congo, various schemes to assassinate Patrice Lumumba, one involving a kit made up of native African poisons, came to naught—although Lumumba was eventually murdered, in horrific circumstances, by rival Congolese and Belgian soldiers in January 1961.[40]

Increasingly error-prone and sordid though the regime change operations of the late Eisenhower era were, the biggest failure was yet to come. In 1959, a group of young guerrillas led by Fidel Alejandro Castro Ruz seized power from Cuba's corrupt dictator, Fulgencio Batista. At first many Americans were charmed by the romantic revolutionary Castro and his bearded followers, but as he began confiscating US property, then requested Soviet aid, the romance soured. At the behest of the Eisenhower administration, the CIA started making plans for his removal. These drew heavily on the Agency's earlier operation in Guatemala and involved many of the same personnel. But the covert techniques that had worked against Jacobo Árbenz—the military training and arming of opposition elements, propaganda, and intimidation—failed to dislodge Castro. Consequently, by the time a new president, the Democrat John F. Kennedy, entered the White House in January 1961, CIA planning had shifted from the relatively light touch shown in Guatemala to preparations for a full-scale invasion code-named ZAPATA. Kennedy wanted to be rid of Castro as much as his predecessor had, but he was, if anything, even more conscious of the need to preserve plausible deniability. Hence when in April 1961 a task force of anti-Castro Cuban émigrés ran into trouble trying to land on a beach in the Bay of Pigs, the president refused to order up additional US fighter planes to protect it, effectively abandoning the men to their fates. Whereas the failures of Syria and Indonesia barely impinged on the American consciousness, the Cuba debacle became a national and international news story.[41]

The immediate cause of the CIA's failure in Cuba—a stark contrast with its earlier success in Iran and Guatemala—was JFK's reluctance to authorize the air cover needed to defend the invasion force. But the fact that overt military support was needed at all speaks to a deeper issue: ZAPATA was not working as a *covert* operation. Why not? In part, it was problems internal to the CIA that were to blame. The aging Allen Dulles was withdrawing from the day-to-day management of the organization, and the demands of waging the rapidly globalizing Cold War were stretching some of his deputies to breaking point (former Office of Policy Coordination chief Frank G. Wisner was literally driven mad by the pressures of the job). The growing emphasis within the CIA on covert action as opposed to intelligence analysis—its founding mission, lest it be forgotten—was another factor. In an echo of the earlier division over Iran between the covert operatives and the analysts, Agency management was so busy concocting regime-change plots against Castro that it neglected the relatively mundane but vital task of assessing actual political conditions on the ground in Cuba.

Had the CIA's leaders been paying more attention, they might have realized that Cuba's political environment was fundamentally different from that of Iran or Guatemala. The Cuban operation was premised on the hope that the invasion force of émigrés would be greeted by a local uprising against Castro, as had occurred in Tehran. However, there was little evidence of anti-Castro sentiment among ordinary Cubans. If anything, they appeared to be rallying in support of their nationalist leader as evidence of US hostility toward him mounted. Unlike the Guatemalan Jacobo Árbenz, a cautious intellectual by temperament, Castro was a man of action, full of swagger and bombast—and therefore less likely to suffer a loss of nerve in the face of US pressure. He had also taken steps to coup-proof his revolutionary government, cracking down ruthlessly on dissenters and purging his army of opponents. It helped that he was getting advice from a comrade who had personally witnessed the Guatemalan coup: his Argentinian-born second-in-command, Ernesto "Che" Guevara.

In other words, a necessary precondition for successful CIA regime change seems to have been the existence of powerful local groups or institutions—the shah and his supporters in Iran, say, or the army in Guatemala—capable of mobilizing against the leader whom the Agency was seeking to remove. Absent such local allies, the constraints imposed on the CIA by the doctrine of plausible deniability rendered it all but useless. The British, long used to controlling distant territories through indigenous agents, understood these limits on the efficacy of covert action. Several UK officials attempted to warn their US counterparts about the dim prospects for success in Cuba in the run-up to the Bay of Pigs. "After all, we have been through it all ourselves," as Harold Macmillan pointed out to Dwight Eisenhower.[42]

This realization raises an intriguing question. When CIA interventions did end in success, was it really the Agency that deserved the credit (or blame, depending on one's perspective)? In the last few years, some historians have argued that the CIA was in fact a bit player in such events and that the principal architects of regime change were to be found in the Global South itself, among colonial and conservative elites. Take, for example, the 1954 Guatemala coup. In addition to offending the United States with his land reforms and other left-wing policies, Árbenz had antagonized powerful locals such as Guatemalan landowners, anti-communist army officers, and Catholic bishops. According to the new interpretation, the main impetus for the

1954 coup came from these institutions and individuals, not the CIA. Indeed, in an echo of British tactics in the Middle East, conservative Central Americans deliberately played on Washington's fear of communism to enlist its support in their campaign against Árbenz. Not only was the CIA's contribution secondary, it was also sometimes comically inept, as when Agency-owned planes accidentally bombed a radio station near Guatemala City owned by American missionaries.[43]

Writing in a similar vein, some scholars have even called into question the authorship of the prototypical CIA coup operation: Kim Roosevelt's triumph in Iran. In several books and articles published since 2010, the CIA plays only a marginal role in the tumultuous events of 28 Mordad. The spark for the violent street demonstrations that culminated in the fall of Mosaddeq, these studies argue, came rather from traditional Iranian elites alarmed by the drift of events under the nationalist prime minister. Foremost among these were senior Muslim clerics who feared that anti-shah elements such as the Tudeh posed a threat to Islam as well as the monarchy. According to this revisionist version of events, Roosevelt's actions in the days after the first coup plot had been detected were aimed less at having a second go at regime change on August 19, as he subsequently claimed, than at activating the CIA's stay-behind networks as part of an Agency withdrawal from Iran. These measures had little to do with what happened on 28 Mordad but later allowed Roosevelt to claim credit for Mosaddeq's overthrow.[44]

There is some substance to this revisionist argument. As his reporting after August 19 indicated, Kim Roosevelt was not averse to depicting the operation as a spy thriller with himself in the starring role. In later years, British intelligence officers who had laid the groundwork for the coup, as well as CIA colleagues who participated in its planning, would chide Roosevelt for slighting their contributions. Also, the operation would clearly not have succeeded without the involvement of several key Iranians: the shah, who precipitated the crisis when he signed the royal decrees dismissing Mosaddeq from office on August 13; Fazlollah Zahedi, who led anti-Mosaddeq elements in the Iranian army and emerged from hiding on 28 Mordad to take over as prime minister; and even, arguably, Mosaddeq himself, who failed to act decisively in the face of the mounting threat to his government and made several critical errors of judgment on the day of his overthrow. Moreover, the recently released US government documents confirm that there were indeed Shiite clerics among those conspiring against the nationalist prime minister. These included popular leaders capable of summoning crowds, such as Ayatollah Abolqasem Kashani and Ayatollah Mohammed Behbahani. The notion that Kim Roosevelt turned up in Tehran and engineered Mosaddeq's downfall on his own—the dominant narrative not only in CIA mythology but also in popular left-wing understanding of the coup—is obvious nonsense.[45]

But to depict the coup as a purely Iranian event is also a mistake. There is simply too much evidence of US involvement to support such an interpretation. The shah had initially been reluctant to move against his prime minister, for fear of provoking a republican backlash, and only agreed to do so after being subjected to relentless pressure by Roosevelt. Likewise, it was Roosevelt who decided when Zahedi should leave his hiding place on August 19 and take to the radio announcing that he was assuming power. Among the newly available CIA documents are some suggesting that the Agency even provided secret funds for Ayatollah Behbahani, and possibly for Ayatollah Kashani as well, to mount street protests against Mosaddeq as part of the massive campaign of political warfare being waged by Roosevelt. Revisionist scholars, some obviously motivated by hostility toward Iran's current religious leadership, have been too quick to discount such evidence in their rush to reassign responsibility for the coup from the CIA to the ayatollahs.[46]

In the final analysis, the CIA's victory in Iran was the product of a combination of moves by American, Iranian, and—earlier—British actors, with covert Western support providing conservative local elites with a crucial margin of advantage in a domestic power struggle.

Another way of saying this is that the 1953 coup operation was a fairly typical imperial arrangement.

Although a furious John Kennedy threatened to "splinter the CIA into a thousand pieces" and Allen Dulles was forced to resign as DCI, otherwise the Bay of Pigs had few immediate consequences for the Agency. Like so many men of his class and generation, JFK nursed a boyish fascination for spies—he loved Ian Fleming's James Bond novels, for example—and his administration continued to reach for the CIA as its preferred weapon in what was now becoming a personal vendetta against Fidel Castro. At the direction of Attorney General Robert F. Kennedy, the president's brother, the Agency entertained a series of far-fetched proposals for doing away with the Cuban—rigging seashells on his favorite diving beach with explosives was one—some possibly suggested by Ian Fleming himself during a Georgetown dinner party.[47]

The campaign against Castro was just the tip of a Kennedy-era iceberg. The CIA plotted to assassinate another Caribbean leader, Rafael Trujillo, whose corrupt dictatorship appeared to be inviting the communization of the Dominican Republic (although, as in the case of Patrice Lumumba, it was not directly involved when Dominican dissidents killed Trujillo in 1961). On the South American mainland, where British Guyana was preparing for national independence, the Agency mounted an influence operation via US labor organizations against the Marxist premier Cheddi Jagan, who was eventually replaced in 1964. The same year, following a similar campaign of psychological warfare in Brazil, a military coup overthrew the constitutional but leftist government of President João Goulart. In relative terms, Kennedy presided over more covert operations in Latin America than Eisenhower had. Older imperialists such as the British were impressed, although they could not resist teasing their American cousins about their earlier sympathy for Third World nationalism. As Harold Macmillan admitted, "It is . . . rather fun making the Americans repeat over and over again their passionate plea to us to stick to 'Colonialism' and 'Imperialism' at any cost."[48]

The same pattern—of presidents having personal reasons to resent the CIA yet nonetheless continuing to use it as, in effect, a secret army—would carry on into the 1970s. Richard Nixon detested the Agency as "a refuge for Ivy League intellectuals" yet gladly availed himself of its covert capabilities, even as he implemented an overt foreign policy of détente with the Soviet Union. In Latin America, the focus of US attention shifted to the so-called Southern Cone, where the CIA carried out influence operations against the Marxist president of Chile, Salvador Allende Gossens (although it was local actors within the Chilean military who eventually overthrew Allende in a 1973 *golpe*). Elsewhere, in the decolonizing world, CIA operations rushed to fill the power vacuum left by the departing Europeans. In Indochina, the Agency intervened constantly in the former French colonies surrounding the war-torn nation of Vietnam in an effort to produce pro-Western governments there. And in one of the last colonies anywhere to acquire its independence, the oil-rich central African state of Angola (previously a possession of Portugal), it fought a particularly vicious "brush war" with supporters of the new nationalist, Soviet-backed government in Luanda—a war soon joined, in the increasingly complex Cold War geopolitics of the day, by Cuba and South Africa.[49]

But it was not until the 1980s, and the arrival in the White House of the unreconstructed Cold Warrior Ronald Reagan, that presidential support for covert operations reached its zenith. On the campaign trail, Reagan had denounced détente and pledged to "unleash" the CIA against the Soviets. Once in office, he placed the Agency under OSS veteran William J. Casey, a throwback to the Allen Dulles "Golden Age." The buccaneering Casey faced a much more restrictive domestic environment than earlier directors: new laws curbing secret government powers, and a less supportive national media. But he cleverly circumvented these obstacles by farming out covert operations, some to government proxies like the charming but mendacious National Security Council staffer Colonel Oliver North, others to external surrogates: private contractors, mercenaries, and foreign intelligence services. By dint of this strategy, Bill Casey's CIA was able to take the lead in an operation originally launched under the previous president, Jimmy Carter: the covert support of mujahideen rebels resisting the Soviet occupation of Afghanistan. Closer to home, in Central America, Casey oversaw a massive, largely illegal effort to overthrow the left-wing Sandinista government in Nicaragua by funding anti-government rebels known as the Contras.[50]

The Contra supply program proved to be the last big CIA regime-change operation of the Cold War era. There had been some impressive Agency victories, to be sure: in Iran, Guatemala, and Afghanistan, where the mujahideen helped compel the withdrawal of Soviet forces in

1989, contributing to the dissolution of the Soviet Union itself in 1991. Through the efforts of officers such as Kim Roosevelt, the CIA was able to accomplish important US strategic goals at a fraction of the financial, reputational, and human costs of conventional military warfare.

But there were many failures as well. Various factors—bureaucratic flaws, the near impossibility of maintaining operational secrecy, and the unpredictability of conditions in the target countries themselves—all meant that the odds were stacked against covert action from the start. After surveying the whole range of US regime-change attempts during the Cold War, including overt military operations, one political scientist has concluded that covert methods worked just 39 percent of the time, as opposed to the 66 percent success rate of overt interventions. The cold statistics hide the often terrible human costs of such failures: the death of hundreds of Cuban émigrés at the Bay of Pigs, for example, or the capture and execution of American mercenaries in Angola (CIA officers rarely suffered such fates themselves). Abortive regime-change operations also often had the paradoxical effect of strengthening the foreign governments concerned, as citizens closed ranks around their embattled leaders, and local security services adopted new measures to avert future coups.[51]

Even CIA successes carried hidden costs. Perhaps the least of these were institutional, affecting the US foreign-policy-making process. Iran and Guatemala encouraged a view among American officials of covert action as a magic bullet. Why bother with diplomacy when one could call up the CIA? This tendency demoralized the US Foreign Service and bred tension between it and the Agency. Foreign leaders were not sure who really represented the views of Washington at the US embassy—the ambassador or the CIA station chief? Even the Agency itself suffered from the unrealistic expectations of successive Cold War presidents, who were angry when operations went wrong—but not so angry that they stopped wanting more. Over the course of the Cold War, several different CIA directors tried to rein in the covert-action side of the Agency and reprioritize its original mission of intelligence analysis. But they all failed. The lure of quick-fix ops proved too strong.

If the cult of covert action was damaging institutionally for US foreign policy, for the nations at the receiving end it was devastating. CIA-backed coups produced repressive regimes, typically military dictatorships, that guaranteed US interests at the expense of their citizens' human rights, economic well-being, and in some cases lives. Consider the most "successful" regime-change operations of the Cold War. In Iran, the shah used his restored monarchical powers, which included the services of his CIA-trained secret police, the SAVAK, to suppress all political opposition. Not content with repealing Jacobo Árbenz's land reforms, Carlos Castillo Armas, the colonel who took over in Guatemala after the 1954 coup, suspended the country's constitution and murdered his political opponents, before himself falling to an assassin's bullet in 1957. In Chile, after Salvador Allende took his own life during the *golpe* of 1973, a junta led by General Augusto Pinochet Ugarte killed at least 3,000 citizens, detained and tortured tens of thousands more, and forced over 200,000 into exile.[52]

The use of the CIA was meant to hide the US hand in this carnage. In reality, the Agency's involvement was an open secret. Various parties helped make it so. Leaders of targeted governments protested signs of US interference on international platforms such as the United Nations or, in the wake of a failed operation, mounted show trials of captured American agents. Communist propagandists were quick to seize on any hint of US covert action, especially the Agency's growing use of mercenaries (or "hired killers," "fascist cutthroats," and "thugs," as they were described). Often, the CIA's own agents gave the game away, especially émigrés such as the Cubans who participated in the Bay of Pigs operation, a notoriously loose-lipped bunch. By the time of the 1980s operation in Afghanistan, covertness had become a sort of charade, acknowledged as such by all sides.[53]

The combined effect of the widespread devastation and open secrecy was to make the CIA into possibly the most infamous organization on the planet. Commentators throughout the Global South denounced its covert influence in the world, sometimes even alleging plots where none existed. This conspiracism was particularly pronounced in postcolonial nations where the old imperial powers had used intelligence as a primary means of colonial governance. In India, for example, Prime Minister Indira Gandhi, whose family had been subject to constant surveillance and harassment by the British intelligence services, saw the CIA's hand everywhere. Fanned by communist propaganda and opportunistic local politicians, this obsession became so widespread that Indian intellectuals joked about it. "How is it that the poet got no applause when he recited his poem on the stage?" asked one contributor to a Hindi literary magazine. "Why is [there] so much tension [between] husband and wife? . . . This is all due to the secret operations of the CIA."[54]

But this was not the only continuity from earlier empires. So too was another consequence of covert US interventionism: a revival of anti-colonial nationalism of the sort that had existed during the age of European imperialism but now was directed at the United States instead. Across the postcolonial world, repressive governments installed as a result of CIA regime-change operations engendered profound resentment toward America—and nowhere more so than in the scene of the CIA's first successful coup plot, Iran.

The irony is that Kim Roosevelt had seen it all coming. Soon after AJAX, the hero of Tehran began to develop regrets about the lessons the Eisenhower administration was taking from his victory and turned down an invitation to lead the nascent Guatemala operation. "Now we'll think we can walk on water, everywhere," he warned the same meeting of officials where he had noticed John Foster Dulles purring. As Dulles reversed his earlier policy of support for Arab nationalism and its unofficial spokesperson Gamal Nasser, Roosevelt's unhappiness grew. The CIA had been working to strengthen Nasser's hold on power in Egypt, yet now was being instructed to take down nationalist governments in the Arab world. This was "bad policy," according to Roosevelt, "adventurist" and "intolerable": "You can't go around overthrowing any government at will." Although he did not face charges of being "more Arab than the Arabs," Roosevelt now found himself in a position reminiscent of T. E. Lawrence's after World War I, watching in dismay as the postwar settlement betrayed the Arab cause.[55]

By December 1957, Roosevelt had seen enough. He resigned from the CIA, going to work first for Gulf Oil, then for his own Middle East consultancy business, liaising between US corporations and Middle Eastern leaders such as the shah. He filled his leisure time with travel, tennis, and hunting—and regaling private audiences with anecdotes about his involvement in the 1953 coup. Usually a "very quiet, private person," he would, so his son Jonathan remembered later, become quite "garrulous" on the subject of Iran. It was his signature Roosevelt family story, his own Spanish-American War or River of Doubt expedition, a true Kipling adventure.[56]

Quite why Roosevelt chose 1976 as the year to start writing a book about the coup is not clear. It might have been that he wanted to repair his reputation following press allegations that he had improperly used his CIA connections in his consultancy work, or that his judgment was impaired by recent heart surgery. Whatever the reason, his timing was disastrous. For one thing, the literary marketplace had changed since T. E. Lawrence and Kim's father, Kermit, had achieved celebrity with their World War I memoirs. In the world of spy thrillers, for example, stories of imperial romance were giving way to more "realistic" espionage novels like John le Carré's claustrophobic, bureaucratic fictions of double agents, cynicism, and betrayal.

More importantly, Iran itself was by now in a state of upheaval. The brutal repressiveness of the monarchy, widespread poverty, and the rise of Islamic fundamentalism were creating a perfect storm of revolutionary conditions. In back of it all was many Iranians' belief that the shah's rule was illegitimate, a neocolonial imposition. Not all of this was down to the 1953 coup but, even after a quarter of a century, the overthrow of Mosaddeq was still a cause of boiling nationalist anger. Why else were anti-shah protesters chanting the former prime minister's name and waving placards bearing his image?

Roosevelt's book project soon ran into problems. First, the shah himself, nervous about its possible impact in Iran, objected to his portrayal in several passages of the manuscript after Roosevelt had shown them to him, holding up publication. Next, Roosevelt got bogged down in the CIA's publication review process, forcing further delays. Then, the British weighed in, with MI6 demanding the deletion of any material acknowledging its part in the coup. At this point, Roosevelt hit on the idea of simply replacing MI6's name with that of the Anglo-Iranian Oil Company (AIOC), the British-government-controlled company that had effectively managed Iran's oil industry. Roosevelt's memoir at last appeared in print in the fall of 1979—but then British Petroleum, as the AIOC was now named, appeared on the scene threatening libel action, causing the publisher, McGraw-Hill, to pulp the first print run.[57]

The final published version of *Countercoup* did not appear until September 1980. By then, of course, the shah had fled into exile, Ayatollah Khomeini had declared Iran an Islamic republic, and protesters had overrun the US Embassy in Tehran, taking its occupants hostage. The Iranian Revolution transformed the reputation of the 1953 coup, once reckoned a Cold War victory for the United States, into a classic case of "blowback"—the term used by CIA officers to describe the unintended adverse consequences of earlier operations. Not surprisingly, many reviews of Roosevelt's memoir took this transformation as their central theme. The Iran expert Richard Cottam (earlier a consultant for the CIA) assailed the book as an "outrageous" tale of "individual adventurism." Intelligence commentator Thomas Powers lamented the "golly-gee-whiz air" that pervaded it. As Kim Roosevelt himself wrote in a rueful foreword uncomfortably acknowledging recent developments in Iran, "What was a heroic story has gone on to become a tragic story."[58]

The blowback was personal, too. If Kim Roosevelt's intention in writing *Countercoup* was to secure his place in history, as *Seven Pillars of Wisdom* had for T. E. Lawrence, he must have been sorely disappointed. If anything, the book had the opposite effect, tarnishing his reputation for the remainder of his life. When Roosevelt died in 2000, all his obituaries remarked on his role in the Iran coup and its unwanted aftereffects; few noted his support for Arab nationalism or his efforts to build up the Egyptian leader Gamal Nasser, an operation that had consumed much more of his time and energy.

Roosevelt himself had ensured that his name would forever be associated with regime change rather than regime maintenance. The latter practice, no less important as a CIA technique for spreading US power in the postcolonial world, would instead be identified with another "legendary" member of the Agency's founding generation. His story, like Roosevelt's one of early success followed by tragic failure, takes us from the Middle to the Far East and the scene of America's worst Cold War defeat, a former French colony in Indochina.

CHAPTER 3

Regime Maintenance

If any CIA officer of the Agency's founding generation obtained celebrity comparable with that of the imperial heroes of an earlier age, that officer would be the counterinsurgency expert Edward Lansdale.

Lansdale's legend began almost as soon as he started serving in the CIA in 1949 under the cover of his rank as a US Air Force colonel, the result of some clever self-boosterism (he had earlier worked as an advertising executive) and his undeniable success helping the newly independent government of the Philippines defeat a communist insurgency. By the time he moved to his next assignment, coup-proofing the embattled regime of South Vietnam's anti-communist premier, Ngo Dinh Diem, his growing legend had moved beyond government circles. Some identified him as the inspiration for Alden Pyle, the American anti-hero of Graham Greene's 1955 Vietnam novel *The Quiet American*, although both he and Greene subsequently denied the link. There was, however, no question that he was the model for Edwin Barnum Hillandale, a much more likable character in William J. Lederer and Eugene Burdick's best-selling *The Ugly American* (1958), a thinly fictionalized depiction of the US effort to "win hearts and minds" in Cold War Asia. Hillandale is a maverick Air Force colonel who does many things that Lansdale was reputed to have done in real life, such as turning up in remote villages and befriending the locals by playing the harmonica. Later, after it became clear that Lansdale's counterinsurgency efforts in Vietnam had failed and he had retired from government service, came another wave of publicity, some of it less positive. His name featured prominently in the Pentagon Papers, the cache of Defense Department documents about the Vietnam War leaked to the *New York Times* in 1971 by military-analyst-turned-whistleblower Daniel Ellsberg (earlier, a member of Lansdale's coup-proofing team). Lansdale and his supporters responded with some publicity of their own: his memoir *In the Midst of Wars*, published in 1972, and an authorized biography by historian Cecil Currey subtitled *The Unquiet American*, which appeared in 1988, a year after Lansdale died from a heart ailment. As recently as 2018, the military historian Max Boot published another admiring biography, *The Road Not Taken*, proposing Lansdale as a pioneer of the sort of population-centric counterinsurgency that, Boot suggests, the United States should be carrying out in the twenty-first century.[1]

Admittedly, none of this attention is on the same scale of celebrity as that achieved by T. E. Lawrence or Hubert Lyautey: there were no statues of Lansdale or feature films based on his life (although characters resembling him did wander into several movies, about which more later). Also, Lansdale himself likely would have rejected any comparisons with the heroes of earlier Western empires. He explicitly described his approach to counterinsurgency as anti-imperial and claimed that what he was doing in the postcolonial world was both original and distinctively American.

Nonetheless, as a review of Lansdale's life and career makes clear, the echoes of earlier imperial heroism were there, not just in his personal legend, with its peculiar, Lawrence-like blend of covertness and publicity, but also in his practice of counterinsurgency, which in several crucial respects harked back to the kinds of colonial pacification campaigns waged by the likes of Lyautey and Ralph Van Deman in the age of the New Imperialism.

Indeed, the whole history of CIA regime maintenance points toward something about the doctrine of counterinsurgency that is rarely acknowledged by those who still advocate for it today: it is imperial through and through.[2]

In fairness to Lansdale, there was plenty about his early life and career to suggest that his approach *was* different, not just from that of earlier European colonials but also from that of CIA contemporaries such as Kim Roosevelt and other members of the Cold War imperial brotherhood. Born in Detroit in 1908 to Christian Scientist parents, Edward Geary Lansdale grew up in financially precarious, peripatetic circumstances, worlds removed from the secure, privileged origins of most first-generation CIA officers. Young Ed eventually fetched up on the West Coast, where he attended the University of California, Los Angeles, then later went to work for a San Francisco advertising agency. If this background was a far cry from the Groton set's, so too were Lansdale's easygoing California manner and his rejection of Old World, imperialist attitudes. Even as a young man, he was conspicuous for refusing to join in with other white Americans' denigration of non-whites, Asians especially. As he later told an interviewer, "I was first of all an anti-colonial."[3]

There was, though, one respect in which Lansdale was typical of his CIA generation: his ardent patriotism and belief in the universality of American ideals. From a young age, he loved to read early US history and was fond of quoting Tom Paine: "Wherever freedom is not, that is my country." During World War II, heeding the same call to national service as his Grotonian contemporaries, he signed up for Bill Donovan's Office of Strategic Services, a good organizational fit for his irreverent, freewheeling style. When the OSS was disbanded at the war's end, he moved over to Army intelligence (G-2) in the western Pacific, assigned to the Philippines, just liberated from Japanese occupation. Now in his late thirties, Lansdale already resembled his later (and rather barbed) description as yet another fictional character, the General, in Norman Mailer's 1991 CIA novel *Harlot's Ghost*: "mild, pleasant, soft-spoken, and not bad-looking—a long, straight nose, good dimpled chin, . . . mustache—but . . . hollow eyes."[4]

Arriving in Manila in 1945, Lansdale found himself part of a crucial test of American power in the postwar world. US rule of the Philippines was just about to end in what Americans regarded as a textbook example of peaceful decolonization, a lesson for the European colonial powers and a "showcase of democracy" for other Asian nations. The problem was, not all Filipinos agreed. Many peasants resisted the corrupt and oppressive policies of the landlord class that had helped run the colony for Washington before the war and then, during it, collaborated with the Japanese. Soon after liberation, the communist-led Hukbalahaps mounted an insurgency against the government of President Manuel Roxas, who, along with his successor, Elpidio Quirino, responded with a clumsy mix of harsh military repression and unfulfilled promises of land reform. By the time of Edward Lansdale's arrival, Americans faced a dilemma in the Philippines: how to quell the Huks while maintaining their image as friends of Philippine nationalism.[5]

It was not long before Lansdale came up with a solution. Leaving Manila behind, he headed out into the rural stronghold of the Huk insurgency in central Luzon island. There, he set about converting rebel peasants into loyal citizens, not by lecturing them about the errors of communism but rather simply by smiling, listening, and sharing his cigarettes and beer. To win over younger villagers, he enlisted the seductive power of American popular culture, using a mobile projector to show Disney movies. The children "ate it up," he recorded in his diary, "inching along the floor until they could get right up to the screen." Lansdale never learned to speak Tagalog, getting by on guileless displays of friendship that contrasted with the overbearing manner of European colonials. It undoubtedly also helped that he had a local guide on his dangerous forays into the countryside: Patrocinio Yapcinco Kelly, a young Filipina widow who became his lover shortly after they met in 1946.[6]

Word of Lansdale's unusual methods soon spread in official Philippine and US circles. In 1947, the Supreme Commander for the Allied Powers in Japan, General Douglas MacArthur, placed him in charge of publicity for the US occupation forces throughout the region. Having already moved from his berth in the Army to the Air Force in search of a less regimented environment, Lansdale landed in the CIA's swashbuckling covert action wing, the Office of Policy Coordination, in the fall of 1949—at just the moment Mao Zedong proclaimed the People's Republic of China, raising US fears of communist-led peasant insurgencies spreading across the whole of Asia.

The United States needed local allies capable of countering this threat and, at least in the Philippines, it found one. Having returned home from Asia, Lansdale was in Washington, DC, in March 1950, when he met a visiting Filipino congressman, Ramon Magsaysay. A vigorous forty-three-year-old former auto mechanic, Magsaysay was drawing flattering comparisons with the Philippine president, the older, infirm Elpidio Quirino. At Lansdale's urging, officials in the Truman administration leaned on Quirino to appoint Magsaysay his defense secretary, making him Washington's point man in the campaign against the Huks. In September 1950, Lansdale went back to Manila in the Joint US Military Advisory Group as, in effect, Magsaysay's personal advisor. The two men had by now developed an extraordinarily intimate, even brotherly relationship, eating, traveling, and bunking together. Meanwhile, Lansdale resumed his passionate affair with Pat Kelly. When Lansdale declared later, "Filipinos and I fell in love with each other," he meant it literally.[7]

For the next three years, Lansdale was in his element. In what would become a characteristic move, he assembled around him a small team of American advisors with a mix of unconventional skills, men like Charles T. R. Bohannan, an anthropology PhD and Army captain who had fought with Filipino guerrillas against the Japanese during World War II. Meanwhile, Lansdale urged Magsaysay to transform the Philippine army from an instrument of fear in the daily lives of ordinary citizens into a force for good, making "the soldier a *brother* of the people." The Filipino responded with a series of imaginative moves, including opening up army hospitals to civilian casualties and providing free legal advice to tenants in disputes with their landlords. In one particularly famous initiative, the Economic Development Corps (EDCOR), Magsaysay ordered army units to clear land in the jungle so that former anti-government insurgents could set up protected farming communities there. By 1951, it seemed that Lansdale's "civic action" operations were working. Under Magsaysay, the Philippine army was building a political base for the government; Huk morale was sagging and defections growing. News of Lansdale's progress carried to Washington and beyond. Foreign officials began arriving in Luzon to observe EDCOR. Even the British, who faced a communist-inspired insurgency of their own in Malaya, sent a team.[8]

The legend of Edward Lansdale was born. But was it merited—did Lansdale's performance in the Philippines justify his reputation as the progenitor of a new, non-colonial, *American* kind of counterinsurgency?

To some extent, Lansdale was indeed channeling specifically American traditions of international engagement during his assignment in the Philippines. One of these was the long prior history of American missionary work in Asia. Religious, spiritual concepts permeated Lansdale's vocabulary; as Admiral Felix B. Stump, commander of the US Pacific Fleet, noted dismissively, "Oh, he just goes around preaching the gospel of love." The concept of international community development, of building nations from the grassroots up, was another powerful impulse in mid-twentieth-century US life, one that also animated idealistic foreign aid programs such as the Peace Corps. Cold War–era Americans felt an especially strong affiliation with Asia, which they expressed in sentimental, even familial terms of affection that defied the racist logic of Orientalist European attitudes. In one famous case, the wildly popular Rodgers and Hammerstein musical *South Pacific*, the story ends with its American heroine overcoming her racism and adopting her French lover's mixed-race children. With his unusual West Coast origins and anti-racist attitudes, Lansdale operated as a powerful vector of these missionary-descended traditions into the early CIA, where they competed with the influence of earlier Western imperialism.[9]

But not even Ed Lansdale could elude the imperial past altogether. After all, American civic action in the Philippines had a colonial as well as a missionary history dating back to 1901 when Governor Taft had inaugurated civilian rule of the islands. For one leading historian of US-Philippine relations, elements of Ramon Magsaysay's flagship program EDCOR, such as its core focus on landownership, came "direct from William Howard Taft's playbook." Both sides in the post–World War II Hukbalahap insurgency acknowledged this continuity. The Huks saw themselves as heirs to the Filipino revolutionaries of the turn of the twentieth century and branded the government agents of their day "running dogs of the American imperialists." Magsaysay himself told a US reporter, "We treat the people as you did when you came here to fight us in 1901." Lansdale, meanwhile, extolled the colonial education efforts of the Thomasites, the American teachers who had arrived in the Philippines during Taft's governorship. Unprecedented though they seemed, the CIA man's solitary expeditions into the Huk backcountry were redolent of colonial-era travels in Moro Province by John Pershing (of later Pancho Villa and World War I fame), who also bothered to learn the folkways and eat the food of the Muslim locals. Even Lansdale's talk of fraternal love had precedent in colonial history: Governor Taft had referred to his Filipino wards as "little brown brothers."[10]

Other features of Lansdale and Magsaysay's counterinsurgency operations were reminiscent of the darker, violent side of the earlier US occupation and European pacification campaigns of the New Imperial era. According to Lansdale team member Charles Bohannan, the postwar Philippine army contained a "Research and Development Unit" responsible for devising "dirty tricks" for use against the Huks, such as a double-barreled automatic carbine and a "home-made substitute for napalm." Some of its techniques were consciously borrowed from the Philippine Constabulary of the early 1900s, such as the deliberate "losing" of sabotaged rifle cartridges near enemy encampments that would blow up in the hands of any Huk who tried to use them. Another army unit, Nenita, a hunter-killer squad led by Lansdale's close friend Napoleon Valeriano, imitated the tactics employed by US forces in the days of Ralph Van Deman as they pursued insurgents across the Luzon countryside, including use of the "water cure" on Huk prisoners. Lansdale himself privately deplored the "cruelty and lust for murder" of Valeriano's men, but he spoke to other US officials of the need for tougher measures against the Huks, including the "more liberal use of napalm." This move from population-centric to "enemy-centric" counterinsurgency, from winning over peasants to killing insurgents, had happened earlier in imperial history, and not just in the Philippines. Half a century before, in Indochina and Africa, Hubert Lyautey had taken off his velvet glove to reveal an iron fist within.[11]

Even Lansdale's most intimate interactions with Filipinos had imperial undertones. His affair with Pat Kelly proved a long-lasting, mutually rewarding relationship, but it also evoked the colonial tradition of Western men seeking erotic adventure overseas. Lansdale was already married to an American woman, Helen Batcheller, whom he effectively abandoned for long periods to raise their two sons on her own while he traveled in Asia. The peculiarly intense male friendships Lansdale developed in the Philippines, although couched in an unmistakably twentieth-century idiom of slangy, tough-guy sentimentality, likewise echoed earlier relationships. In some respects, they conjured the classic US narrative of white and non-white men forming fiercely loyal friendships in an American frontier setting—Tom Sawyer and

Jim, say, or the Lone Ranger and Tonto—except here transposed to the undeveloped Philippines. But there were also hints of Hubert Lyautey or T. E. Lawrence and their search for homosocial comradeship in "the colonies," away from the emasculating domestic routine of the metropole.[12]

Above all, it was Lansdale's intimacy with Ramon Magsaysay that, for all its anti-racist outward appearance, evoked the colonial past. Close pairings of Filipino leaders and American officials had been a recurring theme of US-Philippine relations since 1898, most recently during the 1930s commonwealth period, when Douglas MacArthur (who also had a Filipina mistress) served as President Manuel Quezon's "military advisor." There was also a whiff about Lansdale of an even older figure in colonial history: the British political officer deputized to a princely ruler in the Raj, or the French proconsul ruling "with the mandarin," as Lyautey would have put it. To be sure, the American was, in keeping with his veneration for US democratic ideals, more concerned than his European predecessors with securing popular consent for indirect rule, hence his attraction to the thoroughly un-mandarin-like Magsaysay. Nevertheless, the parallels were there, especially with the Arabist imperial agents Britain dispatched to help establish the Hashemite kingdoms of the Middle East during the mandate period. It was no accident that journalists later took to calling Lansdale "Lawrence of Asia." Like the British Arabist, the American was known for living among "the natives," learning their ways, and leading them to victories they supposedly would not have managed on their own.

This is not to say that Magsaysay was merely a US puppet with Lansdale operating his strings. Like indigenous colonial agents before him, the Filipino brought his own agenda to his dealings with Americans, manipulating their fear of communism to gain their support while building up his position within local political circles. Despite his image as a reformer, Magsaysay was fundamentally a rather traditional Filipino politician. EDCOR was in this regard a fitting legacy of his time as defense secretary: for all its big reputation, it only resettled about 250 Huk families. Its fame was probably due mainly to an accompanying publicity campaign that drew on Lansdale's professional experience in advertising. Lansdale himself admitted that "EDCOR projects were part of these enlightened psychological operations."[13]

It was Lansdale's skills in psychological warfare that also account for his single greatest accomplishment in the Philippines. In 1953, having helped bring the Huks to the verge of defeat, the American set about taking the next step toward legitimizing the Philippine government in the eyes of its people: the election of a truly popular leader. In February, Magsaysay announced he was resigning from Quirino's cabinet and launching a bid for the presidency in elections due to take place in November. With the army and various civilian allies working to prevent Quirino from fixing the race, Lansdale channeled thousands of dollars of CIA funds into his friend's campaign, ghostwrote his speeches, and even helped arrange for the recording of a catchy election jingle, "The Magsaysay Mambo." Several parties voiced their opposition to this rather obvious interference: Philippine nationalists, Quirino supporters, and US Foreign Service officers who objected on principle to CIA king-making. Even the head of the Agency's Far East division had qualms about Lansdale overreaching. But none of it mattered. Between Lansdale's Madison Avenue know-how and Magsaysay's natural political talents, Quirino never stood a chance. Magsaysay won the November election with 68.9 percent of the votes cast, and Lansdale congratulated himself on helping to bring about "a social revolution which would have delighted Thomas Jefferson."[14]

"Colonel Landslide," as he now became known, returned in glory to Washington, where he received the National Security Medal, making him and Kim Roosevelt the only two CIA officers below the level of director so far to have received the honor. Back in the Philippines, the Huk leader Luis Taruc surrendered to government forces the following year, 1954. Lansdale had apparently "saved" the Philippines with a brand-new American version of counterinsurgency—but also with some older techniques borrowed from the imperial past. The last line of his report to CIA headquarters on the 1953 election operation rather gave the game away. "It was a privilege . . . to give the lie to the current adage that the white man is through in Asia," he wrote. "Hellsfire, we're just starting."[15]

The next Asian battlefield awaited him.

In May 1954, communist Vietnamese nationalists, the Viet Minh, overran the French garrison at Dien Bien Phu, bringing a bloody end to France's empire in Indochina. As elsewhere in the postcolonial world, there was a history of American sympathy for Vietnamese independence. During World War II, when Japan had occupied Vietnam, the OSS had supplied the Viet Minh and their leader, Ho Chi Minh, with arms and training. But by the early 1950s, other, more powerful considerations were in play. Washington needed France's support in the postwar effort to stop the spread of Soviet influence in Western Europe; like the British in the Middle East, the French cleverly portrayed the defense of their Indochinese colonies as vital to the Free World cause, pointing toward the weapons and training the Viet Minh were receiving from communist China; and US business interests feared the loss of Vietnamese mineral reserves and rubber. Strong though anti-colonial sentiment was in some American circles, it was offset by the residual influence of Orientalist French stereotypes about the Vietnamese as racially incapable of self-government. When the 1954 Geneva Accords split Vietnam along the 17th parallel into a communist-controlled North and non-communist South—supposedly a temporary arrangement, with national elections to reunify the country scheduled for 1956—US officials resolved on a two-track course of action: working covertly to overthrow the northern government while simultaneously coup-proofing the one in the South.[16]

But there was a problem: whereas the communist leader Ho Chi Minh was a national hero of the anti-colonial struggle, the southern government was still in the hands of the absentee French puppet emperor Bao Dai and his prime minister, Ngo Dinh Diem. In contrast with the charismatic man of the people Ramon Magsaysay, the corpulent Diem, a Catholic in a majority Buddhist society, looked every inch the colonial mandarin. South Vietnam was also an extraordinarily hard place to govern. In addition to the communist threat from the north, the French were lingering in the country, trying to bend the new government in Saigon to their will in another case of the "imperialism of decolonization," while in the countryside powerful religious groups and criminal organizations were competing for control of territory. Diem did have some advantages in the game of postcolonial Vietnamese politics. For all his shortcomings, he was a sincere nationalist with a clear personal philosophy, a mixture of political Confucian thought and modern Catholic theology. He was also a smart operator, skilled at playing rival Vietnamese factions off one another and appealing to American patrons he had courted during an earlier stay in the United States. But none of this necessarily made him a reliable agent of American interests: prior imperial history was littered with examples of clever colonial subalterns manipulating their supposed Western masters to their own ends.[17]

After the Philippines, only one person seemed equal to the task of coup-proofing South Vietnam. In May 1954, Director of Central Intelligence Allen Dulles sent orders for Edward Lansdale to report to Saigon, signing off (perhaps in a nod to Lansdale's missionary-like zeal), "God Bless You." The covert action expert arrived in Vietnam the following month and was soon followed, in a now familiar pattern, by a crack team of specialists operating under military cover, the Saigon Military Mission (SMM). Some members of the SMM, like the roguish French American Lucien E. Conein, focused on regime-change operations in the North. As an OSS officer, Conein had fought alongside Ho Chi Minh against the imperial Japanese. Now, he ran sabotage missions across the 17th parallel, some as far as the northern capital, Hanoi. Others devoted themselves to regime maintenance in the South. The Virginia-raised Rufus Phillips, a strapping, idealistic Yalie, headed into the countryside to help build roads and bridges, hoping through civic action to grow popular loyalty to Diem. A few operations combined the SMM's offensive and defensive functions. Calling again on his advertising experience, Lansdale mounted a psychological warfare campaign designed to scare northern Catholics into fleeing south to escape communist persecution. As well as undermining Ho Chi Minh's regime in Hanoi, the exodus helped swell support for Diem by increasing the ranks of southern Catholics.[18]

When not making psy-war, Lansdale got to work doing what he always did when he traveled: making friends. Shortly after his arrival in Saigon, he turned up unannounced at Diem's residence, bearing a memorandum entitled "Notes on How to Be a Prime Minister of Vietnam." (Such memos seem to have been a common technique of CIA coup-proofers in this period—Kim Roosevelt's CIA team in

Egypt wrote similar papers for Nasser and the other Free Officers.) Diem listened closely to the American's presentation (delivered via an interpreter—as in the Philippines, Lansdale never learned the local language, in this case Vietnamese) and then, in a slightly ambiguous gesture, tucked the document in his pocket. Thereafter, Lansdale became a frequent presence at Diem's side, often dining and sometimes even sleeping at the premier's palace. It was not yet the brotherly romance the American had enjoyed with Ramon Magsaysay—but it was a start.[19]

The Lansdale charm offensive now broadened to other targets. Shortly after setting up house in central Saigon, a few blocks from Diem's residence, the CIA man was throwing parties for the capital's power elite of generals and sect leaders. The unbuttoned atmosphere of these occasions—Lansdale would encourage guests to perform a Philippine bamboo dance, the *tinikling*, as an icebreaker—contrasted sharply with the formal black-tie functions hosted by the US ambassador. Lansdale never entirely won over Diem's prickly brother and advisor, Ngo Dinh Nhu, but this did not matter terribly, as Paul Harwood, covert action chief in the CIA's regular Saigon station, was already in close contact with him. The "love campaign," as Lansdale called it in an October 1954 report to Washington, had "started work[ing]."[20]

Lansdale was not being cynical when he talked about love; he meant it. "I found a warm brotherhood with a great host of people," he wrote later of his time in Vietnam, "an affectionate kinship with people I had once regarded as foreigners." As in the Philippines, there was an almost familial quality about the relationships Lansdale and his CIA colleagues formed with their Vietnamese hosts. In 1956, the American and his longtime Filipina mistress Pat Kelly vacationed with Diem, Nhu, and Nhu's wife, Trần Lệ Xuân (better known in the West as Madame Nhu), at a beach resort near Saigon. The women splashed

Counterinsurgency expert Edward Lansdale, in tropical dress uniform, attending Vietnamese National Day celebrations in 1956. The photograph was taken by his young CIA colleague and friend Rufus Phillips.
Rufus Phillips Collection, Vietnam Center and Sam Johnson Vietnam Archive, Texas Tech University

about in the waves while the American played Scrabble with Nhu and Diem dozed. Back in Saigon, Paul Harwood and his wife grew so close to Nhu's family that they served as confirmation sponsors to his daughter Le Thuy. Like Graham Greene's Alden Pyle, members of Lansdale's SMM team fell in love with and married Vietnamese women. Lou Conein met his Vietnamese French wife, Elyette Bruchot, at a cocktail party in Hanoi on one of his sabotage missions in the North. In the Americans' eyes, this was not sexual exploitation of the sort that happened under the French; it was true love.[21]

Lansdale abhorred European colonialism and advised members of his team to keep their distance from the French officials still in Vietnam. The latter returned his contempt with interest, wishing, so he suspected, "that a truck would run over me." The rivalry did eventually turn deadly. In June 1955, presumably in a botched assassination attempt, assailants shot a Frenchman who resembled Lansdale. Lucien Conein retaliated by lobbing bombs at French homes. Lansdale even suggested to Allen Dulles, apparently in all seriousness, that the CIA sponsor a "military coup in Paris, to make [a] lady out of [a] slut." The sexual metaphor, by the way, was telling. The French and Americans frequently resorted to the language of sexual competition in their clashes over Vietnam. An old French colonial once asked the hulking young Rufus Phillips, employing an image straight from the pages of *The Quiet American*, "How would you feel if you had a mistress, and you were very, very close to her. Finally, after this long relationship, you broke it off because really you couldn't afford to support her anymore. You're sitting in a sidewalk café, and . . . she comes roaring by in this Cadillac with this American. How would you feel?"[22]

Of course, Lansdale could not make his attempts at seduction of the Vietnamese too blatant. Doing so risked not just upsetting the French but also arousing Vietnamese suspicions that the United States was, for all its representatives' talk of anti-colonialism and love, really just another Western imperial power. To allay such concerns, Lansdale resorted to a tactic he had already used in the Philippines—the use of third parties and "front groups" to conceal official US sponsorship—but with a new spin, summed up in the phrase "Asiatics-to-Asiatics." Almost immediately after arriving in Saigon, he began arranging for teams of Filipinos and Filipinas to visit Vietnam so that they could forge new bonds of friendship with their fellow Asians and, at the same time, model the benefits of American tutelage. First to appear in October 1954, ostensibly under the auspices of the Philippine Junior Chamber of Commerce, was a volunteer group of doctors and nurses. The "happy and hardworking crew," as Lansdale described them, immediately set to work treating the thousands of Catholic refugees who had recently fled from North to South Vietnam (thanks in part to SMM propaganda). As an Operation Brotherhood statement explained, medicine was a "universal sign language" that transcended national borders by healing "common ties of suffering." Or, as Lansdale put it in a secret US government report, "The presence of medical personnel furnishes the ideal answer to . . . the initial suspicion that foreigners evoke."[23]

Widely regarded as a tremendous success, Operation Brotherhood inspired similar "nation-building" projects involving groups from the Philippines. Next to arrive was the Freedom Company, a team of army veterans of the counterinsurgency campaign against the Huks. With Lansdale and his old lieutenant Charles Bohannan in the background, the Freedom Company taught guerrilla and psychological warfare methods in South Vietnamese army training programs, creating in the process a network of pro-government, anti-communist officers united by ties of fraternal comradeship. In 1956, the same organization sponsored a visit to Saigon by Filipino lawyers tasked with educating the Diem regime in US constitutional principles such as the separation of powers. Here was Lansdale the psychological warrior at his cleverest, employing Asian nationals to spread American values and practices in the region while simultaneously preaching the principles of anti-colonialism and nationhood.[24]

But the most consequential nation-building operation of the era did not involve Asians, at least not directly. Starting on an emergency basis while Harry Truman was still president, then shifting onto a per-manent, more global footing under Dwight Eisenhower, the US gov-ernment was engaged in an ongoing effort to "modernize" civilian police forces in friendly nations facing anti-government insurgencies. Largely carried out on the ground by the CIA, this program, like earlier pacification campaigns conducted by the military, had two objectives: making police a visible and even welcome presence in the daily lives of citizens (like the Norman Rockwell image of a friendly American beat cop helping a runaway child) while, at the same time, building the repressive capacities of the government concerned.[25]

For expert assistance with this program, the CIA turned in a per-haps surprising direction: the American Midwest. Considered the birthplace of modern rural policing, the region boasted an institu-tion known in the criminal justice world as the "Police West Point," the Department of Police Administration at Michigan State University (MSU). In 1955, a team of MSU advisors and undercover CIA coun-terintelligence officers pitched up in South Vietnam to train Ngo Dinh Diem's provincial constabulary, the Civil Guard. They received a warm welcome. Diem had spent time working on the MSU campus during his stint in America and remained good friends with Wesley R. Fishel, a professor from the university's political science department. Vietnam now became the setting for one of the more curious US experiments in Cold War nation-building: a group of midwestern professors led by the former police chief of Kalamazoo shaping the South Vietnamese Civil Guard along the lines of a rural Michigan police squad.[26]

Using these and other more straightforward methods such as cajol-ery and bribery, Ed Lansdale and his CIA colleagues helped Diem cling to power during the precarious first years of his leadership. In the fall of 1954, Diem headed off an army mutiny; the following spring, he survived an uprising by religious sects and criminal gangs. Lansdale was also busy on another front, using CIA channels to negate possible opposition to Diem among his fellow Americans. When in April 1955 a presidential envoy sent to assess the premier's prospects for survival, General J. Lawton Collins, recommended that the Eisenhower administration end US support for him, Lansdale intervened on Diem's behalf with the Dulles brothers, and Collins's advice was disregarded. By the fall of 1955, Diem felt confident enough of his position to hold a referendum to depose the absent emperor, Bao Dai. Shortly after a landslide victory that echoed the Philippine election results of 1953, Diem proclaimed South Vietnam a republic and himself its president. It was clear by now that the national elections scheduled for 1956 would not take place; the temporary partition of Vietnam at the 17th parallel had become permanent. Lansdale left Vietnam in December 1956, having apparently coup-proofed another pro-American government in Asia.[27]

But to anyone inclined to look for them, there were already signs of trouble ahead. Lansdale wanted Diem to follow Magsaysay's example and build a popular following using democratic methods—to govern with love rather than rule by fear. The new president should ensure that elections were fair and proper, respect the rights of religious minorities, and wave at crowds as he passed by in his motorcade. However, the American's talk of egalitarianism and Jefferson did not impress Diem, whose instincts—now strengthened by his success at neutralizing his opposition—were more authoritarian. Far from rejoicing, Lansdale was dismayed by the scale of Diem's victory in the fall 1955 referendum—98.2 percent of votes cast—as it invited the suspicion that the poll was rigged. He was also disappointed when the president unveiled the constitution of the Republic of Vietnam, which, contrary to the recommendations of his Filipino lawyer friends, gave Diem the power to rule by decree for five years.

In fact, none of the CIA's operations in postcolonial Vietnam proved entirely successful. The US attempt to modernize the Vietnamese police force and make it an instrument of nation-building in the countryside was undermined by Diem himself, who was more interested in using the rural Civil Guard as a military force with which to terrorize his opponents. The front elements of the police training program were also causing problems, with some MSU professors complaining about the secret presence of CIA officers in their midst. Meanwhile, Lansdale's clever plan to enlist other Asians in the brotherly winning of Vietnamese hearts and minds butted up against some distinctly un-fraternal attitudes. Diem wanted humanitarian aid for Vietnam but not the Filipino personnel who came with it. As he explained to Lansdale, "The Vietnamese didn't need the help of a bunch of orators and nightclub musicians." The CIA man had failed to anticipate important national differences within the region, assuming that what had worked in one Asian country could simply be transplanted to another. For all his anti-colonial rhetoric, Lansdale was recycling colonial attitudes about a homogenous "Asiatic" character.[28]

Residues of the imperial past blighted other CIA operations in South Vietnam. Lansdale wanted to befriend the new nation's leader and educate him in what he regarded as the universal values of the American Revolution. But Diem, a dedicated Vietnamese nationalist, understandably resisted what he perceived as another uninvited Western imposition—although this did not prevent him from, in an old colonial maneuver, using US support to bolster his regime. The president's behavior found an echo in the response of Vietnam's rural poor to American civic action. "People in a deplorable situation unhesitat-ingly received the help," a Vietnamese student told a US aid worker, "but bitter experiences the French left behind still keep them suspect-ing the good will of another 'civilized' country from the West."[29]

No matter how much Lansdale personally deplored French colo-nialism, he could not evade its influence. Prior to the Viet Minh victory of 1954, US and French officials had collaborated on counterguerrilla programs in Indochina; even before that, during World War II, the French had been part of the OSS Jedburgh teams supplying resistance elements in France such as the rural maquis. Shortly after his arrival in Saigon, Lansdale himself was assigned to the Training Relations and Instruction Mission (TRIM), a joint Franco-American unit for training South Vietnamese troops. Service in TRIM exposed him and his SMM team to French colonial pacification techniques whether they liked it or not. Some did like it. Lansdale's French American second-in-command, Lou Conein, enthusiastically adopted the notion of mobilizing *mon-tagnards* in the Vietnamese highlands as an anti-communist guerrilla army, a sort of counter-maquis. (SMM participation in TRIM had one other baleful consequence: it enabled Pham Xuan An, a North Viet-namese agent who had penetrated the French army's general staff in Saigon, to spy on the CIA, too. On the surface a cheery, guileless per-sonality not unlike Lansdale himself, An was such an effective spy that Ho Chi Minh would reputedly exclaim on receiving his reports, "We are now in the United States' war room!")[30]

The list of colonial continuities goes on. The Lansdale legend was not confined to his admirers in the United States: a conspiracist version sprang up in Southeast Asia, where, like earlier colonial secret agents, he was credited with having an almost supernatural ability to influence the region's affairs. "His visits [to the region] have never been without consequence for the nations visited," noted a Cambodian newspaper in 1961. "Lansdale . . . is intelligent, very active . . . and dangerous." As in the Philippines, the SMM members' romantic and sexual relationships with Vietnamese women carried overtones of earlier, colonial liaisons, what the French had called *mariages à l'indigène*. Madame Nhu, herself the object of clichéd Orientalist fantasy (historian and Kennedy advisor Arthur M. Schlesinger Jr. described her as "lovely and serpentine"), conjured up this sordid past when she complained about "false brothers," foreigners who were using economic aid "to make lackeys of Vietnamese and to seduce Vietnamese women into decadent paths." Like CIA officers elsewhere in the postcolonial world, Lansdale and his men lived in colonial villas, spoke a colonial language ("bad French," according to Pham Xuan An), and even dressed like colonial officials. When a Saigon tailor made the young Americans of the SMM matching outfits suited to Vietnam's tropical climate, he included the khaki shorts and knee-length stockings of French colonial officers—whether in ironic jest or not is unclear. For good measure, Lansdale even recommended that new American arrivals in the country read the urtext of Anglo-Orientalism, Kipling's *Kim*, because (as he explained later) "Vietnam was so filled with the arcane."[31]

Perhaps none of this would have proved an insurmountable problem for the Diem regime had it not been for events occurring elsewhere. In North Vietnam, a southern-born ideological firebrand by the name of Le Duan was taking over the reins of power from the elderly Ho Chi Minh. Where Ho had prioritized the consolidation of the revolution in the North, Le Duan dreamed of a reunified Vietnamese nation under communist leadership. Pursuing a "South First" strategy, he dispatched cadres across the 17th parallel to organize an uprising in the southern countryside. In December 1960, an alliance of Diem's opponents created the National Liberation Front. The NLF became known in Saigon as the Viet Cong.[32]

Diem faced another threat to this regime but, unlike in earlier moments of crisis, he no longer had Edward Lansdale by his side. After returning home from Vietnam in late 1956, the American had moved from the CIA to a planning role in the Pentagon, where he remained for the next seven years, rising to the rank of brigadier general. Like Hubert Lyautey before him, he used this position to spread his unconventional warfare gospel in domestic circles, lecturing at staff colleges and promoting the cause of other believers such as a young Frenchman by the name of David Galula. In doing so, Lansdale was to some extent pushing at an open door. With Soviet premier Nikita Khrushchev promising Soviet support for "wars of national liberation," Washington proved highly receptive to counterinsurgency (COIN). When John Kennedy occupied the presidency in 1961, the White House became a sort of COIN think tank, devoting numerous task forces and study groups to the subject. There was even talk of sending Lansdale back to Saigon as US ambassador. JFK himself was a fan—before becoming president, he had sent copies of *The Ugly American* to his fellow senators. But Lansdale was less popular with other military and political leaders, who found his manner disrespectful and ideas eccentric. Indeed, there was something about Lansdale in this period of his career that echoed T. E. Lawrence after his return to England following World War I, when, despite his legend as "Lawrence of Arabia," many of his superiors regarded Lawrence as dangerously Orientalized. As Lansdale told a former CIA colleague, he "was cut completely out of any meaningful say on Asian affairs." Instead of Saigon, the Kennedy administration found an assignment for him heading up the psychological warfare campaign against Fidel Castro—an operation whose excesses would eventually embarrass all involved. With Lansdale increasingly out of the picture, other COIN strategists touted his doctrine, but now with less emphasis on civic action than on military force, as seemed to suit the deteriorating security situation in Vietnam.[33]

As Lansdale's star sank, so memory of his signal achievement, the defeat of the Huks and king-making of Ramon Magsaysay, faded, too. This was partly because Magsaysay himself had perished tragically in a plane crash in 1957. But it also reflected the eclipse of Lansdale's Philippine victory by another counterinsurgency case study, this one provided by an old imperial power. Since sending observers to the Philippines in the early 1950s, Britain had managed to suppress the communist rebellion roiling Malaya, employing a clever mix of precision military operations, nation-building civic action, and propaganda (the last, incidentally, handled by Hugh Carleton Greene, brother of Graham). The "Malayan Emergency"—a euphemism that echoed earlier British responses to colonial crises in India and Ireland—soon earned a reputation as a counterinsurgency master class. For Americans in particular, the British had achieved maximum effect with minimum use of force, precisely what was required of Western power in the postcolonial age, and Malaya overtook the Philippines as the preferred counterinsurgency template for Kennedy's COIN experts.[34]

Whether the British operation deserved this reputation is open to question. One historian has described the Malaya counterinsurgency as "nasty not nice," including as it did the coerced relocation of thousands of ethnic Chinese "squatters" to so-called New Villages, military camps surrounded by barbed wire and guard towers. Similar tactics were used more openly by the British authorities to put down another colonial rebellion of the era, the Mau Mau uprising in Kenya, a gruesome operation that tends not to feature in COIN textbooks. Still, the

Americans were entranced by Malaya—"the domino that stood," in Dwight Eisenhower's view—and made a point of seeking British advice about how to manage their own emergency in Vietnam. In 1961, Sir Robert Thompson, a veteran of the Malayan campaign and esteemed British COIN authority, arrived in Saigon on an advisory mission to the Diem government.[35]

Like many an imperial project before it, the Thompson mission did not achieve its intended effect. Diem borrowed some elements from Malaya, but he and his brother Nhu mistrusted Thompson's colonial background, and in any case had some counterinsurgency ideas of their own, which had already found expression in earlier resettlement programs in the Vietnamese countryside. These consisted of the Ngos' "personalist" Catholic philosophy and, perhaps surprisingly given their intense nationalism, tactics borrowed from Vietnam's colonial occupier, the French, dating back to the days of Joseph Gallieni and Hubert Lyautey. Particularly influential was a notion developed by the COIN theorist Roger Trinquier and applied in France's brutal and failing counterinsurgency campaign in its only remaining North African colony, Algeria: *hameaux stratégiques*, fortified villages intended to both defend and corral their inhabitants. Nhu used this concept as the centerpiece for a new program he was crafting to counter the Viet Cong insurgency, the "Strategic Hamlets."[36]

Predictably enough, the result was a mess. Launched in March 1962, the new counterinsurgency program was plagued by shoddy construction, poor security, and corruption. Hoping to redeem the early promise of Lansdalean civic action, former SMM member Rufus Phillips returned to Vietnam later in the year as the head of a new Office of Rural Affairs and was soon busy in the countryside introducing imported varieties of rice and a faster-growing breed of pig. But other

American officials scoffed at such measures, insisting that the correct response to the growing Viet Cong threat was military escalation.[37]

As for the Ngo brothers, they plowed ahead with the resettlement program, hoping that, if successful, it would free them of their dependence on US support. By July 1963, there were 7,200 strategic hamlets housing 8,737,000 South Vietnamese, roughly half of the country's population. The idea was that the new settlements would cut villagers off from the insurgency and grow loyalty to the government in Saigon. In fact, the opposite happened. Uprooted from traditional villages and forced into shantytowns surrounded by moats with wooden stakes, the peasants felt like they were in a new kind of colonial prison camp. The program was also riddled with North Vietnamese agents, who ensured that many settlements were sited in areas of Viet Cong strength, making them impossible to defend. If anything, the hamlets only demonstrated Diem's inability to govern South Vietnam without the help of an outside power.[38]

The relationship between Washington and Saigon was by now understandably frayed. It did not help that, much like Nasser and the Free Officers in Cairo a few years earlier, the Ngo brothers had begun to suspect that the CIA, having previously supported them, was now plotting to depose them. In 1963, after South Vietnam's large Buddhist community joined in the anti-government rebellion and the Ngos responded with another brutal government crackdown, Diem moved from the regime maintenance to the regime change column in America's Cold War playbook. When word reached Washington that generals in the South Vietnamese army were planning to overthrow the president, US officials indicated they would not stand in their way. In another echo of Nasser's Egypt and, for that matter, Mosaddeq's Iran, some CIA officers, such as the recently arrived Saigon station chief

John H. Richardson, opposed the move, either out of personal loyalty to the president or because they could not identify anyone better to replace him. Others, however, pressed ahead. Lansdale lieutenant Lucien Conein, who had known several of the generals concerned since his OSS days, served as US liaison with the plot. The coup came in late October. Despite assurances that they would not be harmed, the Ngo brothers were knifed and shot to death, after having sought refuge in a Catholic church. Quite by chance, the day that news of the coup reached Washington, October 31, Edward Lansdale, aged just fifty-five but disaffected with what he now described as the "giant institution of counterinsurgency," retired from US government service.[39]

Lansdale would return to Saigon in 1965 for one more mission, as a civilian assistant to the US ambassador, working to coup-proof the military junta that succeeded Diem. Accompanied by several familiar faces such as Charles Bohannan and a few new ones like the military analyst Daniel Ellsberg, he was soon hosting high-level social gatherings with his customary brio. But the encore fell flat. The generals proved no more amenable to Lansdale's efforts to democratize Vietnamese politics than Diem had, and other American officials viewed him with mistrust and disdain. Meanwhile, the counterinsurgency campaign continued its conversion into a "big-unit" military conflict featuring fast-growing US troop numbers and massive aerial bombardment. The civic action impulse had not disappeared altogether—CORDS (Civil Operations and Rural Development Support), a new pacification program introduced in 1967, was descended from Rufus Phillips's Office of Rural Affairs—but it now played second fiddle to a more conventional military strategy. An allied CIA effort to destroy the Viet Cong infrastructure, the Phoenix program, degenerated into a bloodbath of assassination and torture reminiscent of French tactics in Algeria and the

British approach in Kenya. By the time Lansdale left Vietnam for good in 1968, the "love campaign" had become a dirty war of the sort that the European colonial powers were waging in their former colonies—only much more conspicuous because of its scale and the extent of the domestic US opposition it was arousing. "Today South Vietnam is no longer a place where arch-colonialist Lansdale can display his talents," crowed the Viet Cong Liberation Radio, in a final echo of empire.[40]

The CIA's failure to coup-proof South Vietnam was repeated elsewhere in Indochina, as anti-communist governments in Laos and Cambodia teetered before communist insurgencies, the Pathet Lao and Khmer Rouge, respectively; both eventually fell, in 1975, the same year that Vietnam was reunified under communist rule. The chaotic US evacuation of Saigon, with its echoes of earlier colonial debacles, seemed to have drawn a line under the Cold War US romance with counterinsurgency.

But the picture elsewhere in Southeast Asia was different. In Vietnam's other Indochinese neighbor, Thailand, the CIA succeeded in shoring up the repressive military rule of Bhumipol, one of the region's pro-Western "friendly kings." With Malaysia stabilized by the British, and Indonesia now in pro-American hands (President Sukarno had eventually succumbed to a creeping military coup, in 1965–1967), the United States was establishing an "arc of containment" around communist China, extending north from the Philippines to Japan. The latter nation served as a sort of US "sub-empire" in the region, its fealty cemented by the millions of dollars the CIA channeled to the ruling Liberal Democrats during the 1950s and 1960s. The Europeans had packed up and gone home, but their rule had been succeeded by a new, "murkier" form of Western imperium.[41]

The story in the rest of the Third World was similar. In the Middle East, the restoration of Western rule had faltered in 1958 when a surge of nationalist rebellion engulfed the region, toppling the British client king of Iraq and nearly sweeping away the Christian president of Lebanon. But Washington, working largely through the CIA, stemmed the tide before it reached the pro-Western monarchies of Iran, Saudi Arabia, and Jordan. Eventually, following Gamal Nasser's unexpected death in 1970 and the succession of Anwar Sadat, even revolutionary Egypt came over to the Americans' side. As in Southeast Asia, the United States also had a special regional partner in the Middle East—Israel. The Israeli secret intelligence agency, Mossad, acted as a kind of regional surrogate for the CIA. Under the terms of KKMOUNTAIN, as this arrangement was code-named, Mossad helped train the shah of Iran's secret police, the SAVAK, aided Kurds rebelling against the new nationalist government of Iraq, and provided security assistance to the staunchly anti-communist emperor of Ethiopia, Haile Selassie.[42]

As the need for Israeli backup in Ethiopia attested, the United States was relatively late in its arrival on the African scene, but even here the CIA had its clients. In the former Belgian colony of the Congo, scene of Patrice Lumumba's murder in 1961, the United States underwrote the kleptocratic government of military dictator Mobutu Sese Seko. In return, Mobutu allowed the CIA to use his country (now named Zaire) as a staging post for cash and arms destined for rebel leaders fighting the Marxist government that had succeeded the Portuguese in Angola. Also involved in the Angola conflict was another recipient of covert American backing, South Africa. Although CIA analysts voiced doubts about supporting the apartheid regime, and new US president Jimmy Carter tried to use the Agency to force change on South Africa, the CIA tended to work with the white supremacist government in Pretoria and against the anti-apartheid movement. The tip-off that led to the 1962 arrest and twenty-seven-year imprisonment of Nelson Mandela came from an undercover CIA officer who suspected the African National Congress leader of being a Soviet agent.[43]

Greater still was the CIA's presence in a more traditional zone of US power: Latin America. Here, the wave of conservative counterrevolution that began with the Guatemalan coup of 1954 had swept into South America during the 1960s as Brazil and other democracies succumbed to military takeovers, then crested in the continent's Southern Cone with the 1973 fall of Chilean president Salvador Allende. The CIA helped coup-proof the resulting regimes, providing them with intelligence about remaining pockets of opposition, security training, and the latest surveillance and communications technologies. The Agency also played a support role when the juntas of the Southern Cone came together in 1976 to launch Operation Condor, an international effort to track down and liquidate leftists who had managed to escape the national crackdowns (among them a former minister in the Allende government, Orlando Letelier, whom the Chilean secret police dared to murder in Washington). As in Africa, the presidency of Jimmy Carter briefly focused official US attention on the human rights abuses of these regimes, but the arrival of Ronald Reagan in the White House in 1981 soon squashed such qualms, at least in government circles. Under Reagan, the counterrevolution returned where it had begun, to Central America. In addition to supplying the Contra rebels trying to overthrow the Sandinistas in Nicaragua, the CIA supported the military-dominated government of El Salvador as it mounted a savage campaign of repression against a left-wing insurgency. Paramilitary death squads reminiscent of the Nenita units in Edward Lansdale's Philippines roamed the Salvadoran countryside, killing leftist insurgents and terrorizing indigenous peasants.[44]

This was not the only echo of Lansdale's earlier actions in the Philippines and Vietnam. More benign Lansdalian techniques, such as the CIA man's constant search for intimate male comradeship in the Third World, were repeated in locales far beyond Southeast Asia. In the international spy hub of Mexico City, the proconsul-like CIA station chief Winston M. Scott deployed a combination of cash and camaraderie to lubricate the special intelligence relationship the United States enjoyed with the ruling Partido Revolucionario Institucional. When Scott's friend President Adolfo López Mateos heard that the American was buying a car for a girlfriend of Minister of Government (and future president) Gustavo Díaz Ordaz, he insisted that Win buy his girlfriend one, too. Thousands of miles away, in Amman, Jordan, another station chief, John "Jack" O'Connell, became the Lansdale-like confidant of the young King Hussein. After O'Connell retired from the CIA, Hussein made him his attorney and diplomatic counselor in Washington. To the south, in Zaire's capital, Kinshasa, Larry Devlin provided President Mobutu with a range of covert support services, including regular breakfast intelligence briefings. For his contributions, Devlin was awarded the Congolese Order of the Leopard, meaning he could not be arrested without the president's personal approval. All these relationships resembled Lansdale's friendship with Ramon Magsaysay and earlier colonial intimacies in their peculiar mix of masculine sentimentality and political self-interest. The latter cut both ways: Mobutu was particularly adept at using the resources at the CIA's disposal to reinforce his dominance of post-independence Zairian politics.[45]

Despite their failure in Vietnam, Lansdalian civic action and other population-centric forms of counterinsurgency also carried over into later operations. Third World military dictators liked the important role that COIN doctrine accorded the armed forces and were excited by the possibility of modernizing their countries along US lines—even if grass-roots community development interested them less than authoritarian social programs imposed from above. Hence, even in 1980s El Salvador, witness to ghastly government atrocities against unarmed civilians, there were US-supported efforts at election reform and land redistribution.[46]

Generally, though it was the more repressive, violent side of COIN doctrine—the iron fist rather than the velvet glove—that was uppermost as it spread across the globe. This was especially apparent in another crucial field of US counterinsurgency operation: policing. In 1962, the same year that the troubled Michigan State University police training mission in South Vietnam was eventually cancelled, the Kennedy administration created a new foreign entity, the Office of Public Safety (OPS). Although lodged within the US Agency for International Development (USAID), the OPS effectively functioned as a CIA covert operation. Both the national security official who shepherded it into existence, Robert W. Komer, and its long-serving chief, Byron Engle, had previously worked for the CIA; the latter's wife, Geraldine L. Engle, another CIA officer, was still serving. Under Engle, "Public Safety Advisors" shifted the police assistance program from a focus on rural to urban policing, prioritizing crowd control and other direct methods of political repression. The OPS expanded rapidly, providing US client regimes around the world with technical support, material aid, and training, either on the ground in the countries concerned or at facilities in the United States. By the time the OPS was terminated in 1975, over 1 million foreign police officers had passed through its portals.[47]

Reflecting a desire to reach into even the most routine aspects of foreign societies, much OPS training covered such mundane matters as urban traffic control. Other elements, though, were more sinister. Drawing on years of research into interrogation methods by CIA scientists (and, as will be discussed later, American psychologists), some Public Safety Advisors taught foreign trainees how to inflict "no-touch" forms of torture such as sensory deprivation or stress positions that caused self-inflicted pain. The most notorious of these instructors was a former Indiana police chief, Dan Mitrione. After demonstrating the effects of such torture on randomly selected street beggars to Uruguayan police officers, Mitrione was himself kidnapped and murdered by Tupamaros guerrillas in 1970. Although publicity surrounding Mitrione's death contributed to the 1975 dismantling of the OPS, the psychological torture methods taught in its programs assumed a life of their own, metastasizing to other locales in Latin America and Asia, such as Ferdinand Marcos's Philippines. The OPS might also have facilitated the diffusion of another characteristic technique of military repression in Latin America: the "disappearing" of political prisoners. The spread of this practice seems to have followed closely the movements of Public Safety Advisor John P. Longan as he traveled between countries in South America during the 1960s and 1970s.[48]

By this point, some Americans, rather than seeing military repression as a necessary evil, had positively embraced it. Grouping together in organizations like the World Anti-Communist League, this motley collection of die-hard conservative intellectuals, veterans of the failed counterinsurgency campaign in Vietnam, and hard-line intelligence officials alienated by the Nixon-era turn to détente, extolled the military dictatorships of Latin America as truer foes of communism than the soft, yielding United States. With the election of Ronald Reagan in 1980, leaders of this shadow network such as the retired two-star general John K. Singlaub enjoyed a new entrée to government circles. Singlaub, a former OSSer, founding member of the CIA, and friend of Reagan's Director of Central Intelligence, Bill Casey, acted as (in the

words of one historian) "the self-proclaimed lightning rod" for Lieutenant Colonel Oliver North's operation supplying anti-government
forces in Nicaragua, providing cover for North's illegal use of money
from illegal arms sales to revolutionary Iran to fund the Contra rebels.[49]

What did Edward Lansdale, the American father of counterinsurgency,
make of the doctrine's repressive turn? The Reagan era found the retired
CIA man living close to his old employer's Langley headquarters in suburban northern Virginia, near such former colleagues as Rufus Phillips
and Lucien Conein. He shared his ranch-style home there with the love
of his life, the Filipina Pat Kelly, having married her in 1973, two years
after the death of his long-suffering first, American wife, Helen. Together,
they hosted gatherings of their US and Vietnamese friends, much as
he had while stationed in Saigon trying to save the Diem regime. In
other words, Lansdale still seemed to be living according to the ideals
of American-Asian friendship and love he had identified as the cardinal
principles of his coup-proofing missions during the 1950s.

It is therefore a little surprising that, shortly before he died at
the age of seventy-nine in 1987, Lansdale responded favorably to a
call from Washington inviting him to advise the Pentagon about US
counterinsurgency strategy in El Salvador. A Special Forces reservist,
Major F. Andy Messing Jr., had been studying Lansdale's career and
grown convinced that he had come up with the template for waging
"low-intensity conflict." Messing introduced Lansdale to Jack Singlaub
and Oliver North, and the three men hit it off. The veteran counterinsurgency expert expressed his pleasure that US foreign policy was
showing "a more aggressive attitude" in Central America. The Sandinistas were a "fascist clique" and the Reagan administration's support for

the Contras was within the "heritage set forth by the American Revolution." Lansdale also approved of North's maverick personal style. Later, after the White House staffer had gotten into trouble for his role in the Iran-Contra affair, Lansdale remarked that "friends of mine have claimed that he is simply a current copy of me in today's government."[50]

This paradox—the contradiction between Edward Lansdale's missionary idealism and his approval of a bloody, even illegal neocolonial counterinsurgency—was not new. It had been present in his career from his first CIA mission in the Philippines, when he had declared his love for Filipinos while tolerating his friend Napoleon Valeriano's use of death squads to hunt down Huks. Indeed, the pattern of "peaceful conquest" alternating with violence was baked into the whole doctrine of counterinsurgency as it had evolved from nineteenth-century French and British imperial antecedents and as it had already played out in precisely the same colonial regions where Lansdale himself had operated. In the early 1900s, Captain John Pershing had achieved such intimacy with Moro insurgents in the southern Philippines that he became the honorary father of the wife of a sultan. In 1913, with the insurgency still continuing, Pershing led an attack on a Moro camp that resulted in the death of over 200 inhabitants, including women and children.[51]

This is why, despite later efforts to resurrect his reputation, Lansdale's counterinsurgency prescriptions are fundamentally flawed. True, he did help stabilize the Philippines, but his success there was due more to military coercion and his skills as a psychological warrior than to his attempts at population-centric civic action. When he tried to apply the same nation-building nostrum in South Vietnam, not even psy-war and enemy-centric repression were enough to overcome the Diem government's lack of legitimacy in the eyes of many Vietnamese.

For that matter, none of the regimes the CIA helped coup-proof during the Cold War era achieved the popular consent to which Lansdale aspired because, as in prior imperial history, those who lived under them tended to resent their dependence on foreign power. Nor was such resentment targeted only at local client elites. It also extended to the foreigners who kept repressive governments in power. Torture victims often remembered the presence in their prison cells of shadowy men with American accents, and this memory bred a powerful and enduring hatred of the United States.[52]

As the British, French, and others had already discovered, the effects of colonial interventions, even ones carried out by local agents, did not necessarily stay in the colonies. Empire had a way of coming home.

PART TWO

AT HOME

CHAPTER 4

Counterintelligence

If the imperial impulse eventually won out in post–World War II US foreign policy, it was not for want of opposition. Ever since the dawn of the Republic, American imperialism has had a twin: anti-imperialism. Even as Thomas Jefferson sought an "Empire of Liberty," another founding father, James Madison, advised against imperial adventure, warning that "no nation could preserve its freedom in the midst of continual warfare." In 1854, confronted by the foreign ambitions of future secretary of state William Henry Seward, Henry J. Raymond, founding editor of the *New York Times*, stated his fear that "we shall sacrifice our liberties to our imperial dream." At the end of the nineteenth century, with imperialists such as Teddy Roosevelt clamoring for the annexation of the Philippines, US senator from Massachusetts George F. Hoar decried "the danger that we are to be transformed from a Republic, founded on the Declaration of Independence, . . . into a vulgar, commonplace empire, founded upon physical force." Again and again, anti-imperialists made the same argument: empire did not just threaten the freedom and well-being of foreigners; it endangered the American Republic itself.[1]

For proof of this, Americans had to look no further than contemporary Europe. There, the main domestic consequence of empire-building was plain for all to see: the growth of great military establishments and colonial bureaucracies. But there were other, less obvious impacts, too. Imperial states propagandized their own citizens to create popular support for costly and often brutal interventions abroad. They also built internal security services that employed policing techniques developed in the colonies to suppress domestic dissent. So profound was the influence of empire on the European home front that it carried on even after decolonization, in the form of immigration from colonial regions—the British Caribbean, for example, or French North Africa. Observing the domestic effects of empire, European and postcolonial intellectuals came up with a term to describe them: the "imperial boomerang."[2]

At first sight, the United States appears to have evaded the imperial boomerang. True, its brief dalliance with formal colonialism after the Spanish-American War did cause some backwash on American shores—for example, the domestic campaign waged by colonial counterintelligence expert Ralph Van Deman against leftist and Black "subversives." For the most part, though, the United States' lack of colonies relative to Europe meant comparatively few outward signs of empire at home: no colonial offices housed in grand government buildings, no statues of imperial heroes, no "Empire Day" holidays with parades and bunting.

But for all the lack of imperial spectacle, a closer inspection reveals that the United States' Cold War–era foreign interventions did have domestic ramifications—and, as was the case overseas, the CIA was

CIA counterintelligence chief James Angleton during his excruciating appearance before the Senate Select Committee on Intelligence in 1975.
Bettmann, Getty Images

at the center of them. Some of these consequences were unintended, such as immigration flows from Third World countries precipitated by Agency regime change or maintenance operations. Others, however, were intentional: covert CIA efforts to influence American public opinion to make it more supportive of US actions overseas, for instance, an especially important undertaking in a nation with a long history of popular anti-interventionism.

These publicity efforts were not altogether successful, however. Although quiescent in the early years of the Cold War, the anti-imperial impulse in American life came roaring back in the 1960s and 1970s, partly because, in another, ironic boomerang effect, the example of anti-colonial resistance to US interventions abroad inspired similar opposition within American society, some of it targeted at the CIA itself. As a foreign intelligence service, the Agency was explicitly prohibited from performing internal security functions. Nonetheless, as the period wore on, the CIA began surveilling and, in doing so, effectively repressing dissident US citizens, putting itself in the middle of the struggle between imperialists and anti-imperialists that had been going on since the founding of the nation. The back-and-forth of this contest, with fortune favoring first one side, then the other, would carry on throughout the remainder of the Cold War.

Just as it had once been the counterintelligence pioneer Ralph Van Deman demonstrating the imperial boomerang effect in the realm of US internal security and state secrecy, so in the Cold War era it was the man responsible for running CIA counterintelligence who personified the most secretive and repressive domestic tendencies of the American covert empire—another Agency legend who conjured the imperial past.

Few figures in the history of the CIA have proved more controversial than James Jesus Angleton. His early life and career were undeniably brilliant, even romantic. His father, a dashing military adventurer and businessman, James Hugh Angleton, was serving in the National Guard on the US-Mexico border when he met and married a young Mexican woman, Carmen Mercedes Moreno (making their offspring almost literally the products of imperial romance). Born in Boise, Idaho, in 1917, young Jim grew up mainly in Italy, where Angleton senior managed a lucrative cash register franchise. His resume thereafter was that of a typically privileged member of the imperial brotherhood: Yale, where he studied English literature and achieved a reputation as a minor but not insignificant modernist poet and editor; a brief spell at Harvard Law School and marriage to a Vassar undergraduate, Cicely Harriet d'Autremont; and distinguished wartime service in the

Office of Strategic Services' top-secret counterintelligence unit, X-2, based first in London, then in Rome.

It was during his service in X-2 that Angleton began to build his legend as a counterintelligence genius, a reputation he burnished after the war when, staying on in Rome, he helped run the influence operation leading up to the crucial Italian elections of 1948. Returning to Washington as a founding officer of the new Central Intelligence Agency, he rapidly acquired other important responsibilities: liaison with sister Western agencies, management of the CIA's valuable Israeli "account," and, in 1954, command of the Agency's new Counter-Intelligence Staff (CIS). With the personal backing of successive directors, Angleton built the CIS into a powerful force both within and outside the CIA, successfully preventing the sort of communist penetration that was afflicting other Western services, in Britain especially. He also cultivated a formidable personal image, a combination of his considerable intellect, increasingly gaunt (some would say sinister) appearance, and obsessive pursuit of solitary hobbies such as fly-fishing and, most famously, orchid-growing.

In the early 1960s, however, Angleton's performance and, with it, his reputation began to deteriorate. Teaming up with controversial Soviet defector Anatoli Golitsyn, he launched a hunt for communist "moles" within the CIA that soon spun out of control, effectively paralyzing US espionage in the Eastern bloc. At the same time, his CIS mounted an operation, MHCHAOS, spying on US campus radicals and Black activists. When in 1974 the investigative reporter Seymour Hersh published details of CHAOS in the *New York Times*, the then Director of Central Intelligence, William Colby, already fed up with what he regarded as Angleton's byzantine approach to counterintelligence, decided enough was enough and forced his resignation. Angleton died the following decade, in 1987, bitterly lamenting what he regarded as the betrayal of his life's work.

Given the dramatic arc of his career, from glamorous young poet to ghoulish mole-hunter, it is not surprising that, like Edward Lansdale, James Angleton has attracted more than his fair share of attention from biographers, novelists, and even moviemakers (Robert de Niro's 2006 feature film *The Good Shepherd* featured an Angleton-like character as its hero, or anti-hero, played by Matt Damon). Angleton's chroniclers have proposed various explanations for his descent into the mole mania of his later years: clinical paranoia (although, as his defenders point out, this was never professionally diagnosed); the profound shock of the 1963 defection to the Soviet Union of his friend Kim Philby, the British mole; and even, in some recent accounts, the lingering influence of the modernist literary movement in which he had participated at Yale. There is doubtless some truth to all these theories, but there is one other factor that has not received quite the attention it deserves.[3]

During his formative years, James Angleton was exposed to British imperial culture more than any CIA contemporary, even Kim Roosevelt. While the likes of Roosevelt received their schooling at faux English public schools such as Groton, Angleton experienced the real thing. From 1933 to 1936, he attended Malvern College, a Victorian-era boarding school nestled in a bucolic region of the English Midlands. His brother, Hugh, went to the even more prestigious Harrow, alma mater of Winston Churchill. Serving in the ranks of the Malvern Officers' Training Corps and school prefects, Jim Angleton imbibed the peculiar British public school ethos of aristocratic entitlement and self-sacrifice. "I learned, at least I was disciplined to learn, certain features of life, and what I regarded as duty," he later told an interviewer. He also became, to all outward appearances, British. Several of his Yale classmates, observing his Anglicized accent, London-tailored wardrobe, and proficiency at soccer, assumed that he actually was English. Even his name changed, from James Jesus Angleton to simply James Angleton. His headmaster, conscious of the teasing his young American charge would likely receive from the other boys, suggested he drop his middle name, a sign of his half-Mexican ancestry, "to avoid the additional ragging that he would have faced had he been known as Jesus—or Hay-Suss."[4]

A few years later, Angleton's Englishness was reinforced by his World War II service in the London base of the OSS counterintelligence unit, X-2. The young American officers of X-2 were relatively unversed in the dark arts of counterintelligence and, according to Kim Philby, then deputy chief of MI6's counterpart unit, Section V, "they lost no opportunity of telling us that they had come to school." The head of Section V, Felix Cowgill, willingly obliged, laying on intensive training courses for the Americans and even granting them access to MI6 counterintelligence records, including the top-secret ULTRA intercepts of German wireless traffic. There was an element of self-interest to Cowgill's openness: as Philby explained later, the British hoped to avail themselves of the voluminous files that the Americans, with their superior resources, were bound to create on their own one day. But, as in the Jedburgh commando teams, the wartime counterintelligence collaboration also featured a good deal of genuine camaraderie. X-2 and Section V shared the same West End office building. Norman Holmes Pearson, the convivial Yale English professor who headed the US unit (and who had recruited Angleton), became an intimate friend of Cowgill's. Angleton himself developed abiding friendships with several MI6 officers, including the charming Philby. English literature provided one bond between the Brits and Yanks: Pearson and Angleton both had literary connections in London, including with the expatriate giant of Anglo-American letters, T. S. Eliot, while the British group featured several writers of later prominence, among them the ubiquitous Graham Greene. Another bond was alcohol. This was the period when Angleton developed a taste for boozy lunchtime meetings that later would slide into alcoholism. After the war, when he acquired his liaison function in the new CIA and Kim Philby was sent to Washington to perform the same duty for MI6, the two men became notorious for their drink-sodden lunches together.[5]

Angleton's biographers have disagreed about many aspects of his life and career, but about one thing there is universal agreement: his London years were crucial in shaping his later approach to counterintelligence. Take, for example, the hypersecrecy surrounding the ULTRA cipher-breaking operation, whose existence was known to only six of Churchill's ministers. The lesson Angleton took away from ULTRA was that counterintelligence must operate as a compartmented service within a service, sealed off from the rest of its host organization by its own dedicated communication channels and special secrecy oaths. Then there was Double Cross, a deception operation in which the British used German agents uncovered by the ULTRA intercepts to send false information to their Nazi controllers—an operation so secret that not even Churchill was informed about it (on the not unreasonable grounds he likely would have interfered had he been). Henceforth, Angleton was always on the lookout for "strategic deception" by enemy services, including the dispatching of false defectors. According to CIA historian David Robarge, Angleton's induction into ULTRA and Double Cross, the most closely guarded secrets of World War II, had a career-defining impact on him similar to the experience of a later generation of CIA officers tasked with hunting Osama bin Laden in the wake of 9/11.[6]

It was not just that James Angleton's London years exposed him to an intelligence culture of extreme secrecy. Even in World War II, British intelligence was still very much *imperial* intelligence. Section V chief Felix Cowgill was a former Indian policeman, as was his predecessor, Valentine Vivian. Cowgill had also served as inspector general of the North-West Frontier—the classic theater of the old Anglo-Russian espionage rivalry, the Great Game, and the setting for the climactic scenes of Rudyard Kipling's *Kim*. He and his colleagues were festooned with imperial orders, decorations, and medals. Even Britons who lacked direct experience of colonial service—Kim Philby, for example—were shaped by the imperial past. Philby had spent his infancy in India, where he acquired his nickname from the fictional hero of the Great Game (incidentally adding to his personal attractiveness for American fans of Kipling). His father, St. John Philby, was an eccentric British Arabist in the mold of the imperial agent T. E. Lawrence.[7]

Service in the colonies left a distinctive mark on British intelligence officers. In addition to a fondness for pink gin and polo, old colonial hands tended to display a condition scholars have termed "imperial paranoia": a shapeless but terrible fear of native conspiracies engendered by the tremendous challenge of managing restive populations in Britain's far-flung empire. At its height in Kipling's Raj, imperial paranoia was still on display in twentieth-century British intelligence. "My own view is that it has something to do with the Arabs," Kim Philby recalled Felix Cowgill saying at a meeting of MI6 section heads. "Wherever I look in this case, I see Arabs!" ("Richard Hannay was with us again" was Philby's acid comment.) And it wasn't only Arabs: the Russians were everywhere, too, harnessing colonial rebellion to their own imperial ambitions, first in the form of czarist expansionism, then as Bolshevik revolution. It was this awful specter that had distracted

British intelligence from the international danger of Nazism during the 1930s; suspicion of a communist conspiracy to inspire "Eastern unrest" persisted even during the Grand Alliance of World War II. The irony was that Soviet agents were in fact operating directly under the noses of the British—indeed, within MI6: the spy ring of Cambridge University graduates that included Angleton's friend Kim Philby, unsuspected because of their establishment credentials.[8]

It is impossible to say for sure that James Angleton contracted imperial paranoia from his wartime British colleagues. What is clear is that he consciously imitated specific counterintelligence practices he had first encountered in London throughout his career, starting with the mundane but all-important business of file-keeping. During the early years of the war, David Petrie, director of the British imperial security service MI5 (and another former Indian police officer), had drafted in a business organization expert, Reginald Horrocks, to reorganize and modernize its sprawling filing system. By the time of Angleton's arrival in London, the MI5 central registry constituted not only an unrivaled collection of wartime intelligence data but also a model of modern information management. The Americans of X-2 took advantage of their unfettered access to British records to copy both the records and the filing system. Angleton's secretary, Perdita Aldington (the daughter, by the way, of the great Anglo-American poet Hilda Doolittle, who wrote as "H.D."), remembered him being "into everything; pulling, leafing, thumbing." Later, in the mid-1950s, when Angleton was establishing a registry in the CIA's new Counter-Intelligence Staff, he again turned to MI5 officers for guidance.[9]

Echoes of the British imperial past could also be heard in other, more controversial CIA counterintelligence practices. In 1955, Angleton took over an operation monitoring a portion of the mail passing through New York between the United States and the Soviet Union. Initiated by the CIA's Soviet division three years earlier, the program was originally intended to identify possible themes for US propaganda. Angleton reoriented HTLINGUAL, as it was renamed, toward the detection of communist espionage. All of the Soviet mail flow was now inspected; a growing proportion of letters was opened and their contents photographed; and a watch list was established based in part on names provided by the domestic intelligence service, the FBI. In return, the Agency sent the Bureau reports about what were regarded as possible internal US security threats, including domestic dissidents such as civil rights campaigners. By the time LINGUAL was terminated in 1973, the CIA had handled over 28 million items and opened 215,000 of them, including the mail of author John Steinbeck, Congresswoman Bella Abzug, and a member of the Rockefeller family. As Angleton himself admitted, all this was legally dubious. Tampering with the mail was expressly forbidden by US law and violated the Fourth Amendment of the Constitution. LINGUAL also overlapped with the FBI's domestic jurisdiction—a realm from which the CIA was excluded by its legislative charter, the 1947 National Security Act.[10]

Mail interception is, of course, a classic technique of espionage with a centuries-long history, but the similarities between LINGUAL and British imperial security practices were striking all the same. MI5's mission involved a similar blurring of the boundaries between the homeland and empire, the foreign and domestic. During World War I, the British security service had opened the letters of suspected German spies, then, in a moment of "mission creep" that anticipated LINGUAL's monitoring of civil rights activists, begun targeting women suffragists as well. Even the surprisingly crude technology employed by the Americans and British was the same: the "kettle and stick" technique, with teams of workers in offices next door to mail rooms steaming open letters as if on a production line.[11]

Finally, there was something distinctly British about James Angleton's counterintelligence *style*. Elsewhere in the Agency, intelligence experts such as Sherman Kent liked to think of their discipline as a science; Kent himself was particularly emphatic on this score, as shown by his ranking of poetry below bookkeeping in his list of preferred professions. Angleton, in contrast, positively boasted of recruiting poets and literary scholars into the OSS, and after his retirement spoke to interviewers of counterintelligence as "the art."[12]

In part, Angleton's cultural approach to counterintelligence was probably a relic of his undergraduate enthusiasm for modernist literature and the Anglo-American school of literary theory known as the New Criticism. As several scholars have noted, there was a marked resemblance between Angleton's intensive sifting of his intelligence files for signs of Soviet espionage and the New Critics' "close reading" of literary texts for hidden meanings. The counterintelligence chief and his staff also handled historical case studies of Russian and communist deception—the Trust, for example, a 1920s false-flag operation run by the Soviet Cheka—as if they made up a sort of literary canon, poring over them endlessly in hopes of gaining insight into current KGB operations.[13]

But Angleton's approach to counterintelligence, characterized in an internal CIA study as "arcane," "intuitive," and "non-systematic," clearly owed something as well to his wartime exposure to the influence of British intelligence, with its emphasis on deep area knowledge as opposed to empirical and technological data collection. In this respect, Angleton was less like his fellow American Sherman Kent than T. E. Lawrence or even a fictional character in a British imperial spy novel. Author Mark

Riebling has pointed out the similarity between the Angleton persona and the intelligence chief Sir Walter Bullivant in John Buchan's Richard Hannay novels, another fly-fisherman for whom angling was not just a favorite hobby but a metaphor for spy-catching as well. Angleton's conceptually self-conscious, skeptical counterintelligence methodology was, arguably, more sophisticated than Kent's unreflective, scientistic approach—but the British influence also exposed Angleton to the germ of imperial paranoia.[14]

It is hard to pinpoint the precise moment when Angleton's suspicion of communist penetration slid into destructive obsession. It seems likely, though, that two events in 1963 were pivotal, and both again had to do with the British. First, there was Kim Philby's flight to Moscow. While Angleton might already have entertained some suspicions about his friend, the British mole's defection still came as a devastating blow. Not only was it embarrassing professionally, but it also contravened the deeply cherished Anglo-American notion of intelligence as a gentlemanly club united by a shared code of honor and mutual personal loyalty. The British counterintelligence officer Peter Wright put it best: "To find that a man like Philby . . . had betrayed everything; . . . youth and innocence passed away, and the dark ages began." If Angleton did have paranoid tendencies, this shockingly intimate act of betrayal might almost have been calculated to bring them to the surface. Later in the decade, as he and Wright talked late into the night about other possible penetrations, a ravaged-looking Angleton uttered a sentence reminiscent of Felix Cowgill's conspiracist musings about Arabs: "This is Kim's work."[15]

The other event in 1963 that confirmed Angleton's belief in a KGB "Master Plan" (or "Monster Plot," as Angleton's critics called it) was his acquiring control from the CIA's Soviet division of the defector Anatoli Golitsyn. The egotistical and voluble Golitsyn had just returned from a year in Britain helping MI5 ferret out possible Soviet agents in its ranks. According to CIA officer Cleveland C. Cram, a former London deputy station chief later tasked with conducting an internal review of Angleton's mole hunt, Golitsyn's sojourn in England crucially strengthened his inclination to "embroider and fabricate." MI5 counterintelligence staff such as Peter Wright who shared Angleton's conviction about top-level penetration—in their case, even suspecting their director, Roger Hollis, of being a mole—fed Golitsyn "a number of conspiratorial ideas which (like an infectious disease) he brought back to CIA." Infected by Golitsyn's suspicions about British leaders, including the soon-to-be prime minister, Labour Party politician Harold Wilson, Angleton teamed up with the MI5 "Fundamentalists" in their investigations, and even hatched a scheme to take over the British internal security service as, in effect, a CIA substation. By now, the germs of paranoia were crossing and recrossing the Atlantic.[16]

"It is from this time on," reckoned Cleveland Cram, "that the Monster Plot burst into full bloom." Golitsyn's hold over Angleton deepened. Another Soviet defector, Yuri Nosenko, who Golitsyn claimed was a provocateur sent to discredit and possibly assassinate him, was subjected to years of hostile interrogation by the CIA's Soviet division. The miasma of suspicion spread further overseas, especially within the British Commonwealth, claiming the careers of senior officials such as a top counterintelligence officer in the Canadian Mounties. Perfectly loyal career officers within the Agency's own Soviet division were investigated by the FBI and some lost their jobs. Eventually the monster turned on its creator and a member of his own staff began to suspect Angleton himself of being a Soviet mole.[17]

In the mid-1960s, Angleton tried to re-create the English-speaking circle of trust that had existed in the war years by launching a secret consortium of "Anglosphere" counterintelligence experts. Known as CAZAB (Canada, Australia, New Zealand, America, and Britain), the venture duplicated the membership of the post–World War II UKUSA signals intelligence-sharing agreement, which during the 1950s had expanded to include the principal English-speaking British Commonwealth countries in the "Five Eyes" alliance. Participants remembered Angleton relaxed and happy in the alcoholic haze of homosocial intimacy that prevailed at CAZAB's highly secretive meetings. But the old, imperial sense of mission was passing, even within the CIA itself, where a new, more socially and ethnically diverse generation of younger intelligence officers was starting to question the gentlemanly values of the Agency's Anglo founders—and, once again, empire was at the bottom of it.[18]

If, in his mission to protect American secrets, James Angleton was trying to replicate the conditions of British state secrecy within the United States, one thing remained beyond his reach. Britain had an Official Secrets Act that made the unauthorized disclosure or receipt of any classified information a felony. Although the US Espionage Act of 1917 contained some similar elements, the First Amendment of the Constitution protected American citizens' freedom of speech and freedom of the press. Combined with Americans' traditional dislike of government in general and spying in particular—a contrast with the "culture of secrecy" that pervaded imperial British society—the First Amendment made the job of counterintelligence that much harder in the United States than in Britain.[19]

Fortunately for Angleton, the two institutions in American society most likely to pry into the secrets of the Central Intelligence Agency— Congress and the press—showed little appetite for doing so, at least during the first years of the Cold War. The anti-communist cause seemed so urgent that few were inclined publicly to question the exceptional government powers that went with it. This "Cold War consensus," as historians have called it, meant that CIA officers like Angleton were able to go about their business with an almost complete absence of public oversight and accountability—in other words, to simulate an imperial state of official secrecy.

It was as the 1950s turned into the 1960s, the same moment that Angleton was starting his slide into mania, that cracks began appearing in America's Cold War consensus. Some of the reasons for the arrival of "the sixties" were obvious: the rise of the African American civil rights movement and a corresponding mood of political restlessness among white middle-class youth. Less immediately apparent but important nonetheless was a sort of *anti*-imperial boomerang effect. Many activists in the Black freedom struggle and the nascent New Left were deeply impressed by the example of nationalist movements in the decolonizing world. African Americans perceived similarities between anti-colonial struggles abroad and their own fight against white supremacy at home. Young whites were captivated by the air of romantic heroism surrounding such revolutionaries as Fidel Castro. Thanks to Castro's charisma and his avowed intention of abolishing racial segregation, the Cuban Revolution of 1958 became an early cause célèbre of 1960s American dissent. Founded in 1960, the Fair Play for Cuba Committee (FPCC) attracted an impressive roster of both white and Black supporters. Among these was the radical Columbia University sociologist C. Wright Mills, whose pro-Cuban polemic *Listen, Yankee!*, published in the same year, rapidly sold an astonishing 400,000 copies. Due to the influence of the Cuban Revolution and similar insurgencies in Africa and Asia, 1960s US protest had a strongly anti-colonial coloration to it that associated it with the longer history of American anti-imperialism.[20]

It was also thanks to Cuba that the CIA became, for the first time, a target of criticism within America itself. In *Listen, Yankee!*, Mills, writing in the voice of an imaginary Cuban revolutionary address-ing a US audience, specifically named the Agency as a likely threat to the Castro regime. "Yankee military aggression will take the form of indirect action," Mills predicted, before proceeding to warn his Amer-ican readers that US "world imperialism" was creating "a state within a state" that "might be turned upon you also." The following year, just after Mills's prediction had come true in spectacular fashion at the Bay of Pigs, W. E. B. Du Bois, Maya Angelou, and other Black members of the Fair Play for Cuba Committee, "still fighting for our own liberation from tyranny," signed a "Declaration of Conscience" protesting the "criminal aggression" of "a gang of ousted white Cuban politicians . . . armed, trained, and financed by the U.S. Central Intelligence Agency." The FPCC also helped organize the first anti-CIA protest events inside the United States, including a two-week vigil and fast outside the Agen-cy's headquarters. Later in 1961, the progressive New York publishing house Marzani & Munsell brought out *Cuba Versus CIA*, a compilation of all the publicly available information about the failed invasion, and one of the first books to list other CIA regime-change operations, too, including Iran and Guatemala.[21]

Much as imperial paranoia boomeranged back and forth between the United States and Europe, so 1960s American anti-imperialism formed a kind of feedback loop with anti-colonial nationalism in the Global South. In 1964, two US journalists, David Wise and Thomas B. Ross, published *Invisible Government*, a book assailing the CIA for its interventions in the developing world and secretive role within

American society. The following year, the postcolonial Ghanaian leader Kwame Nkrumah cited Wise and Ross's work in his own book, *Neo-Colonialism: The Last Stage of Imperialism*, an influential critique of the continuing grip of Western imperialism on the decolonizing world. In it, Nkrumah provided chapter and verse about CIA operations in a variety of postcolonial locations as well as the Agency's influence on America itself. Adding an additional loop to the circuit, *Neo-Colonialism* became a key theoretical text for 1960s African American nationalists and US anti-imperialists generally.[22]

By now, American anti-imperialism had found another cause besides Cuba. President Lyndon B. Johnson's 1964 decision to escalate US military involvement in Vietnam and the launch of the American ground war the following year provoked a spate of protest on US university campuses. Leaders of Students for a Democratic Society (SDS), the premier organization of the New Left, gave speeches denouncing American actions in Vietnam as imperialist and traveled to Hanoi to forge anti-imperial links with the North Vietnamese leadership. The Black Panthers, a militant Black nationalist organization founded in Oakland, California, in 1966, likewise identified with the North Vietnamese, depicting their resistance to American imperialism as part of the same struggle that African Americans, as an "internal colony" of the United States, were waging on the home front.

Meanwhile, another Bay Area countercultural institution, *Ramparts* magazine, was helping to combine the different strands of 1960s anti-imperialism into a common front that one scholar has called the "U.S. Third World Left." One of the main editors of *Ramparts*, Robert Scheer, was a veteran of the FPCC and friend of Fidel Castro who introduced the writings of Che Guevara to an American audience; another was Eldridge Cleaver, the Black Panther most identified with transnational, anti-colonial activism. In addition to denouncing the Vietnam War, *Ramparts* launched a series of team investigations of CIA covert operations. One famous story published in 1966 combined these targets: a detailed exposé of Agency infiltration of the Lansdale-era Michigan State University advisory mission to the Diem regime.[23]

What did the CIA itself make of all this anti-imperial ferment? The picture is incomplete due to the scarcity of relevant documents, but there are enough records publicly available to make it clear that, despite its being barred from operation within the United States, the Agency was actively interested in its growing domestic opposition. In April 1961, shortly after the Fair Play for Cuba Committee had announced its formation in the pages of the *New York Times*, William K. Harvey, the CIA officer then in charge of anti-Castro operations, told his FBI liaison that "this Agency has derogatory information on all individuals listed." The FBI subsequently infiltrated the FPCC and, along with the CIA, attempted to recruit its founders as informants. Other declassified documents show that in 1963, the Agency approached the Bureau requesting copies of FPCC stationery so that it could fabricate "deceptive information" that might "embarrass" the committee in foreign countries. After the assassination of President John F. Kennedy in November 1963, a CIA-backed organization of anti-Castro Cuban émigrés drew attention to the fact that the prime suspect, Lee Harvey Oswald, had represented the FPCC in New Orleans. It is unclear whether the émigrés were acting on their own initiative or on instruction from the Agency.[24]

A similar scenario played out in 1966. Responding to the attacks on it in *Ramparts*, the CIA launched an effort to unearth material "of a derogatory nature" about the magazine, hoping to prove that it was "a subversive unit." Whereas the anti-FPCC campaign had been improvised by the Agency's Latin American division, the operation against *Ramparts* was entrusted to James Angleton's Counter-Intelligence Staff, where it was placed under the command of one Richard Ober. The son of an eminent literary agent and graduate of Phillips Exeter, Harvard, and Columbia, Ober was every inch the first-generation Agency easterner: tall, soft-spoken, and charming, with an impeccable record of dedicated service both in the field and at headquarters. However, this did not stop him from resorting to a variety of dirty tricks against *Ramparts*. Among other devices (how much simpler it would have been if the CIA could just have invoked a US Official Secrets Act), Ober ordered his staff to comb the magazine's tax records for evidence of funding by foreign communists, recruited informants on its staff, and planted hostile stories about it in other publications. The Agency had gone to war with the US Third World Left.[25]

But it had not won yet. Leading newspapers such as the *New York Times* were picking up the Agency stories reported by *Ramparts* and printing their own versions with additional detail, alarming their readers and prompting more unwelcome scrutiny. Anti–Vietnam War demonstrations spread across the nation, threatening the safety of CIA facilities and personnel—or such, anyway, was the conclusion of the Agency's Office of Security, which in February 1967 mounted Project Merrimac, a surveillance program targeting Washington-based peace and Black organizations. Like Project Resistance, launched later in the same year to investigate potential threats to Agency recruiters on US university campuses, Merrimac involved the extensive infiltration of suspect groups and illegal liaison with local police departments. Meanwhile, leading personalities within the SDS, the Black Panthers, and, increasingly, the US women's movement stepped up their contacts with the North Vietnamese and other Third World insurgents. Even white draft resisters now viewed their struggle as a colonial war of liberation from the American empire. As one put it, "We too are the Vietcong."[26]

By now, the US president in charge of the Vietnam War effort, Lyndon Johnson, had had enough of the protests. In August 1967, he summoned to the White House CIA director Richard M. Helms, another career intelligence officer and Agency founder. LBJ wanted the CIA to study the possibility that the peace movement was being sponsored and controlled by hostile foreign powers. Why else were American kids protesting a US war? he wanted to know. Helms, one of the more prudent members of his CIA generation, was hesitant, fearing that such an investigation might lead the Agency even further into the prohibited domestic realm. But he could not ignore a presidential directive, even an implied one, as orders from the Oval Office tended to be because of the doctrine of plausible deniability. On August 15, James Angleton received instructions to establish a capability within the Counter-Intelligence Staff for gathering and disseminating intelligence about foreign involvement in domestic dissent. Command of the Special Operations Group (SOG), as the unit was named, was handed to Richard Ober, who folded his data on *Ramparts* into the new operation. Other information was levied from overseas CIA field stations, which were ordered to keep tabs on "radical students and U.S. Negro expatriates as well as travelers passing through," and, from 1969, a small cohort of dedicated agents, mainly domestic FBI informers who happened to be traveling abroad. The operation acquired its code name the following year: MHCHAOS, the MH prefix indicating its worldwide scope, and the cryptonym chosen at random. It was, perhaps, an unfortunate selection. In the laconic words of one historian of the era, "Somebody with a sense of posterity should have spoken up."[27]

CHAOS failed to uncover the evidence of external communist control that LBJ was expecting. It was indeed the case that the Soviet Union was running "active measures" to foment discord within the United States—for example, KGB officer Oleg Kalugin later revealed that Soviet money had helped keep afloat Marzani & Munsell, the New York publishing house that published the 1961 book *Cuba Versus CIA*. But such connections were rare. As Kalugin's testimony and records from Soviet intelligence archives also show, the KGB regarded African American militants and young New Leftists as ideologically too undependable to use them as agents.[28]

Instead, what the CHAOS reports from overseas stations and traveling agents revealed was a plethora of mainly spontaneous interactions between the 1960s anti-imperial left and the Third (not Second) World—a North-South as opposed to East-West axis. In 1969, members of SDS, the Panthers, and other radical movements began undertaking organized visits to Cuba in a venture that harked back to the FPCC: the Venceremos Brigade. The young American members of the brigade, described by one historian as "a radical Peace Corps," provided volunteer labor on Cuban sugar plantations and construction sites; in return, they got to observe a Third World revolution firsthand. The following year, Eldridge Cleaver recruited his *Ramparts* co-editor Robert Scheer to help lead the US People's Anti-Imperialist Delegation's visit to Southeast Asia. Representing "a cross-section of American social movements," the eleven-person group toured the region for two and a half months, building solidarity with Asian revolutionaries and denouncing alleged acts of US imperialism. After the tour, Cleaver returned to his then-home in the former French colony of Algeria, a North African hub of the global anti-colonial movement where the Black Panthers were establishing an international section. There he

rubbed shoulders with an eclectic cast of world revolutionaries including pan-Africanists, North Koreans, and Palestinians. Performing a
similar function as anti-imperialist staging posts were the increasingly
multiracial capitals of the old European colonial powers. Paris, in particular, long a gathering place for anti-imperial activists from the colonial world (Ho Chi Minh had lived there), saw numerous comings and
goings by US dissenters, including a growing community of Vietnam
War draft resisters and deserters. A declassified CHAOS cable based
on a report from an agent code-named PETUNIA describes a Parisian
"hang-out" frequented by "deserters, SDS activists, resisters, and casu-
als passing through." The transient community's French financial supporters reportedly included philosophers Jean-Paul Sartre and Simone
de Beauvoir and film star Catherine Deneuve. Further CHAOS cables
contain a series of vignettes in the daily life of the US Third World Left:
a Black Panther showing Cuban movies in the Philippines, other Panthers traveling from Algiers to Paris in search of false papers and plas-
tic surgery so that they could reenter the United States clandestinely,
and (as the US media also reported) Hollywood star and activist Jane
Fonda visiting Hanoi.[29]

The CIA could argue that it was doing nothing improper in surveilling these US citizens, as it was doing so overseas. The trouble was
that CHAOS did not stop at the water's edge. Training US agents to
pass convincingly in radical circles abroad meant first "sheep dipping"
them, inserting them into domestic leftist groups so that they could
acquire the right political "coloration" before they left the country.
In the process, the trainees often acquired intelligence about purely
domestic matters—upcoming demonstrations, for example—which
they then reported to their CHAOS case officers. In turn, the CIA officers would pass the information to the FBI, but only after incorporating

it in their own files, alongside other domestic data gleaned from the Bureau, Agency divisions such as the Office of Security, and the communications intelligence organization, the National Security Agency. All this clearly exceeded the CIA's authority.[30]

Moreover, despite initial instructions not to do so, the trainees sometimes took on active roles within their host organizations. Thanks to pioneering research by journalist Angus Mackenzie, we know a surprising amount about one such CHAOS agent. Salvatore J. Ferrera was a Chicago-born graduate student with an academic interest in the history of Marxism and a Beatles haircut. Recruited at Loyola University by the CIA, he developed a career as an underground journalist. In this role, he secured interviews with such countercultural luminaries as "Flower Power" advocate Abbie Hoffman, which he then reported to Richard Ober. He also photographed his subjects, using expensive camera equipment he claimed to have acquired through a trust fund. Moving to Washington, ostensibly to pursue his graduate studies, Ferrera participated in the launch of a major new underground newspaper, *Quicksilver Times*. With its offices also infiltrated by FBI agents, the paper soon descended into factional infighting that caused a temporary suspension of publication in 1970. When it relaunched, the *Quicksilver Times* staff collectivized and lived on-site to repel further penetration. At this point, Ferrera was eased out, apparently to his own relief, as he disliked the countercultural lifestyle of his colleagues. "There is . . . plenty of sex," he told Ober, "and this causes problems." Nevertheless, his fellow editors seem never to have suspected his true interest in the paper, and he was able to return to it to report on the May Day anti-war demonstrations that took place in Washington in 1971. When they learned the truth about Ferrera later, several of his former colleagues felt a sense of intimate personal violation. "I cried," said one. "I really liked him."[31]

It is important to note that, for all its undoubted excesses, CHAOS was not, as a later congressional report described it, "an intelligence mission sought by the CIA." The initiative came squarely from the White House, where LBJ's successor, Richard Nixon, ramped up the pressure on the Agency to deliver evidence of foreign communist support for the American peace movement. "The President has assigned a high priority to this project," presidential aide Tom Charles Huston wrote Langley in 1969. "'Support' should be liberally construed." It was to the CIA's credit that, even in the face of some evidence that Cuba was offering Black Panthers military training and recruiting other Americans for espionage purposes, its reporting stuck consistently to the line that foreign support did not "play a major role" in domestic radicalism. If anything, the Agency underplayed the influence of Third World anti-colonialism on young Americans, insisting that the US left was "basically self-sufficient," moving "under its own impetus." Unimpressed, in 1970 the Nixon White House moved to add new powers, such as the right of forced entry, to the intelligence community's surveillance of American protesters (until, ironically enough, opposition from J. Edgar Hoover scuttled the so-called Huston Plan).[32]

It is also only fair to acknowledge that, despite CHAOS being lodged in the Counter-Intelligence Staff, James Angleton personally had little involvement in the day-to-day running of the operation, with Special Operations Group head Ober reporting directly to DCI Helms. Undoubtedly, the canny Angleton wanted to put some distance between himself and an operation with "flap" potential. CIA documents identify CHAOS as "Dick Ober's project" so frequently that one begins to wonder if the exceptionally loyal and hardworking SOG chief was being set up as a fall guy should the program's existence ever become public. But the main reason for Angleton's relative absence from the records is probably that he simply was not as interested in American protesters and their Third World connections as he was in the communist powers of the Second World. Certainly, his staff had almost no prior experience of the domestic radical scene they had been directed to investigate. Frank J. Rafalko, an officer in the SOG branch covering Black radicalism, later admitted that he had not heard of the Black Panthers before being assigned special responsibility for the group. His section chief was reduced to leafing through *Jet* and *Ebony* magazines searching for names to go in the CHAOS index. One gets the sense that CHAOS's mission creep into the domestic realm was, to some extent, an unconscious, even involuntary process, a consequence of the blurriness of the line dividing the foreign and the US home front in the Cold War—or, put another way, a further manifestation of the imperial boomerang effect. Richard Helms grasped at this problem when testifying before a presidential commission a few years later. "When you are dealing with something that has both foreign and domestic aspects to it," he said, "the line has to be wavy. . . . It is like cutting a man down the middle."[33]

Still, even if Angleton did not seek out CHAOS, there was a clear institutional logic to its housing in the Counter-Intelligence Staff. Earlier campaigns against the FPCC and *Ramparts* had already gotten the CIA into a domestic battle with the anti-imperial left; CHAOS ran along organizational tracks laid by Richard Ober's *Ramparts* investigation. The Special Operations Group also bore various unmistakably Angletonian traits, several identified by tradecraft terminology almost as unfortunate as the code name CHAOS. For example, it had its own exclusive communication channel, CACTUS. Knowledge of CHAOS was confined to as small a circle as possible, and officers learning of its existence were required to sign a secrecy agreement entitled "MHCHAOS INDOCTRINATION," after which their names were added to a "Bigot List." Initially housed in separate offices on the second floor of CIA headquarters, the group moved to a vaulted basement area, where its files were kept in a second vault. At Ober's behest, staff entered all individuals named in sources in a database linked to a powerful IBM 360-67 machine in the Office of Computer Services. The information was password-protected in separate streams of increasing sensitivity, giving the database its (especially regrettable) name: HYDRA. Despite the new technology, all the Angleton trademarks were in evidence: the service within a service, the compartmentation, the files. It was even possible to detect a faint trace of British influence on CHAOS. Frank Rafalko later explained that the Bigot List "was derived from the British practice during World War II." Richard Ober, too, testified that "his security system was based on a British model." In sum, it made sense, institutionally speaking, that Angleton's CIS was doing this. Functionally if not consciously, CHAOS was the imperial brotherhood versus anti-imperialists.[34]

As for the anti-imperialists themselves, Operation CHAOS did not by itself deal actual harm to any of the organizations or individuals concerned; it was just a surveillance program. But, combined with other historical forces working to break up the New Left and Black nationalist movement, it undoubtedly contributed to the sense of malaise that gripped the 1960s generation as the decade ended. At *Quicksilver Times*, fear of infiltration caused the paper's editors to barricade themselves within their office, as we have seen; with the original editorial staff down from ten members to just four, the publication folded permanently in 1972. The Black Panthers too were in terminal decline, hobbled by violent internal disputes caused in part by FBI harassment and suspicions of hostile government penetration. Fear of CIA surveillance pervaded the group—Eldridge Cleaver, for example, suspected that a fellow member of the US People's Anti-Imperialist Delegation was an Agency plant. Vietnam resisters and deserters in Europe caught a particularly bad case of CHAOS-induced jitters. In the Parisian commune described by the CIA agent PETUNIA, the inhabitants were "very suspicious of each other and play[ed] games trying to trip each other up." In Stockholm, Sweden, the American Deserters Committee fell into a state of mutual mistrust that approached collective psychosis. Many of these groups were, of course, already divided along ideological and other lines, but the sense of being watched all the time, by both faceless strangers and intimate friends, undoubtedly hastened their demise. The paranoia was crippling.[35]

Round One to the imperial brotherhood.

But then a strange thing happened. As the US Third World Left expired, its anti-imperialism entered the American mainstream. In 1971, the *Washington Post* published the Pentagon Papers, revealing how one administration after another had misled the public about the progress of the Vietnam War. The following year, the *Post*'s Bob Woodward and Carl Bernstein began unraveling the White House's links to a break-in at the Democratic National Committee's office at the Watergate complex in Washington, DC. In 1973, Congress opened an investigation of the Watergate scandal and passed the War Powers Resolution checking the president's power to take the United States into armed conflicts, a move followed up the next year by an amendment to the Foreign Assistance Act requiring express presidential authorization and reporting of future covert operations. The press and Congress were reining in the "imperial presidency," the phrase historian Arthur Schlesinger Jr. used as the title of an influential book of the era.[36]

So strong was the anti-imperial mood that it even spread to the CIA. The Agency had long been home to a minority tradition of mish kid sympathy for Third World nationalism, a tendency that, if anything, was strengthened by the exposure of Agency family members to post-colonial environments during overseas postings. Now, with the Agency's founding generation approaching retirement, there was a demographic changing of the guard under way at Langley. New recruits tended to be from more diverse social and ethnic, if not necessarily gender or racial, backgrounds than their predecessors. They were also different in appearance. The normally imperturbable Richard Helms was taken aback when he spotted an employee in the Executive Dining Room wearing a black turtleneck shirt with a medallion around his neck.[37]

But the rebellion at Langley was not just sartorial. Beginning with the headline-grabbing example of Daniel Ellsberg, the defense analyst (and former member of Ed Lansdale's Vietnam team) who leaked the Pentagon Papers, the CIA found itself facing a new, existential threat: young converts to the anti-imperialist cause divulging official secrets. The first whistleblower to come from within the ranks of the CIA was Victor Marchetti. A working-class Italian American who had risen through the ranks to serve as executive assistant to the deputy director, Marchetti had grown disillusioned with what he perceived as the Agen-cy's excessive use of covert action abroad and secrecy at home. After resigning in 1969, Marchetti published a spy novel obviously based on his career (*The Rope Dancer*) and began writing a non-fiction critique of the Agency. Meanwhile, word reached Langley that Philip Agee, a Latin American field operative who had quit the same year as Marchetti, was also embarking on an exposé of the Agency.[38]

The behavior of these young men was disturbing on several lev-els. Earlier government whistleblowers had been content merely with calling out isolated cases of inefficiency or corruption. The likes of Agee, however, were raising principled objections, based on their new anti-imperial convictions, to the core mission of the CIA. Moreover, in choosing to go outside official circles with their complaints, they were violating the fraternal code, the ethos of the imperial brotherhood, that had sustained the morale of the Agency since its founding. It was perhaps easy to dismiss the not very prepossessing Marchetti, the "lone ethnic" (to use his own words) in Agency senior management, as an outsider figure; it was harder in the case of the rather handsome Agee, who, if not of the old WASP governing class, came from a wealthy Catholic family and, in his youthful liberalism, epitomized the pre-Vietnam Cold War consensus. Later, stories would circulate that Agee was in fact a Soviet agent; the evidence is unclear, but his most recent biographer thinks that if he had any such connections, they were more likely with Cuban intelligence than with the KGB. Like other members of his generation, Agee looked to the Third, not Second, World as his ideological lodestar. His own explanation for his defiance of the CIA was the lifelong ethical influence of his Catholic upbringing.[39]

Confronted with this internal threat, the CIA placed both Marchetti and Agee under surveillance reminiscent of the CHAOS program. Indeed, when Agee moved to Paris to work on his book, the CHAOS agent Salvatore Ferrera was dispatched to befriend him and monitor his progress. But this did not resolve the basic question: In the absence of an Official Secrets Act, how could the CIA prevent whistleblowers from publicizing the Agency's secrets? On the advice of the Nixon White House, which was busy trying to "plumb" its own leaks, the CIA improvised a legal strategy. Arguing that the secrecy agreement Marchetti had signed when entering employment with the Agency overrode his First Amendment rights, CIA lawyers obtained a court order prohibiting him from publishing his manuscript until he had first submitted it to Langley for review. When *The CIA and the Cult of Intelligence* eventually came out in 1974, it contained 168 blank spaces where the Agency had insisted on deletions. The Marchetti case established a valuable legal precedent for the CIA, but its immediate effect was merely to draw public attention to the book and make the Agency look like a censor. Meanwhile, other writers, publishers, and lawyers came forward offering the whistleblowers financial, legal, and moral support. The CIA had inadvertently fostered the emergence of a dissident community devoted to exposing its secrets.[40]

The new anti-imperial sensibility within the Agency—which, in a way, was not that new, given the earlier anti-colonial impulses of such famous operatives as Kim Roosevelt and Edward Lansdale—spelled trouble for one unit in particular: the Counter-Intelligence Staff's Special Operations Group. By 1973, the SOG had created some 13,000 CHAOS files on subjects or individuals, while the HYDRA computer index contained over 300,000 names and organizations. Despite the ultra-secrecy surrounding CHAOS, many CIA officers outside the CIS suspected its existence, and resented it. Field stations objected to the extra reporting it imposed on them; senior managers feared its flap potential; and junior officers (as Special Operations Group officer Frank Rafalko recalled later) "expressed their concern about . . . student unrest and whether CIA should have a role in the domestic aspect of this issue." There was particular unease about the likely reaction of the Agency's few African American officers should they learn of CHAOS's specific interest in Black nationalism. According to a 1972 inspector general's survey of the program, staff at one field station routinely destroyed CHAOS cable traffic "so as to avoid any possibility of its somehow falling into the hands of a black officer." The Counter-Intelligence

Staff had never been popular with the rest of the Agency, as it had the authority to veto operations it deemed vulnerable to enemy penetration. Coinciding as it did with the destructive fallout of the Angleton mole hunt, CHAOS cemented the CIS's poor institutional reputation. One officer spoke disparagingly of the "counterintelligence clique" as a "high priesthood of secrecy." Another dismissed counterintelligence itself as "paranoia made systematic by a card index."[41]

As for the high priest of counterintelligence himself, the early 1970s was proving a testing time. James Angleton was appalled by the politics of the era, especially Richard Nixon's foreign policy of détente, which he saw as falling into the communist trap of strategic deception. Meanwhile, his marriage to Cicely d'Autremont Angleton, always troubled because of his obsessive behavior, grew rockier still when she declared her opposition to the Vietnam War. In a particularly dramatic instance of CIA family alienation, she moved out of the family home and, along with their two daughters, converted to Sikhism. It was not just Angleton's private life that was unspooling; so too was his professional legend. Compounding its other woes, the CIA was caught by surprise when the Yom Kippur War between Israel and its Arab neighbors broke out in 1973; because of his longtime control of the Israeli account, Angleton earned particular opprobrium. The once-feared counterintelligence chief was becoming the butt of office jokes. If a crowded CIA elevator stopped at a floor and the door opened but no one got on or off, riders would whisper, "Angleton."[42]

As long as Richard Helms was DCI, Angleton and counterintelligence operations such as CHAOS and the mail-opening program LINGUAL were safe. Though not close friends, the two intelligence veterans were united by the shared values of first-generation CIA men, including an expansive understanding of the Agency's powers. Helms defended CHAOS in the face of internal criticism, declaring in December 1972 that it was a "legitimate counterintelligence function of the Agency" that could not be discontinued "simply because some members of the organization do not like this activity."[43]

Two months later, though, Helms's protection was gone. The DCI had angered President Nixon, long an enemy of the "Oh-So-Social" CIA set, by refusing to participate in the Watergate cover-up. Empowered by his 1972 reelection, Nixon fired Helms in February 1973, replacing him with James R. Schlesinger, an economist with no intelligence background. The smart, no-nonsense Schlesinger was under orders to shake up the CIA, to "get rid of the clowns," as Nixon put it, and he performed his task without mercy, eliminating some 1,500 Agency staff. Dismayed by the CIA's recent mission creep, Schlesinger also went after the Agency's domestic counterintelligence programs. The Post Office had been getting jumpy about LINGUAL, which was the first to go, in February 1973, despite Angleton's protestations that it was still providing useful information about Soviet-American contacts. CHAOS was on its last legs anyway because its chief targets, the New Left and Black Panthers, had largely disintegrated; Richard Ober had received orders to refocus SOG on international terrorism instead. The program was run down over the course of 1973, and shut altogether in March of the following year. In its last days, SOG officers including Frank Rafalko launched Project Destruction, a systematic purge of CHAOS records reminiscent of a massive culling of embarrassing colonial files that the British government had carried out in the 1960s. Angleton's counterintelligence empire was collapsing around him.[44]

Worse was to come. After only five months as DCI, Schlesinger left the CIA to run the Pentagon. To Angleton's chagrin, his replacement was an old rival, the long-serving covert action expert William

Colby. Despite both being Agency careerists, the two men were cut from very different cloth: Angleton an idiosyncratic, politically conservative literary intellectual, Colby a liberal Catholic with a clipped, soldierly manner. The enmity between them dated back to the early years of the Cold War, when they had disagreed over which political groups to back in Italy, Colby favoring the Non-Communist Left, Angleton the center-right. 1973 found the new DCI wanting to continue his predecessor's policy of reform and openness, all anathema to the CIS chief. Colby thought Angleton's approach to counterintelligence arcane and even harmful to the CIA's core mission of intelligence gathering. On his side, Angleton brooded over Colby's motivation—was this another twist in the Soviet Master Plot? His suspicions deepened after the director proposed he relinquish control of the Israeli liaison and even consider surrendering counterintelligence itself. When in 1974 Colby learned of the theory that Angleton was himself a Soviet agent (and Anatoli Golitsyn his KGB case officer), he ordered the creation of a blue-ribbon panel to investigate. Although the panel concluded there was no case to answer, the episode only increased the DCI's determination to rid himself of the turbulent counterintelligence chief.[45]

Meanwhile, with President Nixon resigning in August 1974 to avoid imminent impeachment, the US press was on the lookout for more stories like Watergate. One young newsman in particular, an abrasive, even obnoxious thirty-seven-year-old by the name of Seymour Hersh who earlier had exposed the My Lai massacre in Vietnam, was on a hot streak reporting on the CIA. During his investigations, he learned that James Schlesinger had ordered a review of past Agency illegalities and that the resulting list, known as the "Family Jewels," contained details of domestic spying operations. In December 1974, Hersh phoned Colby, who confirmed the broad outlines of the story. Soon afterward, the

DCI summoned Angleton and informed him that his name was about to appear in an exposé of CHAOS. Surely now was the time to give up his responsibilities? Again, Angleton refused. Hersh's report about CHAOS, incomplete and occasionally erroneous but revelatory nonetheless, appeared on the front page of the Sunday *New York Times* on December 22, 1974, under the blaring headline "HUGE C.I.A. OPERATION REPORTED IN U.S. AGAINST ANTIWAR FORCES." Angleton's resignation was announced the following day.[46]

The next morning, on Christmas Eve, 1974, a bizarre scene unfolded at James Angleton's Arlington home. Having obtained the address from a telephone book, the CBS correspondent Daniel Schorr approached the front door and knocked. He was answered by a groggy-looking Angleton, still in his pajamas. The journalist was admitted and, to his surprise, granted a long, meandering interview. After several hours, Angleton excused himself to get dressed. Now clad in a long black coat and fedora, he left the house and walked slowly across the lawn to where a bank of cameras was waiting. There he paused, according to Schorr, "as though hypnotized." No one seemed sure what to do. After a few baffling responses to questions, Angleton climbed into his Mercedes and drove off. Schorr remembered him looking back at the pressmen "with a dazed smile." Clearly, a long career in the most secret compartments of the national security state had not prepared Angleton for the sudden glare of publicity.[47]

But the ordeal was not over yet. During 1975, the "Year of Intelligence," blow after blow rained down on the CIA. The new president, Gerald R. Ford, instructed Vice President Nelson Rockefeller to form a presidential commission to investigate CIA activities within the United States. Although clearly intended to draw a line under the scandal, the Rockefeller Commission confirmed Seymour Hersh's main claims about Agency domestic operations, and, with the likes of CBS's Daniel Schorr still on the CIA's trail, new revelations—about the plots to kill Fidel Castro, for example—followed in its wake. Despite various efforts to prevent its publication, Philip Agee's tell-all memoir *Inside the Company* came out in April. Its cover featured a photograph of a typewriter that Sal Ferrera had helped provide to the whistleblower during his time in Paris and was subsequently discovered to have contained listening devices. Later, Agee thanked the CIA for indirectly enabling him to write his book. Even Hollywood was getting in on the act: released in September 1975, *Three Days of the Condor* depicted a villainous Agency attempting to murder one of its own officers, played by Robert Redford. As the movie ends, the Redford character becomes a whistleblower.[48]

The release of *Three Days of the Condor* coincided with another personal humiliation for Angleton. The Ninety-Fourth US Congress was riding the wave of anti-CIA feeling unleashed by the Hersh report, with both chambers establishing select committees on intelligence. While the House of Representatives pursued a relatively wide-ranging investigation, the Senate committee focused on covert operations, including the counterintelligence programs LINGUAL and CHAOS. Its chair, Idaho senator Frank Church, was known for his opposition to the Vietnam War and moralistic approach to politics (his nickname on Capitol Hill was "Frank Sunday School"). During a press conference, in a probably unconscious reference to Rudyard Kipling, he referred to the CIA as a "rogue elephant" trampling on American liberties. The phrase caught on, despite evidence that, as Otis G. Pike, Church's counterpart in the House, put it, the Agency had been "utterly responsive to the instructions of the President." When it came Angleton's turn to testify, in late September, Church seemed to enjoy the opportunity to grill a maven of the secret state. For his part, Angleton appeared discombobulated, even pitiable—like an old man asking for porridge, as a journalist commented. During one particularly excruciating exchange, Church forced Angleton to walk back an earlier statement that subsequently achieved nearly the same notoriety as Church's own "rogue elephant" analogy: "It is inconceivable that a secret intelligence arm of the Government has to comply with all of the overt orders of the Government."[49]

Meanwhile, back at Langley, Colby was launching a purge of Angleton's staff. Within a week of his departure, three of Angleton's most loyal subordinates—Raymond Rocca, Newton S. "Scotty" Miler, and William J. Hood—were gone, too. His successor as chief of the Counter-Intelligence Staff, George T. Kalaris, set about trying to reintegrate the unit into the CIA mainstream, starting with a review of the chaotic contents of Angleton's office. These turned out to include, among other curious items, the JX Files, a cache of reports from Jay Lovestone, a veteran anti-communist infighter in the international trade union movement, whose role as a CIA agent was not even known to the Agency's labor division. In what would become a post-Angleton cottage industry, senior Agency retirees were rehired to investigate what had gone wrong in the CIS. All concluded that, whatever his earlier contributions, Angleton's late-career performance had done more harm than good. One such study, only recently declassified, used the moment as an occasion to denounce Angleton's intuitive, non-systematic brand of counterintelligence in favor of the social scientific approach and "rigorous analytic techniques" favored by the CIA's intelligence analysts—the Sherman Kent school, in other words. Anti-Angletonianism was becoming the new Agency orthodoxy.[50]

Perhaps the biggest victim of this institutional reckoning was the CHAOS fall guy, Richard Ober. His personal papers reveal a career in free fall. Too hot to handle after the CHAOS revelations—his name had featured in the Hersh *New York Times* story—Ober was seconded to the National Security Council as a senior staff member on intelligence, then shifted into the Agency's internal history staff, the Center for the Study of Intelligence. With various plaintiffs claiming civil damages resulting from CHAOS surveillance, Ober found himself a named defendant in four different lawsuits. In 1977, amid another staff reduction, this one imposed by President Jimmy Carter's appointee as DCI, Admiral Stansfield Turner, Ober learned that his performance had been rated within the bottom 5 percent of his grade, and he was to be "separated" from the Agency. The action was clearly unfair and Ober protested vociferously, citing his career-long history of excellent ratings and "loyalty to CIA as an institution." He was particularly irked that, whereas he had been "rewarded for outstanding service by being selected for firing," the anti-imperial whistleblowers, the men who had "effectively ruined [his] career" and done "irreparable damage to CIA," had "escaped unscathed." Following an appeal, Ober obtained his removal from the separation list, but by now his morale was in tatters. A homemade greeting card mixed in with his papers, presumably exchanged with other members of the Turner purge, featured a cartoon character with a big nail sticking through his body and the caption "Work Diligently with Integrity—You'll Get Your Just Reward!" Ober retired from the CIA in 1980 to manage an herb farm in Virginia.[51]

Round Two to the anti-imperialists.

James Angleton also suffered from the bitter sense of injustice, victimhood, and loss that enveloped the CIA's imperial brotherhood in the 1970s. Not only was his counterintelligence empire disintegrating, but Congress was enacting various checks on the Agency that in his view amounted to a kind of unilateral intelligence disarmament against communist infiltration and strategic deception: permanent select committees in both chambers, a Foreign Intelligence Surveillance Act to prevent future warrantless domestic wiretapping, and, in 1980, an Intelligence Oversight Act requiring presidents to brief the new intelligence committees about proposed covert operations. "It's a nightmare," Angleton wrote his friend and now former CIA colleague Cord Meyer Jr.[52]

But Angleton did not get mad; in a coda to his counterintelligence career that has generally gone unremarked by his biographers, he got even. With former CIS acolytes like Scotty Miler rallying around, he doubled down on his claims about Soviet strategic deception and penetration, even claiming that the likes of William Colby and Frank Church were effectively doing the work of the KGB. While his detractors at the Agency wrote postmortem case studies of the Monster Plot for internal consumption, Angleton put his side of the story to a growing clique of friendly newsmen, revealing a hitherto unsuspected talent for public relations. One member of his new circle, the investigative journalist Edward J. Epstein, became, in the words of one historian, "something of a literary amanuensis" for the retired CIS chief. Previously, the dominant image of Angleton had been of a solitary figure sitting in a darkened office at Langley, surrounded by files and wreathed in cigarette smoke. Now, he was an intelligence éminence grise, holding court in the wood-paneled rooms of Washington's Army-Navy Club. Among other deft publicity moves, he succeeded in popularizing a soundbite of his own to describe the KGB's manipulation of Western opinion: "the wilderness of mirrors." Although the phrase was T. S. Eliot's, it became so strongly associated with the spymaster that many, including, apparently, Angleton himself, came to believe he had coined it.[53]

This comeback should not have come as a complete surprise. During the Year of Intelligence investigations, Angleton had shown an ability to turn even the most challenging of circumstances to his own limited advantage. After the Rockefeller Commission requested his testimony, he wrote the commission a long memorandum criticizing DCI Colby's handling of counterintelligence and setting forth recommendations for CIA reform, including increased support for the CIS, compartmentation, and liaison with domestic agencies such as the FBI. A careful reading of Angleton's generally disastrous testimony to the Church Committee reveals that, even amid his inquisitors' denunciations of CIA overreach, he succeeded in getting in several mentions of his own pet themes of Soviet expansionism and Western intelligence disarmament. "When I left the Army, . . . I believed that we were in the dawn of a millennium," he declared, in one of his best lines. "When I look at the map today and the weakness of . . . this country, that is what shocks me."[54]

Angleton was not alone in this belief. The mid-1970s witnessed a growing reaction in conservative circles against the strategy of détente and, with it, a tendency to criticize CIA intelligence assessments of Soviet intentions and capabilities as naïvely optimistic. The so-called Team B exercise of 1976, an external review of the Agency's Soviet estimate, arrived at a much bleaker, more Angletonian set of conclusions. During the Carter years, against a backdrop of the Turner staff reduction at Langley, this tendency began organizing outside of government. In 1976, Angleton himself joined the American Security Council (ASC), an anti-communist citizen group that dated back to the 1950s, telling an early meeting that "the CIA's counterintelligence division was effectively disbanded, and for all practical purposes covert operations were also shut down." The following year, Angleton became chair of the

ASC's Security and Intelligence Fund, established to assist CIA officers and FBI agents facing prosecution as a result of the Year of Intelligence. When, in 1979, an offshoot of the ASC established a colloquium, the Consortium for the Study of Intelligence, it became a forum for the Angletonian school of counterintelligence recently expelled from the Agency. Participants such as Scotty Miler and Edward Epstein sounded familiar themes about the danger of Soviet deception and the need for an aggressive US counterintelligence response. Sympathetic academics like Roy Godson and Richard Pipes critiqued the scientific, technical model of intelligence promulgated by Sherman Kent in favor of Angleton's more intuitive, literary approach. Like a political party defeated at the polls, the counterintelligence expellees were regrouping, waiting for their chance to reenter government. Angleton himself remained fiercely loyal to the CIA, as one might expect given his early-life indoctrination in the imperial value of service. When Angelo Codevilla, a congressional staffer active in the anti-détente cause, criticized one of the retired spy's "tormentors" at Langley, Angleton reproved him: "My Agency, may it always be right, but right or wrong, my Agency!"[55]

Meanwhile, the CIA itself was fighting a rearguard action, this one against the anti-imperial whistleblowers. The Agency had already established the principle of prior restraint in its legal prosecution of Victor Marchetti, who was financially ruined in the process. ("I shoulda kept my mouth shut [and] never taken on the CIA," he admitted later.) Although it had failed similarly to muzzle Philip Agee, who was now living the life of a political exile in London, the Agency did succeed in securing his deportation from England in 1977, after Angleton visited MI5 with evidence from French intelligence and "a CHAOS agent" (likely Sal Ferrera) that Agee had "sold out." Two years later, Agee's US passport was revoked, rendering him stateless. In 1978, in the third landmark whistleblower case of the decade, the CIA obtained a court ruling against Frank Snepp, the analyst who had written a memoir about the botched evacuation of Saigon in 1975, forcing him to surrender any profits that might result from publication. Like Marchetti, Snepp was bankrupted. At the same time as these widely publicized stories discouraged future whistleblowers, the Agency was busy institutionalizing the "Marchetti principle" in the shape of the Publications Review Board. Henceforth, all employees who had signed a secrecy agreement with the Agency were required to submit for review anything they wished to publish, or else face trial. The application of this requirement varied according to the author's standing with the Agency, but it was sufficiently draconian that even "old boys" in good order such as Kim Roosevelt found their writing projects subjected to excessive interference and delays. The CIA had patched together its own version of the British Official Secrets Act.[56]

As one might expect in the ceaseless conflict between the forces of US imperialism and anti-imperialism, the whistleblowers pushed back. Agee, in particular, made a second career as a sort of professional CIA gadfly, engaging in such provocations as publicly naming serving Agency officers (the CIA blamed Agee for the 1975 assassination of Athens station chief Richard S. Welch, probably unfairly). As in the 1960s, there was an anti-imperial boomerang effect, with Agee's defiance fueled by the support he received from leftist governments in the Global South. In 1980, he obtained a passport from the Marxist prime minister of the small Caribbean country of Grenada, Maurice Bishop; later, when Bishop was killed just prior to the 1983 US invasion of the island, the Sandinista government of Nicaragua provided Agee with a replacement. In return, the whistleblower joined in the transnational solidarity movement protesting CIA attempts to topple the Sandinistas via the Contra guerrilla movement. In an action reminiscent of the Venceremos Brigade's support for the Cuban Revolution, Agee and his son went to work on Nicaraguan coffee plantations targeted by the Contras. Back in the United States, he and other anti-imperial CIA whistleblowers such as ex-Marine John Stockwell (the son, by the way, of Presbyterian missionaries) played prominent roles in protests by activists in the CIA Off Campus movement, who were trying to end Agency recruitment efforts at American universities. Even in the hostile environment of the conservative 1980s, the US Third World Left was alive and kicking.[57]

Overall, though, it was the imperial party who held the upper hand. The first years of the Reagan era witnessed a gradual rolling back of the congressional checks on US intelligence enacted during the 1970s, with Congress providing little opposition. The 1982 Intelligence Identities Protection Act, which made it a federal crime to divulge the identity of covert government personnel, was clearly delayed revenge against "traitors like Philip Agee," as one of its sponsors, the arch-conservative senator from Arizona Barry Goldwater, phrased it. With US journalists as compliant as they had been before the 1960s, the Reagan administration had little difficulty squashing would-be whistleblowers. When, in 1986, a small group of mercenaries tried to expose the White House's illegal support of the Contra rebels in Nicaragua, the press either ignored or denounced them. Leading organizations on the transnational left such as the Committee in Solidarity with the People of El Salvador became the victims of a state-private campaign of surveillance and investigation reminiscent of the CHAOS program of the 1960s and 1970s.[58]

The 1980s saw another important victory for the imperial tendency: the Angletonians reentering government. Allies of the former CIA counterintelligence chief in the Consortium for the Study of Intelligence won places in the Reagan transition team, the National Security Council, and the President's Foreign Intelligence Advisory Board (PFIAB). From these positions, they pressed not just for a revival of Cold War covert action but also for a restoration of the CIA's counterintelligence function along pre-1973 lines. In 1982, they won a major victory: the creation of a Foreign Intelligence Capabilities Group within the CIA's Directorate of Intelligence meant to remedy an alleged lack of counter-deception analysis. Although he stayed in retirement, Angleton himself consulted not only with new allies such as Angelo Codevilla, Senator Goldwater, and the PFIAB but also with the CIA itself. In 1983, a delegation of Agency officers visited him for four hours seeking his views on counterintelligence reform. Chain-smoking throughout, Angleton told his audience that his old employer should "turn the clock back to the period before 1973" and "add powers" that various CIA directors had denied him.[59]

Before he died of cancer in 1987, Angleton earned one other validation that almost made his comeback complete. The year 1985 witnessed a series of revelations about moles in US intelligence agencies, so many that the media dubbed it "The Year of the Spy." These included Edward Lee Howard, an aggrieved former CIA officer who escaped the clutches of the FBI and defected to Moscow. Another Agency officer, Aldrich Ames, began spying for the Soviets in the same year but was not arrested until 1994, by which time he had done untold damage to American espionage networks in the Soviet bloc.

None of this had happened when James Angleton was running CIA counterintelligence. Unlike most other Western intelligence services, the Agency experienced no high-level communist infiltration on his watch. Perhaps Angleton's literary, even poetic, methodology was effective counterintelligence after all. The irony was that Angleton himself could not claim credit because doing so would mean denying the existence of the mole he had spent half of his career hunting.

Other forces were in play, too, of course, but the story of CIA counterintelligence is in many ways a story of empire. Its principal designer owed many of his values and methods—and, possibly, his tendency toward paranoia—to the imperial past. Thanks to the imperial boomerang, what should have been an exclusively foreign effort morphed into a campaign of surveillance aimed at domestic radicals. The latter belonged, partly at least, within the long tradition of American anti-imperialism, and they too were influenced by a boomerang effect, in their case, the inspirational example of anti-colonialism in the Cold War Third World. In the ensuing battles between the forces of imperialism and anti-imperialism, the latter enjoyed several stirring victories, the result in part of the United States' lack of official secrecy relative to older imperial powers such as Britain. By the end of the Cold War, however, the imperial party was on top, having fashioned an American version of the British Official Secrets Act. The earlier vision of counterintelligence too had reasserted itself at the CIA, having temporarily been overwhelmed by the anti-imperial currents of the era.

Moreover, the domestic reverberations of covert empire were not confined to counterintelligence. As in other imperial societies, they also extended into the realm of US popular opinion, and government attempts to manage it: in America, another job for the CIA.

CHAPTER 5

Publicity

S pying is about secrecy, but it is also about storytelling. Many future CIA officers first became interested in intelligence after reading espionage novels and imagining themselves heroes of their own spy adventures. The daily business of intelligence work itself involves making up fictions—false identities and cover stories for covert missions. After leaving their professional lives behind, spies often turn their careers into stories, whether in the form of memoirs, their own stabs at spy fiction, or merely anecdotes they tell their family and friends.

As in other aspects of the intelligence trade, it was the British who did the most to establish the association between spying and storytelling. Graham Greene, Ian Fleming, and John le Carré are perhaps the most prominent writers who mined their real-life experiences as intelligence officers for their fiction. But the United States also has had its share of literary spies, including several who have already appeared in the pages of this book: the poet and editor James Angleton; Kim Roosevelt, the son of a writer and himself the author of three published books; and Edward Lansdale, a constant concocter of psychological warfare narratives whose intelligence reports often read like magazine articles (indeed, some actually became magazine articles). Even the decidedly non-poetic Sherman Kent loved spinning spy yarns in his retirement.

None, though, possessed quite the literary credentials of another founding-generation CIA "legend," Cord Meyer. Not only did Meyer write professionally both before and after serving in the CIA, but during his time with the Agency he oversaw a vast covert campaign to mobilize American writers, artists, and many other US citizen groups to tell the story of the "free world" to foreign populations, including the inhabitants of the postcolonial regions where the Cold War was at its hottest. Nor was the "Cultural Cold War," as this dimension of the superpower conflict later became known, confined to foreign battlefields. As during the era of New Imperialism, when the likes of Rudyard Kipling and Hubert Lyautey consciously set out to strengthen British and French public support for the colonial policies of their respective governments, so CIA officers such as Meyer also engaged in operations intended to generate popular American backing for Cold War–era US interventions in far-off, unfamiliar parts of the world—to tell Americans the story of their new, postcolonial empire.

The difference from earlier empires was that, because of decolonization and American anti-imperialism, this was something the US government largely had to do in secret. For those involved, like Cord Meyer, this entailed a strange existence: wielding tremendous power in American society while, at the same time, having to live in the shadows, unable to tell their own story.

There was little about Meyer's early life that suggested he would end up spending most of his career in self-imposed obscurity. Instead, there was a sense of almost limitless possibility.

Cord Meyer Jr. was born in Washington, DC, in 1920. His father was a Long Island real estate developer and diplomat, his mother from an old, well-off family, the Thaws. After a New England prep school (St. Paul's), he entered Yale, where he followed in James Angleton's literary footsteps, studying English poetry, reading the New Critics, and editing the *Yale Lit*. Unlike the slightly wayward Angleton, though, Meyer was a brilliant student. Tall and blue-eyed, he won prizes for both intellectual and athletic achievement (he was goalie on the Yale hockey team, his twin brother, Quentin, a forward). He graduated in 1942 ahead of the rest of his class, summa cum laude, and enlisted in the Marines. Serving in the Pacific, he compiled a war record of conspicuous bravery, earning a Bronze Star and Purple Heart, the latter after losing an eye to a Japanese grenade and nearly dying in fierce fighting on Guam in 1944. While convalescing in New York, he turned this terrible experience into an intensely moving short story, "Waves of Darkness." Published in the *Atlantic Monthly*, it earned the O. Henry Prize for the best first story and subsequently appeared in numerous anthologies. He also became engaged to Mary Pinchot, an equally talented and attractive Vassar graduate and niece of the conservationist Amos Pinchot. Fittingly, the golden couple's 1945 marriage ceremony was presided over by Reinhold Niebuhr, the nation's most eminent theologian, and a major intellectual influence on postwar American literature.[1]

But Meyer was not ready to lead a purely literary life. Combined with the usual call to service and leadership felt by men of his background, his grievous war wounds had instilled in him a powerful desire to make the world a better, more peaceful place. Immediately after their wedding, he and Mary flew to San Francisco to attend the founding conference of the United Nations, he as one of two veteran assistants to the US delegate, Harold Stassen. The experience was defining. Meyer had high hopes for the new UN but, as he explained in another article for the *Atlantic Monthly*, he was disappointed by what he perceived as its founders' failure to accommodate the calls for freedom of colonized peoples (a belief he shared with several other CIA officers of his generation). He also felt that the new body lacked the powers needed to overcome the anarchic tendencies of an international order still made up of sovereign states. Like a surprising number of other Americans after World War II, not just leftists but also self-described realists such as Reinhold Niebuhr, Meyer believed in the need for a world government strong enough to prevent future wars—now, likely nuclear wars. In 1947, after various groups advocating for such an entity had merged to form the United World Federalists, he became president of the new organization and, in the process, a minor American celebrity, pictures of his visibly wounded but still handsome face adorning the walls of countless campus dormitories. As well as continuing to write—his book making the case for world government, *Peace or Anarchy*, appeared in 1947—Meyer lectured in venues such as Madison Square Garden, was featured in glossy magazine profiles (*Glamour* included him along with John F. Kennedy among ten "Young Men Who Care"), and testified before Congress about the need for a world government. "If Cord goes into politics," wrote a friend, "he'll probably not only be President of the United States; he may be the first president of the parliament of man. And if he becomes a writer, he's sure to win the Nobel Prize."[2]

Although his leadership of the world federalist movement placed tremendous demands on him, Meyer still found time during the late 1940s for one other cause. While attending the 1945 UN conference,

Cord Meyer, pictured in 1948 during his time as president of the United World Federalists, before he joined the CIA and took over leadership of its global publicity operations. Cord Meyer Papers, Library of Congress

he had met Charles Bolté, like him a wounded war hero. Bolté was chair of the recently formed American Veterans Committee (AVC), a liberal alternative to the main US veteran organization, the American Legion. Drawn by the AVC's combination of internationalism and progressivism on domestic issues such as race relations, Meyer joined its National Planning Committee alongside such prominent young liberals as Franklin D. Roosevelt Jr. and Gilbert A. Harrison, future editor of the *New Republic*. The trouble was, the AVC was not only attracting liberals to its ranks. Its membership also included a growing number of American communists looking to harness it to their own purposes, a tactic the communist movement had already used to great effect during the Popular Front era of the 1930s. With backing from anti-communist trade unionists who had resisted similar efforts to penetrate American labor organizations, Meyer and his liberal comrades successfully repelled the attempted takeover and eventually barred Communist Party members from AVC membership, a move repeated across the United States left in the late 1940s as US-Soviet relations deteriorated. Not surprisingly, this earned him a series of personal attacks in communist publications, one, for example, describing him as a "fig leaf of American imperialism." Simultaneously, he came under attack from right-wing anti-communists, the sort who would soon rally around the standard of Senator Joe McCarthy, in pamphlets with titles like *Reds Behind World Federalism*.[3]

Later, commentators would identify these twin moments—the bitter AVC faction fight and the conservative impugning of his loyalty—as crucial in Cord Meyer's transformation from an idealistic world federalist into a CIA Cold Warrior. Doubtless these experiences were important, but they ignore an underlying conservative sensibility in Meyer that predated them. Even in his 1945 *Atlantic Monthly* article calling for a stronger UN, Meyer admitted to doubts that such an ambition was realistic. For a supranational authority to work, there needed to be a preexisting community of belief among nations, yet such a thing clearly did not exist. "We live in a tragic age," Meyer reflected, "where the moral and intellectual resources of our time do not seem adequate to meet either our problems or our obligations." His private views, expressed in an unpublished journal, were even bleaker. "If I was asked to prophesy the next 25 years," he confided, "I should prophesy war and . . . perhaps . . . the end of our civilization, . . . though I would never admit this publicly." No doubt this deeply gloomy view of the human condition had something to do with Meyer's terrible personal suffering during the war (in addition to nearly being killed himself, in May 1945 he received news that his beloved twin, Quentin, had died in fighting on Okinawa). But it was also typical of a certain sort of American intellectual who, as the Cold War unfolded, turned slowly from liberalism to conservatism. Indeed, Meyer's views on world government tracked almost precisely those of Reinhold Niebuhr, the theologian who had officiated at his wedding. Niebuhr too espoused world federalism mainly out of a profound pessimism about humankind's future in the atomic age, then came to view the cause as illusory in the absence of a true sense of international community, before eventually reconciling himself to supporting the United States in the Cold War.[4]

In 1949, Meyer resigned from the United World Federalists to take up a fellowship at Harvard. It was no longer possible, he confessed in his journal, to "urge others on to action, when I now doubt the efficacy of any kind of action." The outbreak of the Korean War caught him in a dilemma, dismayed by the prospect of more "senseless slaughter," yet unwilling "to allow a rough despotism . . . to stamp out that freedom of the mind that is the West's best monument." Then, in early 1951, came an apparent solution. After meeting with Allen Dulles, Meyer was offered a job in the CIA. He hesitated briefly—secret government service meant abandoning the public life he had lived since the end of the war. But, following reassuring conversations with a Yale classmate now serving with the Agency and journalist Walter Lippmann, he accepted. By October 1951, Meyer and his family, which now included three young sons, had moved to a pre–Civil War home in McLean, Virginia, and he was commuting to work at CIA headquarters, then still housed in temporary huts strewn along the National Mall's reflecting pool.[5]

Cord Meyer's shift to the CIA appeared to cut short what had seemed a promising literary career; over the next twenty-five years, as he continued to work for the Agency, he would occasionally admit to regrets about "the novels and plays I wish I could have tried to write." But for Meyer and other aristocratic men of letters who ended up at the CIA—Kim Roosevelt might count as another—secret government service did not altogether put an end to their literary ambitions. Indeed, Meyer now found himself at the center of a massive effort to shape the consciousness of whole populations through covert acts of storytelling—an effort that was already under way.[6]

Rather like the British secret services, with their origins in the "invasion scare" literature of the early 1900s, the CIA began in spy stories. In 1945, the Office of Strategic Services chief, Bill Donovan, casting around for ways to advance his plan for a peacetime intelligence agency, urged OSS veterans to start telling their fellow citizens about the daring missions they had performed during World War II. Donovan's European deputy Allen Dulles and others collaborated on articles about their wartime adventures in mass-circulation, "middlebrow" publications like the *Saturday Evening Post*. The former Jedburghs Thomas W. Braden and Stewart Alsop published *Sub Rosa*, a stirring chronicle of the OSS's contribution to the Allied victory. Some OSS vets even went to Hollywood, consulting on productions such as the Fritz Lang–directed *Cloak and Dagger*. Despite having blazed the trail years earlier, British spies were taken aback by this burst of publicity, fearful that precious Allied secrets might leak out to the US public.[7]

They need not have worried. Once their American counterparts got what they wanted—the creation of the CIA in 1947—they quickly retreated behind a British-like veil of official secrecy. The flow of OSS memoirs dried up. So too did the movies, at least for the moment. Even

Allen Dulles, Director of Central Intelligence from 1953, reined in his natural love of Kiplingesque spy stories. Hence, when in the mid-1950s television executives proposed a CIA-themed TV series similar to productions involving J. Edgar Hoover's FBI, Dulles quietly nixed the idea. He and his lieutenants wanted to preserve both the anonymity and the mystique of their secret service, just as the British and French services did theirs. "Neither has permitted any publicity about its activities," observed Sheffield Edwards, director of the Office of Security. "We never like to be mentioned at all," Dulles elaborated. "Every time we see 'CIA' in print, we tremble a little bit."[8]

For all this publicity-shyness, though, complete secrecy was impossible. The CIA was, after all, dependent on Congress for its budget, and while few US legislators questioned the Agency's mission during the early years of the Cold War—the relevant panel of the Senate Appropriations Committee met just once in 1956 and not at all the following year—there was always the possibility of a change in mood on Capitol Hill. As Cord Meyer had discovered, McCarthyism was a powerful force in American politics in this period and, despite their support for the Cold War, conservative and isolationist Republicans were not naturally disposed in favor of a new government agency dedicated to foreign intelligence. There was also the danger of provoking a reaction from the left among the ever-present if currently dormant forces of anti-imperialism. Like Europeans before them, the US public needed to be educated in the nation's new foreign responsibilities, especially the necessity of prolonged, costly commitments in the colonial—now, the postcolonial—world.

Fortunately for Allen Dulles and his colleagues, they could at this time count on the active cooperation of the institution most capable of shaping American public opinion, the US media, many of whose leaders belonged to the same imperial brotherhood as themselves. "It was started on the principle of the English," recalled Robert Amory Jr., a CIA deputy director during the 1950s; "they have that close community, the government, the agency, the press, . . . all together as one at the top." Emblematic of this phenomenon was the columnist Joseph Alsop. A Grotonian cousin of Kermit Roosevelt's, the flamboyantly patrician Alsop was the living archetype of what his brother Stewart had dubbed the Bold Easterner: New England–bred, Ivy League–educated (Harvard in Joe's case), and prodigiously connected to the intelligence community. The host of a Washington social institution, the "Sunday Night Suppers," Alsop would regularly bring together spies and journalists at his Georgetown home to trade opinion and insider information. Not that he saw the relationship in such transactional terms: for Alsop, helping the CIA was a form of patriotic service. "I'm proud . . . to have done it," he told investigative reporter Carl Bernstein later. "The notion that a newspaperman doesn't have a duty to his country is perfect balls." Not surprisingly, CIA men welcomed the arrangement. A regular guest at Alsop's Georgetown-set gatherings, the covert action chief Frank Wisner "seemed to have had an intimate relationship with almost everyone in the media world," reckoned *New York Times* correspondent Harrison E. Salisbury. "It was all a terribly tight establishment," concluded Robert Amory, "a *bruderbund*."[9]

This is not to say that every reporter was from the East Coast aristocracy. Like the CIA itself, the press corps included recruits from public universities in the Midwest as well as the Ivy League schools. For that matter, not even the Bold Easterners could be counted on to always toe the line. Joe Alsop sometimes pressed too hard in search of a good story; as a guest at his dinner parties, Allen Dulles would apparently take pleasure in starting an anecdote that seemed to presage some intelligence revelation, then suddenly announce it was time for him to go home. "Newsmen use a great deal of ingenuity . . . to acquire accurate classified data," Dulles warned CIA colleagues in 1955. "A certain amount of control over contacts with the press is necessary."[10]

On their side, the journalists, willing though they were to perform national service in return for privileged access to valuable intelligence, were not ready to roll over entirely. Indeed, several were rather cynical about "pipeline journalism" thanks to their recent experience of reporting under the strict regime of government news management that existed during World War II. Hence, when in 1958 Frank Wisner canvassed opinion among his press contacts about a proposed bill in Congress for penalizing editors who allowed reporters to publish classified information—like the draconian Section 2 of the British Official Secrets Act—they opposed it. Even C. L. Sulzberger of the *New York Times*, a close friend of Wisner's, contested the notion that "it is possible to ask the press . . . to censure itself." There was, in other words, the potential for serious press-CIA conflict further down the road.[11]

But, at least during the early years of the Cold War, such moments were rare. Usually, Wisner could rely on a remarkable range of journalistic assets, a veritable "Mighty Wurlitzer," as he liked to call it, in a reference to the theatrical organs that accompanied movies in the silent era of US cinema. Among the keys on Wisner's Wurlitzer were friendly publishers, editors, and correspondents at major newspapers such as the *New York Times*; executives at broadcast networks, CBS's William S. Paley, for example; contacts in the publishing industry like Frederick A. Praeger, whose recently founded company used CIA subsidies to print selected titles, and occasional dealings with publishers such as Cass Canfield at more established houses, Harper & Row in Canfield's case; editorial lines into a variety of magazines, ranging from the popular *Saturday Evening Post* and Time Inc. titles to smaller publications such as the anti-communist labor biweekly *The New Leader* (which the CIA also subsidized); links to syndicated news services, including one created by the Agency itself, Forum World Features; and a large covert presence among the American journalists staffing the international program of the journalists' union, the American Newspaper Guild. Even Washington's National Press Building, home to the prestigious National Press Club, housed a CIA proprietary news service, Continental Press, run for several years by E. Howard Hunt, of later Watergate fame. To monitor the flow of news, Wisner kept wire service tickers across the hall from his office. Colleagues remembered him consulting them with a compulsive, frenetic energy. "A story would come over and he'd get on the phone," recalled William Colby. "Get something out! The Mighty Wurlitzer!"[12]

Although the CIA's first press operations were focused on Europe, the original theater of the Cold War, it was not long before US reporters were filing stories that implicitly supported Agency actions further afield, in the Third World—without, of course, identifying them as such. Joe and Stewart Alsop led the way in their nationally syndicated "Matter of Fact" column, helping prepare US public opinion for specific CIA operations. In the spring of 1953, a few months before Kim Roosevelt set off to topple Mohammed Mosaddeq, the Alsops portrayed Iran as a dangerously unstable place and called for its "pacification" as a necessary step to ensuring order in the surrounding region. In September of the same year, reporting on the crucial upcoming Philippines elections, Joe compared the incumbent president, the "aged, crafty, and insatiable" Elpidio Quirino, with the "dark, vigorous, burning" Ramon Magsaysay—the CIA's candidate in the contest, of course. The only major Agency operation of the era for which the brothers seem not to have smoothed the way at home was the coup against Jacobo Árbenz in Guatemala, PBSUCCESS. Despite knowing about SUCCESS in advance, the Alsops chose to remain quiet about it, presumably so as not to jeopardize its secrecy. Fortunately for the CIA, a host of other outlets filled the silence with depictions of Árbenz as a communist and his country as a potential Soviet beachhead in Central America. After the coup, the *Los Angeles Times* and *Harper's* reported stories of the Árbenz regime torturing its opponents. These subsequently turned out to have been fabricated by the United Fruit Company.[13]

In Guatemala, the Alsops had modeled another valuable service performed by the CIA's journalistic allies: *not* reporting ongoing operations the Agency wanted kept secret. In many cases, the reporters censored themselves. As James "Scotty" Reston, the Washington bureau chief for the *New York Times*, explained to his managing editor, citing Guatemala as an example: "Since we are clearly in a form of warfare with the Communist world, it has not been difficult to ignore information, which, if published, would have been valuable to the enemy." In cases where journalists were not willing to behave "responsibly," other steps might be taken. In one notorious instance, another *New York Times* reporter, Sidney Gruson, was effectively moved off the Guatemala story after suggesting that Jacobo Árbenz's land reforms enjoyed genuine popular support. Allen Dulles, it later turned out, had informed Julius Adler, the *Times*'s general manager and a Princeton classmate, that Gruson's political loyalties were suspect. Similar interventions happened elsewhere. Following a report from Frank Wisner (who was reputedly "paranoid" about Gruson), a 1953 CIA deputies' meeting agreed that an unwelcome *Christian Science Monitor* article "should not be published," and "an appropriate message" was "dispatched to this newspaper." As Wisner's Grotonian deputy Richard M. Bissell Jr. recalled later, "Frank would call his journalistic friends . . . to have them go easy on some pieces of news. . . . He worked that way."[14]

Although the CIA's primary purpose in such dealings was to influence US opinion about the foreign countries in which it was operating, domestic developments such as McCarthyite outbursts in Congress also made it think about its own public image as a taxpayer-funded government agency. The Iran and Guatemala coups were, after all, tremendous Cold War victories; the trick was how to publicize them as such without revealing too much of the CIA's contribution. Despite his desire for Agency anonymity, Allen Dulles displayed a strong interest in this question. Initially, as he told President Eisenhower's psychological warfare advisor, *Time* executive C. D. Jackson, he imagined the Agency sponsoring "a sort of historical novel" about the Guatemalan affair, with an "Uncle Tom's Cabin . . . touch." Subsequently, however, the DCI decided in favor of a non-fiction, journalistic treatment, although one clearly influenced by the literary conventions of the imperial spy thriller genre. The result was a three-part article by husband-and-wife writers Richard and Gladys Harkness, old associates of Dulles's, that appeared in the *Saturday Evening Post* in late 1954. The Harknesses did not reveal operational details, but they left little doubt in their readers' minds that the CIA had offered a "helping hand" in both Iran and Guatemala. They also praised Dulles personally in language reminiscent of a Richard Hannay adventure: he was a "steel spring of a man with an aptitude and zest for matching wits with an unseen foe." It later emerged that Dulles had cooperated extensively with the Harknesses as they wrote the story, granting them access to the relevant CIA files. It was perhaps just a coincidence that the articles appeared at the same time that Congress was considering a proposal for a new CIA oversight committee, but the timing was certainly fortunate. "Whether the squeamish like it or not, the United States must know what goes on in those dark places of the world where our overthrow is being plotted by the communists," the series concluded, in an apt summation of the CIA's publicity approach to the Third World. The oversight bill was easily defeated.[15]

Of course, this was not the first time that the US government had engaged in domestic propaganda. During World War I, for instance, the Committee on Public Information, better known as the Creel Committee, had used every medium at its disposal to combat possible public opposition to American belligerence. But, like wartime intelligence operations, such campaigns had generally ended with the return of peace. For peacetime propaganda aimed at domestic audiences, more obvious parallels came from prior imperial history: the efforts of the British and French governments to generate popular support for their post–World War I mandates in the Middle East, for example. Indeed, both the British and French also carried on foreign publicity campaigns during the Cold War that had significant domestic components. In the British case, MI6 and the Foreign Office's covert propaganda unit, the Information Research Department (with which the CIA cooperated in joint campaigns in the Third World), even conducted operations designed to cater to distinct groups within British society—Afro-Caribbean immigrants, for instance. In doing so, they resorted not just to print media but also to a propaganda tactic more commonly associated with the communists, who had used it since the 1920s: the so-called front group, an apparently independent organization secretly sponsored by another for ulterior purposes. Here, too, there were analogous CIA operations, run by the former writer and world federalist who had joined the Agency in 1951.[16]

As Cord Meyer began his retreat from public life into secret service, one of the organizations he helped lead during the late 1940s, the American Veterans Committee, was undergoing a transformation, too. In November

1949, Gilbert Harrison, Meyer's former colleague on the AVC board, now the group's national chairman, traveled to Paris to attend an international veterans' "peace" congress. As peace happened to be the slogan of a communist-orchestrated propaganda campaign launched the previous year, the CIA wanted an observer at the event and paid for Harrison's passage to France. Harrison was back in Paris in 1950, again with secret Agency sponsorship, this time to collaborate with other national veteran leaders in launching a new, non-communist international veterans' organization. After a founding conference held in November 1950, the World Veterans Federation established permanent headquarters in the French capital in 1951, with another American ex-serviceman, Elliott H. Newcomb, as its secretary-general. Harrison, meanwhile, traveled on the CIA's behalf to Southeast Asia to establish links with veterans there—in the Philippines, Edward Lansdale introduced him to Ramon Magsaysay—then on to a new assignment in West Germany before eventually severing his ties with the Agency and returning to the United States to edit the *New Republic*. Back in Paris, Newcomb carried on running the new veterans' international with funds provided by the CIA.[17]

This scenario, of the CIA secretly providing funds for existing US citizen groups to combat communist front organizations, was not confined to veterans' affairs. In student circles, the US National Student Association, like the AVC a recently formed mix of anti-communist internationalists and liberal activists, worked secretly with the Agency to establish the International Student Conference as a Cold War counterweight to the communist-dominated International Union of Students. In the union world, anti-Stalinist labor organizers in New York—the same sort of people who had aided Meyer in his faction fight with communists in the AVC—helped split the Popular Front–style World Federation of Trade Unions and channel CIA monies to anti-communist unionists in Europe (with James Angleton's old friend Jay Lovestone, an American Federation of Labor official, and his lieutenant Irving Brown acting as the principal intermediaries). In 1950, in a sequence of developments almost identical to those in the veteran field, anti-communist writers and philosophers responded to a series of communist peace rallies by convening a conference in Berlin, the Congress for Cultural Freedom, which then became a permanent organization headquartered in Paris. Paying for it all was the CIA, its hand hidden partly in imitation of communist front tactics, but also because it feared that overt US government patronage would discredit the groups concerned. Whereas the central concept of the Soviet propaganda offensive was peace, in the American case it was freedom—and freedom did not go well together with state control.[18]

At its start, the American campaign was an improvised, ad hoc response to the Soviet peace offensive. The private citizens involved enjoyed a lot of discretion in the spending of the CIA's covert grants, which tended to reach them disguised as donations from rich well-wishers. Gradually, however, the program was professionalized. Dummy charitable foundations took over from individuals as funding channels. Management of the various fronts, previously spread over the Agency's regional branches, was consolidated in a new International Organizations division (IO) under the control of the OSS veteran Tom Braden, who had joined the CIA as Allen Dulles's personal assistant in 1950. Another card-carrying liberal (he would later appear as a regular host "from the left" on CNN's talk show *Crossfire*), Braden reinforced the tilt in the CIA campaign toward what Washington officials had taken to calling the "Non-Communist Left" (NCL). Conservative intellectuals in the Congress for Cultural Freedom were shunted off to the side; in the labor field, social democrats in the Congress of Industrial

Organizations were favored over the crudely anti-communist "business unionists" of the AFL. The Cold War fervor of the early days had passed in favor of a cooler, intellectually sophisticated liberalism—the values of the Georgetown Set writ large. This was another reason for the covertness: as Braden put it later, in a reference to a famous conservative advocacy group, the chances of Congress funding such causes overtly in the early Cold War era were about as strong "as the John Birch Society's approving Medicare."[19]

Braden's operation was the perfect fit for Cord Meyer when he entered the CIA in 1951. Joining the IO division as Braden's deputy, Meyer was soon handling student and labor affairs for the CIA. It was not just that his politics suited his new role; so too did the extraordinarily wide range of cultural and political contacts he had developed as a public figure during the late 1940s. His papers at the Library of Congress contain correspondence and journal entries indicating personal friendships with, among many others, the novelist Herbert Gold, *Washington Post* publisher Philip Graham, cartoonist Herb Block, labor official Mike Ross, and publisher Cass Canfield. As well as explaining his usefulness to the CIA, Meyer's social network accounts for the intense dislike McCarthyite elements in the national security bureaucracy felt toward him. In August 1953, he was suspended without pay after becoming the subject of an FBI loyalty investigation. Fortunately, this proved only a blip in his Agency career, as Allen Dulles, who strongly supported the NCL strategy (according to his CIA biographer, it "engaged his personal attention . . . as much as, if not more than, any other activity of the Agency"), made a point of defending victims of McCarthyism on his staff. Meyer was back at work by Thanksgiving, his pay reinstated, having used his time off to write a play about his Kafkaesque experience. The following year, after Braden left the CIA to edit a newspaper in Oceanside, California, Meyer took over as chief of IO.[20]

By now, CIA front organizations were operating in the Global South as well as Europe. Using money that had reached it via pass-through foundations, the Congress for Cultural Freedom held music festivals, founded cultural centers, and launched literary magazines. The National Student Association sponsored seminars, scholarships, and leadership training projects. Anti-communist labor fronts such as the American Institute for Free Labor Development spread the principles of "free trade unionism" and fomented strikes against nationalist governments. To these world-spanning organizations the CIA added several regionally focused societies with names like the American Friends of the Middle East and the American Society of African Culture. In keeping with the NCL strategy, the point of these groups was less to fight communism directly than to promote a positive sense of cultural exchange and community between Americans and the inhabitants of the regions concerned.

Precisely what the impact was of this huge campaign, which involved religious, women's, and lawyers' groups as well, is hard to say for sure. Some have seen the CIA's participation in the Cultural Cold War as a brave and necessary response to communist efforts to win over world opinion to the Soviet cause. Others have denounced it as a particularly insidious form of neoimperialism, a latter-day version of the cultural domination to which Europeans had long subjected the non-Western world, with organizations such as the Congress for Cultural Freedom taking over as covert versions of the British Council or Alliance Française. Arguably, both these views miss a third possibility: that foreign recipients of the disguised CIA subsidies accepted them with a pretty good idea of their actual origin, then used them for postcolonial projects that had little or nothing to do with the Cold War. Regardless, the subject still has the power to arouse bitter controversy. In 2021, for example, the Nigerian Nobel laureate Wole Soyinka published a 165-page book angrily denouncing two Western scholars who had dared to bring up his several early-career entanglements with CIA-front cultural organizations operating in Africa. Theirs was, he fulminated, an "act of generational pseudo-intellectual hubris" produced by "a species of academic thuggery."[21]

But CIA fronts were not only active overseas; they also operated domestically. As with Wisner's press Wurlitzer, this was not merely a matter of accidental "blowback" from foreign operations. Several of the organizations targeted at specific regions abroad were deliberately designed as interventions at home as well. In part, their purpose was to foster among US citizens cultural understanding of and thereby, it was hoped, sentimental attachment to areas of the world that had so far been the domain of the old European powers. Put another way, they were intentional efforts to spread the internationalist consciousness of the East Coast foreign policy establishment, the imperial brotherhood, to the rest of American society.

Take, for instance, the American Friends of the Middle East (AFME). Founded in New York in 1951, AFME would later focus on educational exchange and development projects in the Middle East itself. Initially, however, it put equal emphasis on activities intended for a domestic audience: glittering annual conferences held at top Manhattan hotels, heavily publicized lectures by Middle Eastern visitors, and a thriving English-language publishing operation. This program reflected the Arabist values of the organization's founders, a mix of the few Americans with direct personal experience of the region, principally mish kids and oilmen. The missionary-descended OSS veteran

William Eddy, for example, who went on to work for the Arabian American Oil Company (ARAMCO), wanted to dispel the inherited Orientalist notions that most Americans had about Arab culture, replacing them instead with a sense of "interest and fellowship in the Near East." Another motive was to combat the growing influence on US public opinion of pro-Israel advocacy groups—"piping down . . . the radical Zionists," as AFME's president, journalist Dorothy Thompson, put it. The presence within the organization of a small minority of prominent anti-Zionist Jews strengthened this impulse and helped ward off Zionist accusations of anti-Semitism.[22]

Uniting these various strands, but staying firmly in the background, was CIA officer Kim Roosevelt, who had campaigned for the Arabist, anti-Zionist cause before joining the Agency in 1949. Scattered evidence in the archives and a recently declassified internal Agency study confirm that Roosevelt was the moving force behind AFME, bringing together its public leadership and arranging the regular CIA subsidies it received, via fake foundations, from 1952 on, as part of an operation called ZRTINDER. "One of his 'little boys' was up here on Tuesday, and he tells me that Kim is involved more than ever," wrote one of the organization's leaders to another in December 1951, referring to a junior officer in Roosevelt's Near East division, probably AFME's case officer, Mather Greenleaf Eliot. While not necessarily pro-Arab like Roosevelt, many US government officials shared his conviction that popular American support for Israel was harming the nation's strategic interests in the Middle East.[23]

This tendency only grew stronger in 1953 when the new Eisenhower administration announced a shift away from the Truman White House's pro-Israel stance in favor of a policy of "friendly impartiality" in the Middle East. With Kim Roosevelt working to coup-proof the new nationalist government in Egypt, CIA-friendly media outlets in the United States began to portray a favorable image of the Egyptian and Arab leader Gamal Nasser. In 1955, *Time* magazine featured a cover story about Nasser depicting him as "a dedicated soldier of only 37" with the build of "a big, handsome, All-America fullback." The American Friends of the Middle East featured prominently in this campaign. Dorothy Thompson wrote a glowing introduction to the first English-language edition of Nasser's nationalist tract, *Egypt's Liberation*. Working undercover as an AFME staffer, CIA officer Mather Eliot spent time in Washington, DC, "lobbying" members of Congress and reporters. Zionist opponents began to talk of an "Arab Lobby" with shadowy government connections foisting Nasser onto an unsuspecting American public.[24]

By now, AFME had been joined by another apparently independent citizen group touting a Third World leader to domestic audiences. This second effort began in 1954 when Joseph Buttinger, a wealthy Austrian émigré, visited Vietnam and befriended its embattled new prime minister, Ngo Dinh Diem. Buttinger was in Indochina representing the International Rescue Committee (IRC), a refugee relief organization with roots in the New York labor left, to aid the North Vietnamese Catholics then fleeing south in massive numbers (driven in part by the psychological warfare operations of Edward Lansdale). On his return to the United States, Buttinger teamed up with the New York publicist Harold L. Oram to launch a new organization, the American Friends of Vietnam (AFV). With Oram managing the business side of the operation, AFV embarked on a pro-Diem publicity blitz reminiscent of AFME's lobbying on behalf of Nasser, involving as it did extensive press coverage, newsworthy public events, and publications such as a history of Vietnam written by Buttinger and published by Frederick Praeger.

As an Oram Inc. brochure explained, the point of these activities was to prevent "an inadequately informed public opinion" from interfering with the new US policy of support for Diem.[25]

The AFV was not a CIA front group in the sense that it received regular subsidies from the Agency; Harold Oram was employed directly by the Diem government, which paid his firm $3,000 a month plus expenses. Nonetheless, the AFV had so many links to the Agency it effectively functioned as a front. It received grants for specific projects from CIA funding conduits, such as the Asia Foundation, another major Agency philanthropy with a budget even larger than that of the Congress for Cultural Freedom. Harold Oram acted as a reporting channel between Joseph Buttinger and Allen Dulles (Oram Inc. was connected with several other CIA front groups). Oram's business partner and a member of the AFV's executive committee was Elliott Newcomb, the former American veteran leader last seen moving to Paris to manage the World Veterans Federation for the CIA. There is even a possibility that the idea for a US group boosting Diem's stateside image originated with none other than Edward Lansdale. When in Saigon in 1954, Joseph Buttinger learned of a suggestion from an "American officer" for a "Committee of Friends of Vietnam" to swing US public opinion behind Diem.[26]

Whether or not Lansdale was the American officer in question, there is no shortage of other evidence that the former adman and psy-warrior was deeply interested in US public perceptions of Diem and of Southeast Asia more generally. In 1955, for example, when the Vietnamese leader was facing a set of critical threats to his government, including wavering White House support, Lansdale wrote a paper proposing a *Time* cover story about him. Frank Wisner conveyed the idea to the Time Inc. offices, and a photograph of Diem enjoying a rapturous reception from crowds in central Vietnam duly appeared on the cover of *Life* magazine. Similar stories followed in the *Saturday Evening Post* and *Reader's Digest*, two other middlebrow publications well suited to Lansdale's populist, sentimental style.[27]

Reader's Digest also played an important role in another Lansdale operation: the promotion of the celebrity "jungle doctor" Thomas A. Dooley as an exemplar of ideal American behavior toward Asians. After Lansdale's friend William Lederer, a Navy publicity officer, had worked on the manuscript, the magazine abridged *Deliver Us from Evil*, Dooley's moving account of his experience as a naval medic treating Catholic refugees in Vietnam. The young doctor also featured in fictional form as a tough missionary, Father John X. Finian, in Lederer and Eugene Burdick's famous novel *The Ugly American* alongside a thinly veiled Ed Lansdale. As letters between them show, Lederer and Lansdale consciously saw themselves as working to educate their fellow Americans about the need for, in Lederer's words, "meeting and making friends" in Asia, even if that meant "creature comfort sacrifices."[28]

With Tom Dooley continuing to model this approach—in 1956, he established a jungle hospital in Laos and began recording a weekly radio broadcast from there for American listeners, *That Free Men May Live*—Lansdale busied himself with other Vietnamese publicity projects. Among these was "The Village that Refuses to Die," a *Saturday Evening Post* story by "an American officer" about a heroic Catholic priest leading villagers in a successful fight against communism. The piece, which had originated as a secret report from Lansdale to the Kennedy White House, subsequently became a TV documentary funded by Desilu Productions, the production company of famous comedian Lucille Ball.[29]

Clever though these various ventures undoubtedly were, none measured up to the ingenuity of Lansdale's most impactful intervention in US public opinion. In 1956, the movie director Joseph L. Mankiewicz visited Saigon researching locations for a film adaptation of Graham Greene's just-published *The Quiet American*. During the trip, Mankiewicz met with Lansdale and the two men discussed the director's idea for a possible twist to Greene's anti-American plot, with the clueless US intelligence officer Pyle becoming the movie version's hero, and the British narrator Fowler a communist stooge. Subsequently, with backing from the American Friends of Vietnam, Lansdale smoothed the production's path with the South Vietnamese government. When the shoot wrapped, Mankiewicz showed his gratitude by throwing a cocktail party for Lansdale's military advisory group and, for good measure, the Michigan State University team helping to coup-proof the Diem regime.

Mankiewicz's adaptation of *The Quiet American* premiered in January 1958 at the Washington Playhouse Theatre. The event was organized by Harold Oram, who laid on champagne, cold pheasant, and "prancing Oriental dragons," with the proceeds going to the American Friends of Vietnam. Among the changes to the novel in the movie, Pyle (played by the World War II hero Audie Murphy) was no longer a spy; now he worked for the Friends of Free Asia, a fictional entity that sounded like a cross between the AFV and the Asia Foundation. Lansdale was delighted, writing Diem that the movie would "help win more friends for you and Vietnam in many places in the world." Graham Greene, in contrast, was furious. "Far was it from my mind, when I wrote *The Quiet American*," he stormed, "that the book would become a source of spiritual profit to one of the most corrupt governments in Southeast Asia."[30]

Lansdale's various psychological interventions on the US home front—a sort of domestic analogue of his psy-war operations in Southeast Asia—were perhaps an extreme example of boomerang CIA publicity. Most Agency front operations were chiefly concerned with influencing foreign, not American, audiences. The American Society of African Culture (AMSAC), for example, a true Agency front in that it received regular covert subsidies via foundation pass-throughs, was primarily oriented abroad. Founded in 1957 by a group of prominent Black Americans as the US section of the international Société Africaine de Culture, AMSAC's main, if unstated, purpose was luring postcolonial African intellectuals into the Western camp in the Cold War. To that end, it carried out an extensive program of cultural exchange in Africa emphasizing the artistic achievements of African Americans. An AMSAC-sponsored festival held in Nigeria, for instance, featured performances by the jazz musicians Lionel Hampton and Nina Simone.[31]

But even AMSAC had a domestic-facing program, consisting of lavishly staged annual conferences, handsomely produced publications, and starry holiday events. The point of these activities was, in part, positive: informing Americans, Black as well as white, about Africa's rich cultural heritage at a time when lazy stereotypes about the "dark continent" were still in wide circulation, the implication being that the place was therefore worth "saving" from communism. At the same time, however, AMSAC was also performing a negative function. There was a prior tradition of interest in Africa among American Blacks, based on a politics of left-wing anti-colonialism rather than Cold War realpolitik. Embodied by two giants of African American culture, W. E. B. Du Bois and Paul Robeson, this form of pan-African socialism had, by the 1950s, moved beyond the pale politically for most Americans. AMSAC, by giving leadership positions to Black liberal anti-communists like its president, the political scientist John A. Davis, was helping to marginalize further the anti-imperial tendency within African American thought. A particularly graphic example of this silencing effect came after the famous playwright Lorraine Hansberry delivered a confrontationally anti-colonial address at a 1959 AMSAC conference on Black writers; although it drew a standing ovation, the speech was omitted from the volume of conference papers selected for publication by John Davis the following year.[32]

Just how successful this double-edged strategy was in the end is unclear. As in the debate about the impact of CIA cultural operations overseas, some historians have detected evidence of Black American artists gladly taking AMSAC's money despite suspecting its covert origins and then using it for purposes unintended by the Agency. Events such as the 1961 Nigeria festival that featured Nina Simone may even have contributed indirectly to the growth of 1960s political radicalism among African Americans. "I started to think about myself as a black person in a country run by white people and a woman in a world run by men," Simone later wrote of her CIA-funded trip to Africa.[33]

Clearly, the sudden injection of large sums of covert government cultural patronage into the African American community had some consequences that were unforeseen by the CIA. As the man in charge of the Agency's front operations was about to find out personally, there were limits to his ability to control the narrative.

On March 30, 1967, Cord Meyer woke to discover that he was no longer the storyteller; he was the story. That day, the *New York Times* published "A Hidden Liberal: Cord Meyer Jr." Accompanied by a photograph of him taken in 1948, when he was campaigning for the United World Federalists, the article named Meyer as the CIA officer responsible for managing student, labor, and other professional organizations. This contrast between Meyer's youthful idealism and his subsequent career as a secret bureaucrat was the piece's dominant theme. "He was one of the most promising guys," said an unnamed "friend." "Very sensitive, very intelligent. . . . He got cold warrized." The article concluded by noting a series of personal tragedies that had shadowed Meyer's life: the loss of his brother in the war; then, more recently, the death of his second son, Michael, struck by a car in 1956; his subsequent divorce from Mary Pinchot Meyer; and her death in 1964, in an unsolved murder.[34]

How had Cord Meyer gone from being the man controlling the narrative to having details of his professional and personal life splashed across the pages of the nation's best-known newspaper, itself supposedly part of the CIA's secret storytelling apparatus?

The reality was that the CIA had never been in complete control. Both its press and front operations were dependent on the cooperation of private citizens who brought their own values and agendas to the relationship. As with AMSAC, it was not always possible to predict just what would happen to the CIA's secret subsidies once they had made it into recipients' hands. And, this being the United States, there was the ever-present threat of anti-imperial pushback. In contrast with European states in the age of the New Imperialism, the US government felt compelled to hide its hand in domestic imperial publicity. Like the legally questionable counterintelligence programs HTLINGUAL and MHCHAOS, the CIA's covert publicity campaign was a buried bomb, ready to go off with the slightest disturbance.

An early sign of impending trouble came in the 1950s courtesy of the American Friends of the Middle East. The Arabists and anti-Zionists of AFME had struggled from the outset to tell the story of the Arab nations to US audiences. The Arab American community was too small and disorganized to back them up, and they faced a formidable domestic opposition in the shape of the emerging "Israel lobby," US Zionist groups operating with discreet encouragement from Israeli government information or *hasbara* officers based in New York and Washington. Indeed, it was American Zionists who first began to probe AFME's murky sources of funding via CIA pass-through foundations, although they did not identify the Agency by name. In 1956–1957, with the organization's security compromised and the Eisenhower administration abandoning its policy of support for Gamal Nasser, there was an overhaul of the AFME leadership, and a shift of focus away from domestic publicity work to citizen diplomacy and technical services such as industrial training in the Middle East. It was probably no coincidence that this also happened to be when Kim Roosevelt announced his intention to leave the CIA. The Washington foreign policy establishment had tried to win public support for its preferred strategy in the Middle East and then, in the face of indifference or active resistance from the American public, gave up.

More effective at promoting their favored Third World leader were the American Friends of Vietnam. The organization enjoyed advantages AFME did not: a natural base of support in the shape of US Catholics interested in the fate of their co-religionist Ngo Dinh Diem, and the absence of an organized opposition like the Israel lobby. Perhaps most importantly, its leaders were media-savvy in a way the rather highbrow Arabists of AFME were not. For all these reasons, AFV succeeded in helping make the Vietnamese president America's "miracle man" in Southeast Asia long after Washington's flirtation with Nasser had ended.

But no amount of PR fancy footwork in the United States could solve Diem's fundamental problem: his illegitimacy in the eyes of many ordinary Vietnamese. As he resorted to increasingly repressive measures to maintain his hold on power, liberals in the American Friends of Vietnam began losing confidence in him, some eventually quitting in high-profile resignations. In 1960–1961, Diem in turn sacked Oram Inc. as his PR firm. Around the same time—the precise circumstances are unclear—the CIA increased its funding and control of AFV, prompting further complaints from some members (the Agency had "fastened itself onto our vitals," claimed Supreme Court justice William O. Douglas). With Diem's assassination in 1963, the group lost its principal raison d'être. The death blow came two years later when the CIA's anti-imperial nemesis, the West Coast magazine *Ramparts*, published a damning exposé of what it called the "Vietnam Lobby."[35]

By now, it was not only publications like *Ramparts* that were daring to challenge the CIA. Even mainstream media—formerly keys on Frank Wisner's Mighty Wurlitzer—were joining in, too. As in other areas of Agency operation, the Bay of Pigs was the watershed moment. Coming not long after other missteps to which reporters had turned a blind eye—the abortive attempt to depose the Indonesian president Sukarno, for example—the failed invasion of Cuba made it impossible for the press corps to continue with its strategy of feigned ignorance. Many of the nation's newspapers criticized the operation heavily, less on the anti-imperialist grounds that it was immoral than that it had been executed so poorly. For their part, the spies themselves blamed ZAPATA's failure on the irresponsibility of newsmen such as the *New York Times*'s Tad Szulc, who had broken with convention to report rumors of military preparations he had heard in Miami in the run-up to the landings. When Allen Dulles visited the *Times*'s offices soon afterward and remonstrated that the printing of "untrue information" was jeopardizing the Agency's very existence, the journalists declared it "a very poor case." The hint of mistrust, even paranoia, implicit in relations between the CIA and the press from the beginning was coming to the fore. Agency officials suspected the Polish-born Szulc of being a foreign agent. On their side, journalists began to shun colleagues regarded as too cozy with the CIA—*New York Times* Middle East correspondent Sam Pope Brewer, for example (the man who lost his wife to Kim Philby). In 1963, in a move that anticipated the intelligence scandals of the late 1960s and early 1970s, the Kennedy White House instructed the CIA to wiretap the National Press Building office and homes of two reporters suspected of receiving classified information, Paul J. Scott and Robert S. Allen. The operation was code-named Project MOCKINGBIRD, a moniker that later would return to haunt the Agency.[36]

The CIA made various efforts to halt the slide in its public image. In addition to authorizing MOCKINGBIRD, Allen Dulles's successor as DCI, John McCone, met personally with journalists to pressure them into giving the Agency more favorable coverage, including David Wise and Thomas Ross of *The Invisible Government* fame. In the latter case, McCone took extraordinary measures to prevent the book's appearance, appealing to its publisher, Random House, not to print it, then, when that ploy failed, encouraging negative reviews of it in a campaign that an in-house CIA historian described as "the Agency's most forceful ever against anyone other than former employees." Frank Wisner also worked to combat the influence of *The Invisible Government* and bolster the position of his friends in the newspaper world, trying to arrange a book deal for Cyrus Sulzberger, for instance. But, troubled as he now was by the mental illness that would eventually cause him to take his life in 1965, Wisner was unable to repair his Wurlitzer. As his influence faded, McCone's deputy director for intelligence, the Harvard- and Oxford-educated analyst Ray S. Cline, gradually took over his role. According to an internal memorandum, Cline's mission was to counteract the "rising clamor impairing public confidence in the

Agency as an institution." In addition to regular consultations with Joe Alsop (now as much a critic as an ally of the CIA, due to what he saw as its wavering resolve in the Cold War), Cline met periodically with a group of journalists that featured Stewart Alsop, Cy Sulzberger, Walter Lippmann, Tad Szulc, and Katharine Graham, publisher of the *Washington Post*. From his enforced retirement following the Bay of Pigs fiasco, Allen Dulles tried to work his old magic, appearing in TV documentaries, lending his name to a ghostwritten treatise titled *The Craft of Intelligence*, and editing an anthology, *Great Spy Stories*, which predictably included selections from Kipling and from Dulles's favorite modern British spy writer, Ian Fleming.[37]

But Dulles had lost his touch. As Kim Roosevelt would discover later when he published his memoir of the Iran coup, public taste in spy literature was changing, from romance to realism. Dulles's 1960s appearances and publications generally met with tepid reviews, just as an attempt to interest Hollywood in adapting his OSS book, *The Secret Surrender*, for the screen came to naught. Nor was the reaction from within the intelligence community much better—some CIA officials thought Dulles was placing public relations above the need to protect official secrets, while British and French spies reportedly found the spectacle of a former Director of Central Intelligence having to pander to American public opinion "amusing." Meanwhile, CIA-press relations hit a new low in 1966 when the *New York Times* published an in-depth, five-part investigation of the Agency based on a lengthy survey of the newspaper's foreign correspondents. The spies were horrified. James Angleton, who had been sent a copy of the survey questionnaire by contacts within the newspaper, suspected the hand of the KGB. A management memo summed up the CIA's view of its old ally: "NEW YORK TIMES Threat to Safety of the Nation."[38]

The worst, though, was still to come. In the fall of 1966, the CIA learned through its ongoing surveillance of *Ramparts* that the California-based magazine was following up its story about the Michigan State University mission to South Vietnam with an investigation of another Agency front: the US National Student Association. Tipped off by a former fundraiser for the student group, the editors had mobilized New Left supporters on the East Coast to research the association's finances, starting with the pass-through foundations that were its main source of income. This assignment proved all too easy. Due to their tax-exempt status, the foundations were obliged to file public records with the Internal Revenue Service, and several exposures had already occurred, one during a 1964 congressional investigation that was reported in the *New York Times*. Despite these scares, and repeated warnings from its lawyers, the Agency had failed to take steps to improve the operation's security; Cord Meyer, in particular, seemed mired in a state somewhere between complacency and denial. Using their own version of espionage tradecraft to practice a kind of reverse surveillance, *Ramparts*'s young reporters quickly unraveled the CIA's front network. Despite last-ditch attempts by the Agency to defuse it, the story came out early the next year amid a blaze of publicity, followed by a slew of reports by major newspapers confirming the Agency's secret assistance to a huge range of other apparently private entities.[39]

The 1967 "*Ramparts* revelations," as they became known, elicited a variety of responses. Europeans who had not suspected the full extent of the CIA's front network were cynically amused ("Les Américains sont formidables," joked one French diplomat). In contrast, outraged observers in the postcolonial regions targeted by fronts such as the Congress for Cultural Freedom and the Asia Foundation charged the United States with "academic colonialism." In the United States itself, the revelations brought forth widespread condemnation not just, as one might expect, from the left, but also from conservatives who objected to the CIA's selection of the NCL as the main beneficiary of its covert largesse (a leader of the Young Americans for Freedom wrote DCI Richard Helms sarcastically explaining that his organization felt that it "might also qualify for aid from the Central Intelligence Agency, and would appreciate an application form for such a request").[40]

As for the front groups themselves, they imploded in a storm of arguments about who was aware of the true source of their funding and who was not. A hastily formed White House commission that included Director Helms (assisted by Cord Meyer) tried and failed to contain the damage. For many in the exposed fronts, the revelation that old friends had concealed the truth from them was a shatteringly intimate betrayal of personal trust, not unlike the emotional damage wrought by the penetration of New Left groups in MHCHAOS. Although a few organizations that had earlier focused their programs entirely overseas—AFME, for example—survived, dozens of others, like AMSAC, did not. It was, reckoned a former member of the CIA's history staff, "one of the worst operational catastrophes in CIA history."[41]

For Cord Meyer, the fallout from the *Ramparts* revelations was personal as well as professional. The *New York Times* profile of March 1967 was the first of several such articles that appeared over the next few years, all rehearsing the same narrative that, as Meyer himself put it, "my career and personality represented a kind of Jekyll and Hyde development." Friends rallied around and the Agency affirmed its confidence in him with the award of a Distinguished Intelligence Medal (one of three he received over the course of his career), the citation making particular mention of his "accomplishments in the establishment and development of cooperative relationships between government and private organizations." Later in the year, he was promoted to assistant deputy director of plans—effectively, number two in the clandestine service. But then, in 1972, came more unwelcome press attention: Seymour Hersh learned that Meyer had asked his old friend at Harper & Row, Cass Canfield, to send him the proofs of a book by a Yale graduate student, Alfred W. McCoy, that charged the CIA with complicity in the Southeast Asian heroin trade. This time the Agency was less understanding. "You can be forgiven one public goof, but two—I don't think so," a retired colleague told the *New York Times*. Against a backdrop of the Watergate and Family Jewels investigations, Meyer moved to London as station chief, the same post that Frank Wisner had occupied earlier after his mental breakdown.[42]

There was no escaping the adverse publicity, though. The London media were fascinated by the political turmoil enveloping Washington, and Meyer rapidly became a notorious figure, the focus of allegations about CIA infiltration of the British trade union movement and secret US operations in Britain's former colonies in Africa. The stateless whistleblower Philip Agee got in on the act, claiming that Meyer was partnering with UK intelligence against the nationalist paramilitary organization fighting British forces in Ireland, the Irish Republican Army. When *The Guardian* published the station chief's London address, he began taking extra security precautions, like jumping into his moving chauffeur-driven car as he left home for work each morning.[43]

Despite his having made a successful second marriage, to Starke Patterson Anderson, Meyer continued to suffer family woes as well. His two surviving sons dropped out of Yale; one subsequently became a Christian evangelical, the other a gambling addict in Las Vegas. Both blamed their father for their difficulties navigating adult life, although family letters suggest he was a rather loving and concerned parent, and that the tragic losses the boys had suffered during their early lives—of their brother and mother—were the more likely causes. Meyer endured his various trials stoically, but his private correspondence suggests that by the time his tour in London came to an end in 1976, he was near the end of his tether. When the new DCI, Stansfield Turner, indicated to Meyer that his "well-publicized association with covert action programs" made promoting him impossible, he tendered his resignation. A "victim of the times," as Turner described him, Meyer quit secret government service in 1977, just over a quarter of a century after he had entered it.[44]

The 1970s witnessed a collective humbling of the CIA's imperial brotherhood. But, as the example of James Angleton and counterintelligence showed, this was not an end to their story. During the later years of the decade, they regrouped, some in new conservative organizations outside of government, and launched a counteroffensive. In addition to Angleton's counterintelligence influence operation and the Publications Review Board's crackdown on anti-imperial whistleblowers, this included a public relations component reminiscent of the concerted publicity campaign waged by Wild Bill Donovan just after World War II.

Ironically, given his dismal reputation with many members of his CIA generation, it was the reformist DCI William Colby who initiated this campaign. Colby was as secrecy-minded as any of his contemporaries, but he understood that the Agency would need to project an image of greater openness if it was to survive the existential crises of the era. In his reasoning, improved public relations might even enable the Agency to protect vital secrets more effectively. In October 1975, conscious that the CIA's image was badly damaged—a January 1976 national poll revealed only 50 percent approval of its performance—Colby convened an ad hoc group to come up with recommendations. The resulting list, "Telling the Intelligence Story," placed strong emphasis on one technique in particular: "judicious assistance to selected former Agency employees and retirees who want to defend the CIA in books, articles, or public appearances."[45]

First to respond to this call was the Agency's chief of Latin American operations, David Atlee Phillips. A former actor and newspaper editor, the craggily handsome and slightly stagey Phillips was perfectly suited to a publicity role; he even had experience in running a propaganda campaign, having managed the psy-war offensive against Jacobo Árbenz. In 1975, at age fifty-two, Phillips announced he was leaving the Agency with the intention, as he told his colleagues, of "working on your behalf just as many hours a day after retirement as I do now." He was true to his word. Almost immediately after his departure, he founded a new organization, the Association of Retired Intelligence Officers (ARIO), which by the end of the year could boast a membership of 1,000. He authored pro-CIA magazine articles, lectured and appeared on talk shows debating whistleblowers such as Philip Agee and Victor Marchetti, and, in an echo of Frank Wisner, quietly collaborated with reporters like his friend Joseph C. Goulden. Most importantly, in another, implicit rebuke to Agee and Marchetti, Phillips published a memoir celebrating the CIA, 1977's *The Night Watch*. In this book and his other public pronouncements, Phillips constantly restated certain talking points—for example, that the CIA operated only on presidential orders, and that excessive congressional oversight would hobble its ability to perform its mission. Spying could be a dirty business, Phillips admitted, but it was necessary to protect the nation's security. By undertaking it, and thereby putting their own morality at risk, CIA officers were sacrificing themselves to the public good. The title of Phillips's memoir was taken from a saying of Richard Welch, the Athens station chief murdered supposedly because his identity had been revealed by whistleblowers, that summed it up: "that the night watch can be lonely, but that it must be stood."[46]

Phillips was not alone in his work. Joining him was Ray Cline, the veteran analyst who had earlier helped manage CIA relations with the US press. Since retiring from government service in 1973, Cline had built a scholarly reputation as an intelligence expert, teaching international relations at Georgetown University and authoring works such as the 1976 *The CIA: Reality Versus Myth*. To preserve his scholarly standing, Cline turned down a request from Phillips to head ARIO; he did not want to look like an Agency apologist or "CIAnik." Nevertheless, he too went on talk shows debating whistleblowers—one such appearance drew an admiring letter from Cord Meyer, who thought that he had made the "opposition look extremely foolish"—and testifying in defense of the Agency before congressional committees. Meanwhile, in another echo of James Angleton's trajectory during the same period, Cline became known for his hard-line pronouncements on communism and rejection of détente. A founding member of the premier anti-détente lobby, the Committee on the Present Danger, he joined his Georgetown colleague Roy Godson in the Consortium for the Study of Intelligence and founded his own think tank, the National Intelligence Study Center. Coordinating this alphabet soup of organizations in the so-called Common Interest Network, Cline acted as a pivotal figure in the era's revival of Cold War conservatism.[47]

In 1977, the publicity counteroffensive returned where it had started, to the CIA itself. Jimmy Carter's appointee as DCI, Stansfield Turner, was determined to carry on the policy started by Bill Colby, that is, professing openness while preserving secrecy. That year, he brought in a "jovial" Navy captain and PR expert, Herbert Hetu, to head a new Public Affairs Office within the Agency. Hetu's credentials were not limited to his naval background, attractive though that was to Admiral Turner. During the 1950s, he had helped ready Tom Dooley's *Deliver Us from Evil* for publication and shared an office with William Lederer when he was writing *The Ugly American*. Now he brought a Lansdalian touch to CIA PR, organizing a barrage of publicity across a range of media designed to build a sense of emotional connection between the Agency and the public. Not that he was unmindful of the need to guard secrets: in addition to his job running the Public Affairs Office, Hetu chaired the new Publications Review Board—further evidence of how publicity and secrecy were, for the CIA, different sides of the same coin. Wearing these two hats, Hetu was able to repress writings by some former CIA officers while greenlighting others.[48]

Among the projects approved in this fashion was Cord Meyer's autobiography. Literary agents had begun approaching the CIA man immediately following his exposure in the *Ramparts* revelations, encouraging him to write a book, but, constrained by his secrecy oath, he had been unable to oblige. Now, freed from secret service, and with the Agency positively inviting favorable publications by former employees, Meyer was ready to tell his own story. Several other parties were on hand to help. Georgetown University, where he had begun teaching a course on intelligence with Roy Godson, offered him office space and research assistance. So too did the anti-communist intellectual Irving Kristol, a former employee of the Congress for Cultural Freedom, now attached to a neoconservative think tank, the American Enterprise Institute.[49]

These offers of help from the growing neoconservative apparatus confirmed what many already suspected: that the former poster boy of the NCL had turned right. Again, observers hypothesized different reasons for this development. During his years at the CIA, Meyer had developed a deep personal friendship with his fellow Yale *littérateur* James Angleton; indeed, the two men had grown so close that Angleton served as guardian to Meyer's errant sons. "Jim sucked Cord Meyer in," Tom Braden reckoned. "Cord became not only a great admirer, but also a believer." Then there was the conservatizing influence of Meyer's 1970s posting to London, where he clearly enjoyed rubbing shoulders with colleagues in the UK security services, among them (as he wrote later) "many old friends" who shared his determination to foil "the world-wide operations of the ubiquitous KGB." The anti-colonialism Meyer had expressed in the late 1940s was gone, replaced by hard-line Atlanticism. Finally, there was the accumulated effect of the many misfortunes and professional setbacks Meyer had suffered over the years, layering onto the profound sense of Niebuhrian pessimism he had felt ever since World War II. Whichever of these factors was decisive, there is little question that by the time he came to write his autobiography, Meyer had joined the ranks of conservative Cold Warriors. Stories abound from this period of him angrily confronting fellow guests at cocktail and dinner parties who failed to show the same anti-communist fervor as himself.[50]

When it was published by Harper & Row in 1980, *Facing Reality: From World Federalism to the CIA* earned plaudits from CIA colleagues and conservative commentators; Ray Cline's National Intelligence Study Center awarded Meyer its annual book prize. Other reviewers were less kind. In the *New York Times*, Thomas Powers described the book as "argumentative, confused, disingenuous, self-important and often boring." He had a point. The writing was as elegant and graceful as anything Meyer published during his brief literary career in the 1940s, but for an autobiography it revealed surprisingly little about its author's personality, and scarcely anything that was not already known about the CIA. Instead of confession or revelation—the dominant modes of whistleblower memoirs—there were lengthy defenses of past Agency actions and tortuous exegeses of the Soviet threat. Most of all, Meyer used the opportunity to refute the dominant media narrative about himself—that his life story was one of a tragic transformation from golden boy of world federalism to gray Cold War apparatchik—pointing out, with some justification, that even at the height of his 1940s idealism he had nursed Niebuhrian doubts about the prospects for global government.[51]

Still, if this was Meyer's literary comeback, it was a letdown. It also proved to be his last book. Most of the remainder of his writing career was taken up with a column that appeared in a new conservative challenger to the big liberal newspapers, the *Washington Times*, which also featured David Atlee Phillips's journalist friend Joseph Goulden. Meyer died from lymphoma in 2001, at age eighty.

Like the CIA's earlier effort in the Cultural Cold War, the effect of the Agency's PR drive in the late 1970s is hard to quantify. David Phillips suspected that he and other CIA "Old Boys" were preaching to the anti-communist choir. But perhaps this did not much matter. The likes of Cord Meyer had at last gotten to tell their side of the story. And the political winds were shifting in the Old Boys' favor anyway, as shown by an unexpected development in the 1980s that serves as a coda to CIA Cold War–era publicity: the revival of the Agency's pre-1967 media and front operations, only in a more conservative, frankly imperial form.[52]

In June 1982, William Casey, the unreconstructed Cold Warrior whom Ronald Reagan had chosen as his DCI, summoned one of his senior officers. Walter Raymond Jr. held the same position in the Agency that Cord Meyer had when he was running its front groups, but the similarities between the two men ended there. In contrast with the glamorous Meyer, Raymond was a quiet bureaucrat who reminded people of the John le Carré character George Smiley, a spy who "easily fades into the woodwork." Combined with his experience of waging political warfare, this trait qualified Raymond well for the mission Casey now described to him. President Reagan had just given a major speech in London announcing a renewed US effort to strengthen democracy globally and compete ideologically with the Soviet Union. The problem was that, due to the intelligence scandals of the previous decades and the resulting congressional curbs on its powers, the CIA could no longer perform the sort of psychological operations it once had. Hence Raymond's mission: he was to leave the Agency for the White House's National Security Council and run the campaign from there. This he duly did, taking up the position of director of the Office of International Communications and Public Diplomacy at the NSC.[53]

Over the next five years, Raymond coordinated a massive, multifaceted, interagency campaign reminiscent of the 1950s heyday of Wisner's Wurlitzer and Meyer's fronts. To name just one initiative, the Raymond years saw the creation of the National Endowment for Democracy, a huge international philanthropy for pro-democratic, anti-communist causes around the world, not unlike the Congress for Cultural Freedom except that it was funded from overt sources—a combination of the United States Information Agency (USIA) budget and private donations.

This overtness was not the only difference from the earlier CIA offensive. The involvement of wealthy private donors and the natural ideological leanings of the Reagan administration ensured that

Raymond's campaign had a conservative coloration to it that the Mighty Wurlitzer, with its emphasis on the NCL, did not. In a way, the Reagan years were the revenge of the elements that had been excluded from the CIA's patronage after the tilt to the NCL: anti-communist hard-liners in New York intellectual and labor circles, for example, who would go on to become leading neoconservatives based in institutions like the American Enterprise Institute.

Linked to this, 1980s "public diplomacy" had an aggressive, adversarial quality to it that the soft-sell tactics of the CIA had lacked. This was especially evident in the Raymond network's dealings with the US media. Wisner's Wurlitzer featured some elements of press-CIA tension but, overall, it displayed a remarkable degree of consensus, based on the shared values of the imperial brotherhood. By the 1980s, perception managers in government relied as much on coercion as on cooperation to control the media message. Under Bill Casey, the CIA's Public Affairs Office lectured newspaper editors who dared to criticize Reagan administration policies. Casey himself made threatening phone calls to journalists.

Still, there were also some striking continuities between the CIA's pre-*Ramparts* publicity program and the Reagan-era campaign. Several of the organizations involved were the same—the Asia Foundation, for example, a post-1967 Agency "orphan" that was folded into the new program, with Walter Raymond arranging for the USIA to take on its funding. In fact, the influence of the CIA had never really gone away, despite such ruses as Raymond's move from the Agency to the NSC. Documents produced during congressional hearings on the Iran-Contra scandal revealed that, just as in Oliver North's Contra supply operation, Bill Casey was in the background, talking regularly with Raymond to plan the next moves in the White House's media barrage.

The Reagan campaign even had the same febrile energy as Wisner's, with NSC staffers pivoting from one media operation to the next "at a breakneck pace."[54]

Given these continuities with what had gone before, it was not surprising that the Reagan administration's overseas democracy promotion efforts shared one other important characteristic with earlier Cold War propaganda campaigns: their tendency to spill over into the domestic sphere. If anything, this effect was even more pronounced in the 1980s. After Vietnam, the American public was wary of US interventions in the Third World. Reagan's policies toward Central America, in particular, inspired widespread opposition, not least from remnants of the anti-imperial elements that had earlier protested US actions toward Cuba. For Reagan supporters, especially those who believed that America had only lost in Vietnam because of the domestic anti-war movement, the solution was obvious: the administration needed to do a better job of managing public opinion and quelling possible anti-imperialism.

Such was the background to Walter Raymond's most concerted campaign yet. In the summer of 1983, he created a new unit, housed in the State Department but reporting to him: the Office of Public Diplomacy for Latin America and the Caribbean (S/LPD). There was little pretense that this was a foreign operation. As internal memos made clear, its purpose was rather "to engage in a campaign to influence the public and the Congress to support increased funding for the Administration's Central American policy." As such, it coordinated its program with the Contra supply operation, making it, in the words of Latin American historian Greg Grandin, "the homeland branch of Casey and North's 'enterprise.'" It also employed a variety of propaganda experts, from external public relations consultants to psychological operations detailees provided by the Pentagon. Among its considerable output were books, pamphlets, op-ed pieces, speeches, radio broadcasts, and television documentaries—in short, every form of publicity, all designed to reinforce the administration's central claims that the Nicaraguan Contras were "freedom fighters" and the Sandinista government they were trying to overthrow a terroristic tool of the Soviets (or Cubans).[55]

When not coming up with measures intended to manufacture popular consent for administration policies, the S/LPD was trying to repress dissent. Otto Reich, the right-wing Cuban émigré who ran the unit for Raymond, adopted, in his own words, "a very aggressive posture vis-à-vis a sometimes hostile press." In an echo of the earlier Sidney Gruson incident, a *New York Times* reporter who broke the story of the Salvadoran army's massacre of civilians at El Mozote in 1981 was pulled out of the country. Meanwhile, PR firms under Office of Public Diplomacy contracts attacked congressmen who opposed the Reagan line. Reviewing the S/LPD's performance in 1986, the same year that Congress ended its moratorium on funding for the Contras by approving an aid package worth $100,000, the NSC concluded: "The Office . . . has been successful in shaping public support to give US policy the opportunity and resources to work."[56]

"If you look at it as a whole," an S/LPD staffer admitted to a reporter in 1987, "the Office of Public Diplomacy was carrying out a huge psychological operation, the kind the military conduct to influence the population in denied or enemy territory." Coming from a US government official, it is hard to imagine a franker description of the imperial boomerang effect.[57]

As in the sphere of counterintelligence, the Cold War era ended with the publicity experts of the imperial party, men like Bill Casey's CIA covert operations deputy Walter Raymond, in the box seat. However, as the career of Raymond's predecessor Cord Meyer illustrated, this outcome had been far from guaranteed. Like the pursuit of an imperial state of official secrecy by his friend James Angleton, Meyer's efforts to rally public support behind his government's Cold War foreign policies had encountered growing resistance, at home as well as abroad. Even supposed allies in the US media and the front groups he managed for the Agency had eventually challenged its authority. Perhaps, therefore, it should have come as no surprise that the CIA's overseas operations in the Cold War era would cause other unanticipated developments on the domestic front—including the emergence of a new genre of unauthorized storytelling about the Agency that defied not only Meyer's ability to control it but also official definitions of reality itself.

CHAPTER 6

Unintended Consequences

I f readers wanting to learn more about the CIA officers featured in the pages of this book went online to conduct their own research, they might make some surprising discoveries. According to some sources they might encounter, James Angleton was running Lee Harvey Oswald as a CIA agent in the lead-up to Oswald's assassination of President John Kennedy in November 1963. In other accounts, Angleton's friend Cord Meyer was also involved in the plot against Kennedy—the same plot that a year later would take the life of Mary Pinchot Meyer, Meyer's ex-wife and, it turns out, a lover of the dead president who had introduced him to LSD. Elsewhere, Meyer pops up as Deep Throat, the mysterious source for Carl Bernstein and Bob Woodward's investigation of the Watergate scandal—or should that be Richard Ober, the counterintelligence officer responsible for MHCHAOS? Back with JFK, the CIA publicity expert David Atlee Phillips is revealed as "Maurice Bishop," the real mastermind

Police lead away three "tramps" from the scene of John F. Kennedy's assassination in
Dallas, Texas, in November 1963. According to some conspiracy theorists, the suited
man walking in the opposite direction, his face not visible to the camera, is Edward
Lansdale. Fort Worth Star-Telegram Collection, Special Collections, University of Texas at Arlington Libraries

of the Kennedy plot, while E. Howard Hunt, Agency propagandist and
Watergate burglar, turns up in Dallas disguised as one of a group of
vagrants detained near Dealey Plaza, the scene of the assassination. And
who is the man photographed behind "Hunt" and the other hobos, walking away from the camera, if not the Quiet American himself, Edward
Lansdale? Before long, even the most cautious of researchers is sucked
into a dizzying vortex of Agency conspiracy theories.

Some of these theories have been proven false, and none of the
others is likely true—but, in a historical era in which the US government carried out much of its foreign policy covertly while, at the same
time, secretly surveilling and propagandizing its own citizens at home,
they contained just enough basis in fact that, as opinion polls showed,

a majority of American citizens came to prefer versions of them to the official explanation of the events that took place in Dallas in 1963.

We will return to the various conspiracist scenarios involving legendary CIA officers later in this chapter. But conspiracy theory was not the only unintended domestic consequence of the Agency's overseas operations. Like Europe's imperial metropoles, the United States experienced several other unforeseen repercussions from its covert interventions elsewhere in the world. These ranged from profound geographic and demographic impacts on specific regions such as the suburban hinterland surrounding Washington, DC, to transformations that affected the intellectual life of the United States as a whole. Together, these boomerang effects made the CIA into a looming presence in the domestic life of the nation during the second half of the twentieth century—an ironic fate for a supposedly secret foreign intelligence agency.

Even at the height of post–World War II decolonization, a visitor to metropolitan Europe might be struck by the visible traces of the imperial past: grandiose colonial ministries and monuments, classical and Orientalist motifs in the domestic architecture, streets named for famous generals and battles. The people too might conjure up empire. The postwar period saw a surge of migration to Europe from former colonies, not just returning colonial officers and settlers but millions of immigrants of color as well, following imperial routes back to the metropole: Afro-Caribbeans and South Asians to Britain, North Africans to France, and Indonesians to the Netherlands. The one thing that would not have been clear to the casual observer was the physical location of the secret intelligence services that had helped run the European empires. MI6, whose very existence the British government did not officially admit until after the end of the Cold War, was housed covertly in an obscure London office building, 54 Broadway, remembered by its denizens for its dark cubicles, peeling paint, and antiquated elevator.[1]

Signs of imperial adventures overseas were much less apparent in the postwar United States, even as the nation built its dominion in the colonial regions from which the Europeans were withdrawing. America's was a covert empire, one that sought to conceal its existence from foreigners and its own citizens. But it is hard to hide an empire entirely, even on the home front, not least because American anti-imperialists insisted on public accountability for the covert institutions the US government had created to perform its new global role. The CIA, for example, could not count on the willingness shown by most Europeans to turn a blind eye to the doings of secret intelligence organizations. The domestic traces of covert empire were visible to those who cared to look, a sort of open secret in Cold War American society—"hidden in plain sight," as one observer has put it.[2]

Nowhere were these contradictions more apparent than in Langley, Virginia, site of the huge new CIA headquarters that opened for business in 1961. To be sure, the Agency did not advertise its existence. Ten miles from downtown Washington, it sat in a natural enclosure, surrounded by trees and set back from the George Washington Memorial Parkway, its entrance identified only by a sign reading "Bureau of Public Roads." But, equally, this was not the dreary hiding place of a European spy agency. The massive, modernist structure, the product of the same architectural firm that had designed the United Nations building in New York City, bespoke the global scope of the CIA's power. Its cornerstone was laid at a 1959 ceremony personally planned by DCI Allen Dulles and attended by President Eisenhower, an event hard to imagine outside the United States.

Nor was the domestic footprint of the CIA confined to its Langley campus. The Agency had a way of spilling over into its rural northern Virginia surroundings, slowly transforming the region into a sort of secret annex of the overt government in Washington—a "covert capital," in the telling phrase of one scholar. The CIA's growing workforce purchased or built homes there; Kim Roosevelt, Edward Lansdale, James Angleton, and Cord Meyer were all residents. Local restaurants and bars functioned as spy hangouts, some serving foreign food comfortingly familiar to CIA men and their families returning home from overseas postings. Agency veterans took leading roles in the area's suburbanization, developing it as they had agricultural societies in the Third World. One official-turned-developer who had served in Vietnam named a new subdivision in McLean, Virginia, for Saigon, Vietnam. Like colonial administrators repatriating to Europe, US intelligence officers came home carrying cultural baggage from the covert empire, the American equivalent of pink gin and curry.[3]

But it was not just northern Virginia that was experiencing the effects of the imperial boomerang. Further down the eastern seaboard, another American region was undergoing profound cultural and economic change due to a CIA covert operation. By the time of the October 1962 missile crisis, nearly a quarter of a million people had fled revolutionary Cuba for the United States, the great majority settling in South Florida. This immigration was largely spontaneous. Most of the new arrivals were from the Cuban elite and expected to return to the island when Castro was toppled from power, something they assumed would happen sooner rather than later. But there were other factors involved, too. It was common knowledge among Cuban émigrés that the CIA was organizing an exile army in Miami to retake the island and paying recruits good money: $175 a month, with additional payments for dependents. In addition to this pull factor, the CIA was taking deliberate measures to push Cubans into emigrating, with the dual intention of depriving the Castro regime of valuable human capital and strengthening the exile counterrevolutionary movement. As chief of CIA psychological operations in the run-up to the Bay of Pigs invasion, David Atlee Phillips used radio broadcasts and other means to spread rumors on the island that Castro was planning to brainwash young Catholics into becoming communists. The resulting panic fueled Operation Pedro Pan, an airlift of unaccompanied Cuban children to the United States mounted by the Catholic church in Florida. There is no definite proof, but it seems likely that the CIA was involved in the airlift operation, which bore a strong resemblance to Edward Lansdale's earlier efforts to undermine the Viet Minh and strengthen the Diem regime in Vietnam by scaring North Vietnamese Catholics into fleeing south. Lansdale himself helped plan and eventually ran the US psy-war campaign against Castro. In 1962, he spoke to other US officials of the need to "exploit the emotional possibilities of the 8,000 children that were under the protection of the United States." Soon after, the USIA released a moving documentary about a lonely refugee Cuban boy, *The Lost Apple*, reminiscent of the TV shows about Vietnam made at Lansdale's instigation in the same period. When the missile crisis effectively ended Operation Pedro Pan, thousands of young Cubans were left stranded in the United States.[4]

By this point, the CIA's campaign against Castro had, in the words of a local journalist, "transformed the face of South Florida." The Agency's local station, JMWAVE, housed on the University of Miami's secluded South Campus under the cover name Zenith Technical Enterprises, was the largest outside of Langley. It boasted a budget of $50 million, 300–400 resident officers, and, according to the estimate of its chief, Theodore "Ted" Shackley, 15,000 Cuban exiles "connected to us in one way or another." Radiating out from JMWAVE were hundreds of other semi-covert sites: boatyards to service the CIA-owned craft that ferried exiles to and from Cuba (the Agency was reputed to run the third-largest navy in the Caribbean, after the United States and Cuba's own), law offices that dealt with the voluminous legal paperwork generated by all the CIA's front companies in the area, even a boardinghouse in Miami's Little Havana catering to the American mercenaries the Agency recruited to train its exile army (CIA officers fondly referred to its proprietor, Nellie Hamilton, and her grizzled charges as "Mother Hubbard and her commandos"). The training itself took place in remote corners of Florida's national parks, which doubled as locations in Cuba, literally turning portions of US territory into the Third World for the duration of the exercises. Park rangers and tourists would occasionally stumble across bands of émigrés invading beaches or laying explosives in mock-ups of Cuban targets. Long after the CIA had stood down its Cuban brigade, South Florida abounded with local legends of hidden arms caches, a sort of latter-day pirate treasure.[5]

The operations against Castro left other legacies in Florida, some of them positive. The infusion of CIA dollars caused a boom in the local economy, helping turn Miami from a sleepy resort town into a regional powerhouse, the "Capital of the Caribbean." The Agency also assisted wave after wave of Cuban immigrants in adjusting to life in the United States, providing them with, in effect, a temporary employment program as they established their own livelihoods. According to one Florida historian, the CIA even helped bring Disney World to Orlando. Paul Helliwell, a Miami-based Agency officer and lawyer who specialized in creating proprietary companies, also advised Walt Disney as he acquired his vast Florida holdings.[6]

But not all the effects were benign. As the CIA downsized its presence in Florida during the late 1960s, swapping its JMWAVE base for smaller premises, it cast off most of its Cuban assets. The majority carried on their civilian lives peacefully enough, but some persisted in the paramilitary struggle, often against local Cuban businesses or organizations deemed insufficiently counterrevolutionary, making bombings and assassinations tragically common occurrences in Miami's Cuban community. Others continued to work with the CIA officers and mercenaries who had trained them to overthrow Castro in operations aimed at different targets: the Watergate break-in; the 1976 killing of the Chilean exile Orlando Letelier in Washington, DC; the Contra supply operation of the Reagan years. The covert routes used to transport arms were also used to smuggle narcotics, making Miami a center of the region's drug trade. In sum, the CIA's Cuba operations spawned a host of unintended consequences. Small wonder that conspiracy theories about the Kennedy assassination would feature rogue intelligence officers and right-wing Cubans.[7]

And it was not just abortive attempts at foreign regime change that left a domestic imprint; so too did failed regime maintenance operations. The 1975 collapse of South Vietnam was followed by a surge of Vietnamese immigration as officials of the fallen government and local employees fled communism; a few years later, in 1979, came another wave of refugees, known in the West as the "boat people," bringing the total number of Vietnamese in the United States by 1990 to over half a million. Many of the newcomers ended up in northern Virginia, alongside American operatives they had known in Vietnam, who often went to great lengths to help them settle in the United States, possibly out of guilt for having abandoned Vietnam in such ignominious circumstances. Edward Lansdale's McLean home, in particular, became a refugee halfway house and venue for reunions that conjured poignant memories of the intimate parties he had hosted in Saigon only ten years earlier.

Despite this help, the Vietnamese exiles struggled to cope with their loss of status and the racism they encountered from other neighbors. Some were haunted by their political pasts: reporters descended on a pizza parlor in Burke, Virginia, when they realized that its owner, Nguyen Ngoc Loan, was the former South Vietnamese police chief famously photographed in 1968 executing a Viet Cong prisoner in the street. A few, refusing to surrender hopes of liberating their homeland from communism, organized themselves into paramilitary groups and, encouraged by Lansdale and his old associate Lucien Conein, concocted Cuban-like plans for invading Vietnam. The majority, though, gradually reconciled themselves to their new lives. The Eden Center, a suburban mall in Falls Church, Virginia, became the unofficial capital of the emerging Vietnamese American community, with the names of Saigon stores emblazoned across storefronts and the flag of the Republic of South Vietnam waving proudly next to the Stars and Stripes.[8]

Then, in 1979, came another regime collapse and a new wave of immigrants from America's covert empire, totaling over 100,000 by 1986. Like the Vietnamese before them, Iranians fleeing the Islamic Revolution in their homeland made northern Virginia their first port of call in the United States. There, they too reconstituted intimate friendships with CIA officers and other officials they had known in imperial Tehran. Thanks, though, to the relatively orderly nature of their departure from Iran, and in some cases previous experience of exile in European metropoles, these émigrés came to America with assets that the Vietnamese lacked. The son of the deposed shah, Reza Cyrus Pahlavi, was able to build a mansion in Great Falls, ten minutes from Langley, which functioned as a sort of imperial court-in-exile. Other members of the influx joined in a new surge of development in the covert capital that accompanied the CIA's revival during the Reaganite 1980s. Bahman Batmanghelidj, an intimate of the shah's and "habitué of U.S. imperial circles," undertook construction projects in Fairfax, Virginia, where he acquired the nickname "Batman."[9]

But northern Virginia was not the only part of the United States touched by the regime failures in Vietnam and Iran. Immigrants from those countries went elsewhere in the nation: Texas, California's Bay Area, and, above all, Southern California. Attracted in part by the region's sunny weather, Iranians congregated in Los Angeles's Little Tehran, or "Tehrangeles," south of Westwood Village. There they established businesses, organized protests against the Islamic Republic, and, in a few cases, spied on their homeland for the CIA. Meanwhile, to the south, in Orange County, Vietnamese immigrants, lured by a combination of relatively affordable real estate and a surprisingly warm welcome from local churches and conservative politicians, formed a community that soon rivaled the one in Virginia in size and cultural clout, a bustling enclave of devout Catholicism, thriving nightclubs, and defiant refugee songs. Less desirably, California's Little Saigon was also, like other exile refuges in America, home to revanchist paramilitary groups led by men with old links to the CIA who used threats and violence to silence their critics. Beginning in 1981, five Vietnamese American journalists were murdered, crimes that remain unsolved today. As in Florida, volunteer units trained to liberate their homeland in California's national parks. Novelist Viet Thanh Nguyen depicts these events in thinly fictionalized form in his brilliant 2015 debut novel, *The Sympathizer*, the story of a Vietnamese communist mole in Southern California who, to prove his loyalty to a South Vietnamese general turned liquor store owner, assassinates the general's political enemies, then joins in a guerrilla raid on Vietnam. A Lansdale-like CIA officer, Claude, pops up periodically in the narrative.[10]

And so the pattern repeated itself, as CIA operations overseas stimulated further boomerang flows of immigrants. In the 1980s, it was the turn of Central Americans, whose numbers within the United States more than tripled over the course of the decade. Not all the immigration from that region was a result of covert US intervention: endemic poverty and inequality were problems there long before the CIA even existed. But it is undeniable that American actions aggravated such conditions, creating violence that left many inhabitants feeling that they had no choice but to move: Guatemalans fleeing the civil war that followed the 1954 overthrow of Jacobo Árbenz, or Salvadorans escaping the conflict that engulfed their country during the 1980s as the US-backed military government waged a brutal counterinsurgency campaign. Again, the newcomers arrived with human capital that benefited the United States, in the same way postcolonial migration flows enriched Europe, but a few were also shadowed by the imperial violence that afflicted their homelands. The notorious street gang MS-13 crossed and recrossed between the United States and El Salvador, creating a transnational continuum of criminality.[11]

Not that such effects were confined to immigrant communities: during the Reagan era, boomeranging imperial violence bled into US culture generally, creating a curious but powerful subcultural phenomenon. From the Cuba campaign of the early 1960s to the Contra supply chain of the 1980s, CIA operations had often employed mercenaries or "soldiers of fortune." Initially, such men were considered disreputable, even criminal. However, as hard-line anti-communism enjoyed a revival in the 1970s, the mercenary became a cult figure, the hero of magazines and movies. In part, this was an expression of wider forces in American culture: a reaction against recent national setbacks and humiliations—the so-called Vietnam syndrome—and a reaffirmation of traditional notions of masculinity in the face of such perceived threats as the rise of feminism and the welfare state. But the elevation of anti-communist guerrillas and "freedom fighters" was also part of a deliberate campaign carried out by a loose coalition of hard-line Cold Warriors with links to the intelligence community: former CIA officers who had lost their government jobs in the Agency purges of the 1970s, and right-wing exiles such as Cubans and Vietnamese agitating for renewed efforts to free their homelands from communism. In this sense, 1980s mercenary chic—a seedbed of future American militia movements—was another manifestation of the boomerang effect. If the British and French had venerated imperial generals as their culture heroes, the American equivalent was the muscle-bound special forces renegade John Rambo.[12]

"We are here because you were there," Sri Lankan migrant and intellectual A. Sivanandan once explained to a British audience. America's covert empire might have been less obvious to the observer than its European predecessors, but it shared the imperial tendency to ramify at home as well as abroad, and not just in urban immigrant communities. The groves of American academe also bore the domestic bootprint of the CIA.[13]

In February 1964, a seminar convened on the campus of Michigan State University, the institution that had sent an advisory mission containing undercover CIA officers to South Vietnam the previous decade. Organized by student groups coordinated by Wesley Fishel, the MSU political science professor who had befriended Ngo Dinh Diem, the event took as its theme "Winds of Change in the Emerging Nations" (an echo, presumably intentional, of a famous statement about decolonization made by British prime minister Harold Macmillan when visiting Africa four years earlier: "The wind of change is blowing through this continent"). On the first morning, another of Fishel's friends, Edward Lansdale, led a panel discussion titled "Political Change and the Challenge of Subversive Insurgency" and featuring his longtime associates Napoleon Valeriano, chief of the Philippines counterinsurgency Nenita unit; aid worker and CIA officer Rufus Phillips; and COIN warrior Bernard Yoh. Lansdale reminisced fondly about past adventures with his comrades and urged the need for a population-centric strategy in Vietnam, a "people's war." Other sessions of the conference featured a keynote lecture by Leo Cherne, chair of the heavily CIA-associated International Rescue Committee, and Roger Hilsman, an OSS veteran and influential advocate of counterinsurgency in the Kennedy White House. Among the student organizations sponsoring "Winds of Change" was the US National Student Association, the CIA-funded group that would be exposed in the pages of *Ramparts* three years later.[14]

Fishel's conference was, admittedly, a particularly egregious example of the CIA's presence in American universities in the post–World War II era. Not all US campuses were as deeply interlinked with the national security state as MSU, whose ambitious president, John A. Hannah, once declared, "The world is our campus." Nor were all professors as ready as Fishel to invite the Agency to their institutions. Even at the height of the Cold War consensus in the 1950s, there were those who resisted such interactions either on anti-imperialist grounds or because they feared their intellectual freedom might be compromised—a tendency that would become more outspoken as the postwar period progressed.[15]

But even with these qualifications, it is hard to argue with the judgment that the CIA wielded an outsize influence on American campuses in the 1950s and 1960s. Other universities besides MSU, among them several with world-famous names, hosted "area studies" research programs with intelligence ties. The first of these sprang up immediately after World War II, as continuations of the Office of Strategic Services' research and analysis effort, focused, not surprisingly, on the Soviet Union. Both Columbia University's Russian Institute and Harvard's Russian Research Center replicated features of the OSS and received grants that, while originating with private foundations such as the Carnegie Corporation and Rockefeller Foundation, reflected the priorities of defense and intelligence officials. In 1950, the Massachusetts Institute of Technology (MIT), this time directly employing CIA money, hosted Project Troy, a multidisciplinary summer study group devoted to exploring ways of penetrating the Iron Curtain. Two years later, again with CIA sponsorship, MIT established its new Center for International Studies (CENIS) under the direction of Max Millikan, a former Agency analyst.[16]

By now, the range of area studies was expanding beyond the original focus on the Soviet Union to new regions of interest to the Cold War US state—the Middle East, for example. National security considerations were not the only driver here: Near East studies had its origin in the pre–World War II era and was disproportionately peopled by missionary-stock educators. But the establishment of new programs at institutions such as Princeton after the war followed along tracks laid by the OSS and received encouragement from government officials who wanted to draw on area-specific expertise that matched the United States' growing commitments in the Arab and Muslim worlds. This agenda was less explicit than at comparable British and French academic institutions—the University of London's School of Oriental and African Studies, for example—and the language used was different: the self-consciously modern, social scientific one of "modernization theory." Nevertheless, the echoes of European Orientalism and its mission of supporting colonial conquest in the Middle (and Far) East were unmistakable. Several of the emerging field's most prominent scholars were British-trained, the School of Oriental and African Studies graduate Bernard Lewis, for example.[17]

None of this was a coincidence: there were multifarious connections between US social science and the national security state in the early Cold War. In part, this was because of the predictive powers of scientific disciplines—the qualities valued by Sherman Kent and the CIA's analytical branch. But this was not the only intelligence application of the social sciences. The purported ability of disciplines such as economics, political science, and sociology to reveal the inner workings of foreign societies was also useful for purposes of covert action. Such knowledge was important to counterinsurgency doctrine, the winning of populations' hearts and minds. Psychological warfare, too, demanded scientific expertise, insight into the motivations of human behavior and technical means of influencing it. A secret memorandum of understanding laying out the terms of the relationship between MIT's CENIS and the intelligence community implicitly likened the role of social science in the Cold War to that of the natural sciences during World War II, when new inventions had made a vital contribution to the Allied victory: "It is imperative that we mobilize our resources for research in the broad field of political warfare as has been done ... with the development of more conventional weapons of war."[18]

A striking example of such weaponization is provided by Cold War–era anthropology. As a discipline, anthropology lent itself peculiarly well to intelligence work. With their language skills and access to remote locations, anthropologists had obvious value as espionage agents; moreover, their research into the traditions and structures of "primitive" societies could also feed into nation-building, counterinsurgency, or regime-change operations involving religious or tribal leaders. A complete picture of the CIA's influence on the discipline is probably unattainable due to continuing official secrecy but, thanks to research by anthropologist David H. Price, we already know a good deal. In 1951, the Agency assisted the American Anthropological Association (AAA) in compiling a membership roster, presumably so it would have access to a definitive list of US anthropologists for operational purposes; later in the decade, likely for similar reasons, a grant from the Asia Foundation enabled the AAA to offer Asian anthropologists heavily subsidized membership in the organization. Agency-funded institutions such as MIT's CENIS sponsored major pieces of anthropological research, including the 1950s Modjokuto Project, described by Price as "the classic postwar multisite ethnography project." Under the auspices of Modjokuto, young American researchers, some rising stars in the discipline, traveled to Indonesia—the site of a major regime-change operation at the time—to study such phenomena as the response of villagers to modernization. One of the researchers, Clifford Geertz, whose classic "thick description" of a Balinese cockfight dated from this expedition, was unwitting of CENIS's covert links at the time but later admitted to "a certain mild paranoia among us." The MSU advisory team in South Vietnam also employed anthropologists; one, Gerald Dickey, would later study French colonial pacification tactics in Darlac Province for the premier Cold War think tank, the RAND Corporation. Meanwhile, some CIA officers assumed the identity of traveling anthropologists as cover, fueling suspicions in postcolonial societies that all Western researchers were spies. As revisionist accounts of the history of European anthropology have shown, the discipline's development was inextricably bound up with the advance of Western colonialism; Price's work has shown a similar relationship between American anthropologists and the covert US empire.[19]

Lest it be assumed that it was only social sciences such as anthropology that were brushed by the hidden hand of intelligence, the CIA's relationship with the humanities needs reckoning with, too. As the careers of James Angleton and Cord Meyer both showed, there were intimate personal and intellectual connections between English literature and two intelligence fields: counterintelligence and propaganda. But English literature was not alone in this regard. If intelligence analysis had a parent academic discipline, it would be history. Sherman Kent was a historian, and an extraordinary proportion of senior analysts in the early CIA had history PhDs—five of the eight original Board of National Estimates members, to be precise. The relationship cut both ways. Seven postwar presidents of the American Historical Association (AHA) had served in the Office of Strategic Services and most maintained intelligence connections after the war. Kent's personal papers held at Yale make the postwar AHA look like an OSS old boys' club. Historians of this generation seem to have regarded their discipline and intelligence work as almost identical in their methodology and purpose. It was said of Kent's undergraduate primer, *Writing History*, that one could substitute the words "intelligence officer" for "historian," and it would still make perfect sense. Even that most innocent-seeming and impractical of the humanities, creative writing, was on the CIA's radar. Under the direction of the poet and cultural Cold Warrior Paul Engle, the Iowa Writers' Workshop, probably still the best-known graduate creative writing program in the nation, attracted grants from the Asia

Foundation and the Agency's principal funding conduit to the Congress for Cultural Freedom, the Farfield Foundation.[20]

Still, for all these connections, the CIA's links to the humanities look like a mere flirtation compared with its most disturbing and fateful academic relationship, one that violated the ethics of the field in question, tarnished the reputations of several of its most eminent practitioners, and caused untold human suffering.

The CIA's interest in psychology began almost as soon as the Agency was created, in the late 1940s. This was when reports started reaching the United States that foreign communists had discovered some means of controlling the minds of non-communist prisoners: first a Hungarian cardinal, then American POWs in Korea. Edward Hunter, the journalist who in 1950 invented a new word to describe this phenomenon—"brainwashing"—even suggested that the fall of China to communism was attributable to some sinister, Oriental form of mass hypnosis. It later emerged that Hunter was a former OSS officer who undertook psychological warfare assignments for the CIA, raising the possibility that his stories were themselves Cold War propaganda. But this did not matter. Intelligence leaders, especially Allen Dulles, took the reports seriously, and began investigating ways of defending potential US detainees against brainwashing.[21]

Initially, the most promising avenue appeared to be human subject experimentation involving psychotropic drugs. US Navy researchers had already started down this route, following in the footsteps of Nazi scientists who had forced concentration camp inmates to take the psychedelic substance mescaline. In 1950, the CIA launched BLUEBIRD, a mind-control research project under the charge of a brilliant but eccentric research scientist, Sidney Gottlieb, who soon focused his attention on the consciousness-altering properties of lysergic acid diethylamide

(LSD). BLUEBIRD was later renamed ARTICHOKE and then, in 1954, MKULTRA, because of what Dulles called its "ultra"-sensitive nature. By this point, the CIA's interest had shifted from defensive to offensive purposes, that is, developing techniques US interrogators could themselves use on communist prisoners.[22]

Gottlieb conducted much of his research in-house, at an Army biological weapons unit at Fort Detrick, Maryland, using military personnel as subjects (some of whom later developed depression and epilepsy). From early on, however, the Agency farmed out parts of its research program to non-government experts, among them some of the most eminent researchers of the day. Harvard's Henry K. Beecher, for example, a leading anesthesiologist and medical ethicist, traveled to Europe in pursuit of a "truth serum." There he consulted with scientists working for the British government (as in so many other aspects of the covert Cold War, there was a pronounced Anglo-American dimension to CIA mind control research) and carried out experiments, some reputedly lethal, on communist-bloc prisoners at a CIA safe house in Germany. Other experts, such as Harold G. Wolff, a senior neurologist who had treated Allen Dulles's son Allen Macy after he suffered brain damage in Korea, conducted MKULTRA research involving human subjects at their home institutions (Cornell, in Wolff's case). "Between 1953 and 1963," writes journalist Michael Otterman, "the CIA funded human experiments by 185 non-governmental researchers at eighty institutions, including forty-four universities and twelve hospitals."[23]

Meanwhile, Sidney Gottlieb's experiments involving his CIA-Army team grew ever more reckless. In 1953, one Fort Detrick scientist, Frank Olson, fell to his death from a New York hotel window after having unwittingly ingested LSD, apparently in an experiment gone tragically wrong (although there has been persistent speculation that

Olson was about to blow the whistle on government biological weapons research and was murdered before he could do so). A federal narcotics agent and friend of James Angleton's, George Hunter White, set up CIA "safe houses" in New York's Greenwich Village and San Francisco where prostitutes lured clients and spiked their drinks with LSD. White and Gottlieb observed what the men did next from behind a two-way mirror and, for good measure, sometimes had sex with the prostitutes themselves.[24]

Perhaps in part because of these excesses, during the mid-1950s MKULTRA began shifting its experimental focus from drugs to behavioral methods of interrogation. Donald O. Hebb, a distinguished psychologist at McGill University in Canada, had pioneered such techniques in the early 1950s with backing from the Canadian, UK, and US governments ("We and the Americans were joined at the hip in such matters," British psychologist William Sargant explained later). In experiments involving McGill student volunteers, Hebb had discovered that confining human subjects to cubicles and depriving them of sensory stimulation for just one or two days could cause them to hallucinate as if they had taken psychotropic drugs. Further CIA-funded research into communist interrogation methods by Cornell's Harold Wolff confirmed the effectiveness of Hebb's methods and added another element: the psychologically devastating impact on subjects of pain caused by forcing them to adopt stress positions such as sustained standing. Wolff also performed an additional service for the Agency: he administered the Human Ecology research fund, an MKULTRA conduit that supported a remarkable range of projects, some of them probably intended merely for cover purposes but others reflecting the CIA's growing interest in behavioral methods. One recipient of such funding, Donald Ewen Cameron, another McGill research scientist and friend of Allen Dulles, conducted "psychic driving" experiments involving drug-induced comas, electroshock treatment, and long periods of isolation that left dozens of patients with amnesia and epilepsy. The Scottish-born Cameron was a widely respected practitioner, president of both the American and Canadian Psychiatric Associations, who had pioneered several major advances in the treatment of the mentally ill.[25]

By 1960, it had become clear that there was no truth serum, and in 1963, after a damning CIA inspector general's report, MKULTRA was defunded. This, however, did not prevent the program from unleashing another unintended consequence, this one a countercultural legacy of Sidney Gottlieb's bohemian interest in consciousness-altering drugs. Several young volunteers in Stanford University drug experiments had experienced what they felt were spiritual revelations when taking LSD. One, the Beat poet Allen Ginsberg, was already well-known (and would later go on to become a prominent anti-imperial critic of the CIA). Another, the novelist Ken Kesey, would achieve notoriety as author of *One Flew over the Cuckoo's Nest* and conductor of his own "acid tests" with his band of Merry Pranksters. A third, Robert Hunter, would go on to pen lyrics for the rock band the Grateful Dead. In other words, MKULTRA drug experiments had unwittingly helped give birth to Bay Area psychedelia.[26]

The other track in the CIA's mind-control research program, the behavioral one, does not appear to have left a similar domestic legacy, apart from the trauma of its unfortunate experimental subjects. Its afterlife occurred abroad, where its methods, encoded in a 1963 KUBARK Counterintelligence Interrogation manual (KUBARK being the Agency's cryptonym for itself), were employed by Office of Public Safety police advisors such as Dan Mitrione in Uruguay. As recounted by historian Alfred McCoy, its core elements, isolation and sensory overload, were also adopted by the police forces of repressive US allies—the Marcos regime in the Philippines, for instance, and Honduras in the 1980s. Even the British, this time at the receiving rather than originating end of a trans-imperial circuit, used a version of the US-derived "no-touch" method, teaching it to the Royal Ulster Constabulary for use on Irish Republican suspects in 1971. As a form of torture, self-inflicted pain was peculiarly well suited to the covert nature of empire in the postcolonial era, leaving as it did only invisible, psychic scars.[27]

Other police methods propagated abroad by MSU and OPS advisors did have a boomerang effect. Much as surveillance and classification techniques crafted by Ralph Van Deman in the Philippines earlier in the century had returned to the United States in the form of new countersubversive campaigns, so America's Cold War foreign police assistance program reverberated in late-twentieth-century domestic urban policing. In the mid-1960s, when US inner cities were engulfed by race riots, the Johnson administration sought the advice of the OPS chief, former CIA officer Byron Engle. Some Americans had already begun to think of the domestic urban unrest of the era in terms of a Third World–style insurgency—Senator Karl Mundt referred to "a 'Saigon offensive' in our country here"—making the logical response a home-front counterinsurgency campaign. As one journalist put it, "Our ghettos, too, need a Lansdale, . . . a whole army of Lansdales." Testifying in 1967 before the presidential commission created in the wake of the disturbances, Engle recommended the importation of "non-lethal" riot control techniques that had been employed in Vietnam, including "chemical munitions" such as CS or "tear gas." (Engle might also have noted that the British had used tear gas to disperse rioters in Cyprus and British Guiana.) Within a year, CS was being used heavily by the US Army, National Guard, and police, often alongside rather than instead of firearms. In Los Angeles, future police chief Daryl F. Gates, employing the same Third World analogy—"the streets of America's cities had become a foreign territory"—developed a paramilitary, tactical police team, SWAT, that evoked the mobile counterguerrilla units of counterinsurgency doctrine. Using COIN tactics, SWAT engaged in firefights with the Black Panthers, accompanied, to quote one historian, "by copious clouds of CS." The CIA itself, according to a 1973 Family Jewels document, lent out "surplus technical equipment," presumably originally intended for foreign deployment, to local police departments, "briefing them as to its use." Ironically, one of the targets of the new police tactics, the terrorist Weather Underground, was using a similar boomerang logic when it coined its famous slogan, "Bring the War Home."[28]

But, as US forces overseas could attest, quashing insurgencies was easier said than done. At the same time that Third World nationalists were resisting American foreign policy as a neocolonial imposition, anti-imperial elements in the United States began protesting CIA interventions in their nation's civic life. Thanks to the Agency's funding of various academic disciplines, young white students on the New Left had to look no further than their university campus for targets to denounce. Scholarly organizations such as the American Anthropological Association succumbed to bitter intergenerational controversies. Student demonstrators gathered outside MIT's Center for International Studies and conducted a mock tribunal of Max Millikan and other professors. Anti-CIA activists worked to drive Agency-sponsored researchers and recruiters off campus at institutions ranging from large public universities to liberal arts colleges. "In 1968 alone," writes reporter Daniel Golden, "there were seventy-seven instances of picketings, sit-ins, and other student protests against CIA recruiters."[29]

Even MSU, that most biddable of Cold War US universities, became the scene of intense unrest when its Vietnam program was exposed by *Ramparts* in a 1966 story heralded by one of the great magazine covers of the era: a cartoon of Madame Nhu dressed as a Spartans cheerleader. Thanks to its CIA links, the school was a focus of organizing by Students for a Democratic Society, and home to one of the nation's first radical student newspapers. Wesley Fishel, architect of the 1950s MSU mission to South Vietnam, was denounced variously as a CIA agent, "the Biggest Operator of them all," and one of the "para-military professors." He died in 1977 at the age of fifty-seven, some colleagues blaming stress caused by the protests for his premature passing.[30]

The "Winds of Change" in the title of Fishel's 1964 MSU conference was meant to refer to decolonization and nation-building in the Third World. The phrase might equally well have applied to the United States itself.

Anti-CIA campus protest was the most obvious form of domestic backlash against the United States' overseas covert empire, but it was not the only one. The unintended consequences of Agency interventions abroad also included the growth in American society of a less explicit and coherent but, over the long term, more influential body of criticism: CIA-centered conspiracy theories.

Conspiracism had long been a feature of imperial history, with colonial populations suspecting the hidden hand of Western agents like T. E. Lawrence in every local event. More recently, in the postcolonial era, such suspicions had focused on CIA officers like the latter-day imperial adventurer Kermit Roosevelt. When Kim turned up in Beirut in 1957, the Egyptian ambassador to Lebanon reportedly began "taking bets on when and where the next U.S. coup would take place." Meanwhile, in Southeast Asia, Prince Norodom Sihanouk of Cambodia became so obsessed with Edward Lansdale, believing that the CIA man was out to assassinate him, that in 1968 he wrote, directed, and starred in a movie, *Shadow over Angkor*, in which he bested and killed an American character called Lansdale.[31]

But postcolonial conspiracism did not stay in the postcolonial world. Much as Lawrence of Arabia became the focus of Orientalist suspicion in post–World War I Britain, so conspiracy theories trailed CIA officers home to America. To be sure, the United States had a homegrown history of conspiracism, famously described by historian Richard Hofstadter as "the paranoid style in American politics." Generations of Americans had seen their republic as in peril from "alien" forces inside the nation: Masons, Catholics, Mormons, Jews, and communists. However, several factors made the Cold War United States peculiarly susceptible to conspiracy theories, which now tended to focus less on minority groups threatening the government than on the government itself. One of these was the massive growth of official secrecy that the period witnessed, as US officials asked the American people effectively to surrender democratic control of American foreign policy to covert state entities such as the CIA in exchange for defending the nation against communism. Another was the poorly hidden fact that, also in the name of national security, the government was simultaneously monitoring and propagandizing American citizens, again via the CIA. A third was foreign influence, with postcolonial conspiracism boomeranging to the United States via the anti-imperial left, and communist propagandists seizing on the paranoid tendency in American political life to sow dissension in Cold War US society by deliberately spreading disinformation.[32]

The total effect of these various forces was to produce, in addition to fears about nefarious government plots against Americans, a widespread skepticism about the official version of events, a postmodern blurring between fact and fiction, and a crop of popular stories about the CIA that bore only a tangential relation to reality (ironically enough, given the Agency's own fondness for telling stories). CIA officers tried to regain control of the narrative, responding to the conspiracy theories circulating about them with counterallegations (sometimes justified, sometimes not) that such theories were the product of communist propaganda or pathological paranoia. But their efforts were hampered by the conditions of secrecy in which they had to work, meaning that their counternarratives had to be disseminated, Mighty Wurlitzer style, by proxies, as well as by the propensity of the stories themselves to mutate, virus-like, into ever more fictional versions of reality.[33]

Although several of the conspiracy theories that swirled around the CIA were self-evidently preposterous and earned only limited credence—that it faked the moon landings, for example—a few gained wider, longer-lasting popularity. According to one of these, the Watergate scandal was the work not, as it appeared, of the Nixon administration but rather of the CIA, looking to frame the White House in what amounted to a coup against a sitting president. Initially propounded by Nixon loyalists such as Chuck Colson, this theory got a second lease on life in 1979 when, in a biography of *Washington Post* owner Katharine Graham, journalist Deborah Davis alleged, among other things, that *Post* editor Ben Bradlee was part of a CIA-press conspiracy, Operation Mockingbird, run by Cord Meyer (Bradlee's brother-in-law); that the Watergate break-in was orchestrated by Agency counterintelligence officer Richard Ober; and that Ober, performing a favor for his Harvard classmate Bradlee, was the *Post*'s Watergate source, Deep Throat.[34]

As with most conspiracy theories, Davis's claims did contain some truth: there was a CIA Project MOCKINGBIRD, for example, but rather than being a vast, ongoing plot, it was a wiretapping operation conducted against just two journalists in 1963 at the instruction of John Kennedy. Other claims, such as Davis's identification of Ober as Deep Throat, were invention, and confirmed as such in 2005 when former FBI associate director Mark Felt told *Vanity Fair* that it was in fact he who had passed information about Watergate to the *Post*. After Bradlee hinted at legal action and a lawyer acting for Ober described his characterization as "defamatory and libelous," Davis's publisher, Harcourt Brace Jovanovich, withdrew the book from sale (although Davis subsequently won a sizable settlement from HBJ and reissued a revised version of the book with another publisher). This was not, however, an end to her theories. The notion that Watergate was a "silent coup" by the "deep state" would resurface years later, during the presidency of Donald Trump.[35]

A second set of CIA conspiracy theories, this one inspired by MKULTRA, had equally long legs. Thanks to journalist Edward Hunter and *The Manchurian Candidate*, a popular 1959 novel (and 1962 movie) about a brainwashed assassin, the concept of mind control had already gained a firm purchase on the US imagination even before details of the CIA's drug and behavioral experiments emerged during the congressional investigations of the 1970s. Astounded by the stranger-than-fiction disclosures, some Americans began speculating that real-life assassins such as Robert Kennedy's murderer, the robotic-seeming Sirhan Sirhan, had been programmed to perform their heinous acts by the CIA. The vocal conspiracy theorist and serial presidential candidate Lyndon LaRouche, whose paranoid followers included former members of the Vietnam War deserter community on whom MHCHAOS had spied in the 1960s, alleged the existence of an Agency plot to brainwash America, while himself using psychological techniques to "ego-strip" his recruits. As recently as 2019, a widely reviewed account of the 1969 Tate-LaBianca murders proposed not only that Charles Manson was a graduate of a successful San Francisco CIA drug experiment but also that the gruesome killings were part of an MHCHAOS operation to discredit the counterculture and drive a wedge between liberal Hollywood and the Black Panthers.[36]

A third theory, this one with a more substantial foundation in fact, had its origins in the 1980s Contra supply program and revelations that the Nicaraguan insurgents had traded in cocaine destined for US cities, Los Angeles in particular. African Americans were already inclined to suspect the worst of the CIA thanks to the revelation that the Agency's drug tests had disproportionately involved Black subjects, an unfortunately common pattern in government-sponsored medical experimentation. Hence, when in 1996 Bay Area journalist Gary Webb broke the story that the Contra operation had "boomeranged back to the streets of America," many African Americans saw evidence of a government plot to ensure, as they told pollsters, "that drugs are easily available in poor Black neighborhoods to harm Black people." The CIA pushed back—Director John M. Deutch even attended a town hall meeting of angry South Central LA residents—and supportive newsmen denigrated Webb's journalism, portraying him and his Black readers as pathological conspiracy theorists. Webb committed suicide in 2004, but the association between the CIA and the crack cocaine epidemic then ravaging inner-city neighborhoods was by that point thoroughly established in the minds of many African Americans.[37]

Deeply entrenched though these conspiracist stories about the CIA were, none gained the popularity and durability of the mother of

modern US conspiracy theories: the JFK assassination. Many professional historians now acknowledge that the official account of the events
leading up to Kennedy's November 1963 murder, the 1964 Warren
Commission Report, was deeply flawed. All the main parties assisting
the inquiry—the FBI, CIA, and White House—had reason to withhold
potentially vital information. Kennedy administration members feared
exposure of the dead president's chronic illnesses and sex addiction. J.
Edgar Hoover, who thought the commission unnecessary in the first
place, wanted to conceal the incompetence of G-men in Dallas who had
failed to keep track of Lee Harvey Oswald. And the CIA, for obvious
reasons, wished to preserve the secrecy of its attempts to eliminate Fidel
Castro. Finally, everyone involved feared that revealing foreign responsibility for the assassination, whether Cuban or Soviet, would drive the
US government into an international confrontation that might end in
nuclear war. Consequently, the official inquiry was less an investigation than a prosecution, its main finding—that a disaffected lone gunman killed the president—a foregone conclusion. The resulting report,
while extraordinarily voluminous and detailed (literary intellectuals
ironically hailed it as "an accidental American classic"), abruptly closed
down several lines of inquiry, including the possibility suspected by
several top officials, among them Lyndon Johnson, that the assassination was a preemptive strike by Castro against the US president who
was trying to murder him—or, put another way, that JFK's death was
the ultimate boomerang effect, an act of imperial violence winging its
way back to America.[38]

While some other Americans saw the assassination in these
terms—the Black nationalist Malcolm X, for example, notoriously
described it as a case of "chickens coming home to roost"—the Warren Report otherwise inspired little skepticism, at least at first. *Time*

magazine described it as "utterly convincing," and opinion polls indi-cated general public confidence in its findings. Gradually, however, a community of doubters began corresponding among themselves and publishing in left-wing magazines such as *Ramparts*, quick to JFK con-spiracy theory as to so many other stories. Their motives were vari-ous. Some wanted to find meaning in Kennedy's apparently senseless killing, others to ensure Oswald a posthumous fair hearing. Foreign influence may also have been a factor: articles critiquing the official narrative of the assassination were appearing in the European press, some probably planted there in a KGB disinformation campaign. A few Third World leaders were joining in the questioning, too. When the US ambassador to Ghana showed Kwame Nkrumah a copy of the report, Nkrumah pointed to the name of one of the commission's members, former DCI Allen Dulles, and said simply, "Whitewash." Initially dismissed as a "housewives' underground," the "Warrenolo-gists" attracted national attention in 1966 with the appearance of two major books challenging the report: *Rush to Judgment* by civil rights lawyer Mark Lane, and *Inquest* by Cornell graduate student Edward Jay Epstein (later James Angleton's journalistic amanuensis). By December of the same year, fully 50 percent of Americans suspected that Oswald had not acted alone. Like anti-imperialism, JFK conspiracy theory was crossing into the mainstream.[39]

Although not yet identified as a possible conspirator, the CIA was unnerved by this turn of events. Such questioning of the commis-sion's findings "cast doubt on the whole leadership of American soci-ety," lamented a 1967 Agency memorandum. To counter it, the memo continued, the CIA should mobilize "friendly elite contacts" to suggest that "parts of the conspiracy talk appear to be deliberately generated by Communist propagandists." Mark Lane was a particular focus of such attention, with informers passing on to Agency figures such as Allen Dulles scurrilous gossip about the lawyer's political contacts and sex life.[40]

But the attempt to rally pro-CIA forces came too late. The previous fall, New Orleans district attorney Jim Garrison had launched a new investigation of the Kennedy assassination (he was able to do so because Lee Harvey Oswald had lived in New Orleans over the summer of 1963, during which period he had taken it upon himself to organize a local chapter of the Fair Play for Cuba Committee). Garrison was a flamboyant self-promoter who initially toyed with the idea of arguing that Oswald belonged to a local gay sex ring that killed the president for thrills. Then, however, inspired by the foreign coverage of the murder, he changed tack. In March 1967, the same month that *Ramparts* published its exposé of the National Student Association (JFK conspiracy theory and anti-imperial opposition to the CIA were now moving in tandem), Garrison arrested local businessman Clay Shaw, claiming that he was part of an Agency and Pentagon conspiracy. According to the new scenario, Kennedy had planned to withdraw from Vietnam and wind down the Cold War but the "military-intelligence complex" had murdered him before he had a chance to do so. Echoing earlier anti-imperialist warnings about the domestic dangers of foreign adventurism, Garrison portrayed an America dominated by "an arrogant, swollen bureaucratic complex totally unfettered by the checks and balances of the Constitution."[41]

The CIA was discomfited enough by Garrison's attentions to circulate to station chiefs a guidebook containing talking points defending the Warren Report, and might also have taken further steps, including infiltrating the DA's staff. The investigation ended in abject failure when the jury voted to acquit Shaw after less than an hour's deliberation. However, Garrison's conspiracist narrative, of a peacemaking president cut down by secret warmongers, lived on. The steady drip of revelations about government misdeeds in the early 1970s contributed to its persistence. So too did the first US TV network showing in 1975 of the Zapruder film of the Kennedy assassination, which seemed to cast doubt on the Warren Commission's lone-gunman finding. The public's response contributed to the Church Committee's investigations and then, in 1976, the establishment of a House Select Committee on Assassinations (HSCA) to investigate the death of President Kennedy and the 1968 killing of Martin Luther King Jr. anew. Although HSCA eventually concluded in 1979 that the CIA was not involved, its inquiries did reveal anomalies in the Agency's monitoring of Oswald prior to the assassination, including during a trip by him to Mexico City where he visited the Cuban and Soviet embassies. The committee also muddied the waters by, at the eleventh hour, declaring that there probably was a conspiracy to kill Kennedy on the basis of acoustic evidence that was later discredited (of a police channel Dictabelt recording that appeared to indicate the existence of a second gunman).[42]

By now, the feverish speculation was beginning to feature the names of individual CIA officers—Howard Hunt, for example, and the former Latin America desk chief turned Agency publicist, David Atlee Phillips. This was not perhaps surprising for several reasons. As Phillips himself put it later, he had "asked for it" by becoming "a public figure" after leaving the CIA, as part of the coordinated late 1970s campaign to improve the Agency's image. There was also the fact that, by his own account, he had played an important role in the earlier "regime change" operation against Jacobo Árbenz. Finally, although this was less generally known at the time, during the early 1960s Phillips had run propaganda ops against Castro and his supporters, including the Fair Play for Cuba Committee—now, of course, a name indelibly associated with Oswald.[43]

Phillips's travails as a conspiracy theory "person of interest" began in September 1976. This was when a Church Committee researcher, the investigative journalist Gaeton Fonzi, turned up to interview him at the annual convention of the Association of Retired Intelligence Officers in a Virginia hotel, accompanied by a Spanish-speaking foreigner. It subsequently transpired that Fonzi's mysterious companion was Antonio Veciana, a Cuban former CIA agent, who was now claiming that his Agency case officer, "Maurice Bishop," had introduced him to Lee Harvey Oswald in Dallas shortly before the assassination. Fonzi had brought Veciana to the meeting to establish whether, as he suspected, "Bishop" was in fact Phillips.[44]

Phillips was not, at this point, very concerned: Veciana failed to provide a definitive identification, and his story was discounted by the Senate investigators. But then, in 1980, it resurfaced in an altogether more disquieting form. Fonzi had spoken with an Irish researcher, Anthony Summers, who that year published a book about the Kennedy assassination, *Conspiracy*, along with excerpts in the *Observer* newspaper, repeating Veciana's claims and identifying Phillips as "Bishop." A few months later, Fonzi came out with his own version of the story, "Who Killed JFK?," an 80,000-word article in *Washingtonian* magazine (coincidentally, earlier a publishing venue for Phillips himself) featuring composite sketches of "Bishop" alongside photographs of the CIA man. Meanwhile, other researchers claimed that Phillips was also involved in the 1975 assassination of Orlando Letelier. The allegations proliferated on US TV shows and in mainstream publications. Like Cord Meyer before him, Phillips was going from being the storyteller to the subject of others' stories, an experience he compared to undergoing a Kafkaesque metamorphosis into a different species.[45]

Phillips fought back against his accusers, suing the *Washingtonian* for libel and, at the same time, appealing to CIA allies in the media world, who printed articles suggesting that the allegations were part of "a disinformation campaign," or in other words, communist propaganda. His close journalist friend Joseph C. Goulden, who had once worked with Fonzi, privately shared salacious details about his former colleague's sex life. The stories would not go away, though, springing up whack-a-mole-like throughout the decade. The 1980s conspiracy theory scene was noticeably more sensationalist and scattershot than the relatively sober, earnest tone of earlier investigations. A headline in the spoof newspaper *The Onion* captured the mood: "Kennedy Slain by CIA, Mafia, Castro, LBJ, Teamsters, Freemasons: President Shot 129 Times from 43 Different Angles." Still, in all Phillips's public statements and private correspondence about the allegations against him, he was strikingly silent about the assassination itself, suggesting perhaps a greater degree of knowledge about the event than he was prepared to admit.[46]

Phillips obtained some measure of satisfaction in 1986, when the *Observer* retracted Summers's allegations and paid him £10,000 in damages. By now, however, he had been joined by other CIA officers as individuals named in Agency-JFK conspiracy theories. Several of the stories in question coalesced around a second tragic death that had occurred less than a year after Kennedy's own: the October 1964 slaying of Cord Meyer's ex-wife, Mary Pinchot Meyer, on a remote Georgetown canal towpath.

The murder of Mary Meyer—by the time of her death, a well-known Washington figure in her own right and a highly regarded artist—has never been solved. The chief suspect, Raymond Crump Jr., an African American man arrested near the murder scene, was later acquitted after the legendary civil rights attorney Dovey Johnson Roundtree persuaded the jury there was not enough evidence to convict him. Rumors about the killing circulated in the nation's capital until in 1976—a signal year for JFK conspiracy theories—a close friend of the murdered woman, former *Washington Post* vice president James Truitt, told supermarket tabloid the *National Enquirer* that between January 1962 and November 1963 she had conducted a passionate affair with John Kennedy. According to Truitt, the couple met thirty times in a White House bedroom, once smoking marijuana together, and Meyer kept a journal of the relationship. Seven years later, in his 1983 memoir *Flashbacks*, the Harvard psychologist turned psychedelia guru (and, according to some accounts, MHCHAOS agent) Timothy Leary furnished more detail. At the time of the affair, he claimed, Mary Meyer had confided in him a plan to use drugs to convert "powerful men" in Washington to world peace. After Kennedy was killed, she had phoned Leary, sobbing, "They couldn't control him any more. He was changing too fast." Finally, in his 1995 autobiography *A Good Life*, Meyer's brother-in-law Ben Bradlee confirmed that she did indeed have an affair with Kennedy (without, though, saying anything about the alleged drug use) and added another element to the story: shortly after the murder, Bradlee had surprised James Angleton breaking into Meyer's home and art studio in search of the diary in which she was supposed to have recorded details of her affair with the dead president.[47]

No evidence has ever emerged in support of Leary's claim about Meyer's plan to convert Kennedy to pacifism with drugs, which sounds like an addled combination of MKULTRA and Jim Garrison's narrative about the president as murdered peacemaker. Similarly, the most recent conspiracist account of the murder, Peter Janney's 2016 *Mary's Mosaic*, while right to acknowledge Meyer's fine qualities as an artist and independent woman in a patriarchal era, fails ultimately to prove its claim that she was the victim of a CIA conspiracy (allegedly involving the author's own father, Wistar Janney) to prevent her from exposing falsehoods in the Warren Commission report.[48]

That Mary Meyer had an affair with Kennedy, though, is beyond dispute. In 2016, a letter written by the president to his lover in October 1963, a month before his death, sold at auction for $89,000. In it, he implored Meyer to visit him. "I know it is unwise, irrational, and that you may hate it—on the other hand you may not—and I will love it," Kennedy had written.[49]

Similarly, although aspects of Bradlee's account of Angleton's role are problematic (he had failed to mention both his surprise encounter with the CIA man and the existence of a diary while testifying at Raymond Crump's 1965 trial), the main thrust of his claims—that Angleton was professionally interested in Mary Meyer's murder—rings true. Meyer had, after all, been married to a senior CIA official responsible for global covert operations, then had an affair with a US president. Later, Angleton linked her murder with his hunt for the mole that the Soviet defector Anatoli Golitsyn claimed had infiltrated the highest reaches of the US government. "Did the death of a woman in whom the late president might have confided have anything to do with the Soviet penetration that Golitsyn had warned about?" he asked correspondent Joseph J. Trento. "Had someone in Kennedy's inner circle been compromised?" Later still, suspicion fell on Angleton himself. Timothy Leary, among others, believed he had ordered Mary's murder because she knew too many of the CIA's secrets. The paranoia surrounding the counterintelligence officer was infectious. It seems that even the normally phlegmatic Cord Meyer eventually developed conspiracist beliefs about his ex-wife's murder. When, just six days before his own death, the writer C. David Heymann asked him who he thought had killed Mary, Meyer replied, "The same sons of bitches who killed John F. Kennedy."[50]

Meanwhile, James Angleton was also emerging as a prime suspect in the Kennedy assassination itself. His name began to feature during the congressional investigations of the 1970s when it was revealed that his Counter-Intelligence Staff had handled liaison between the CIA and the Warren Commission during its inquiry the previous decade. Rather than providing commission staff with all the Agency's records on Oswald, Angleton had concealed the existence of a file that his staff had opened on the assassin in 1960. He also hid the fact that Oswald's mail had been monitored as part of the HTLINGUAL operation. Most concerningly, Angleton failed to reveal potentially significant details that the Agency knew about Oswald's 1963 visits to the Cuban and Soviet embassies in Mexico City, actions that pointed toward the possibility of Oswald being a foreign agent. Why had Angleton sat on the CIA's pre-assassination records on Oswald? Was it part of the Agency's general reluctance to reveal anything about its Castro operations? Or, some assassination buffs wondered, was it because Angleton had an operational relationship with Oswald? As the counterintelligence chief's most recent biographer, Jefferson Morley, puts it, "Was Angleton running Oswald as an agent as part of a plot to assassinate President Kennedy?"[51]

The answer to this question is probably not. Among the different conspiracy theories about the Kennedy assassination, Oswald as a Cuban agent seems far more plausible. However, it is not hard to see why Angleton, with his habitual secrecy, obsession with strategic deception, and imperial paranoia, should have attracted such attention. He was, after all, a conspiracy theorist himself.[52]

Nor, finally, is it difficult to see why Edward Lansdale should also have appeared in JFK conspiracy stories, given his diabolical reputation in much of Cold War Asia, his identification as a character in not one but two classic political novels of the era (erroneous in the case of *The Quiet American*, correct in *The Ugly American*), and his own fondness for devious psychological stratagems.

Lansdale's first appearance as a Kennedy conspirator came courtesy of an old associate, L. Fletcher Prouty, a former Air Force colonel who had served as chief of special operations for the Joint Chiefs of Staff during the Kennedy years. After his retirement from government service, Prouty became an outspoken critic of the CIA while at the same time undermining his own credibility by consorting with the Church of Scientology, the far-right Liberty Lobby, and Lyndon LaRouche. His interpretation of the Kennedy assassination was much like Jim Garrison's—the president was a victim of the military-intelligence complex—except that his version featured his old colleague Lansdale as the chief conspirator. As evidence, Prouty produced a photograph of police leading three tramps from the Dealey Plaza (whom other conspiracy theorists claimed to be a disguised Howard Hunt and two co-conspirators) that also showed, or so Prouty claimed, a rear view of Lansdale. Like David Phillips, Lansdale might not have been much bothered by Prouty's pronouncements had they not been taken up by others, among them the Hollywood filmmaker Oliver Stone. Stone's blockbuster 1991 movie about the Garrison investigation, *JFK*, in addition to featuring a character obviously modeled on Prouty—"Colonel X," played by Donald Sutherland—included scenes showing partial, shadowy glimpses of a "General Y." The audience learns that General Y ran operations against Castro and knew Allen Dulles well; he sports a mustache, wears sunglasses, and has a nameplate on his desk with some letters visible: "U.S. Air" and, above them, "M/GEN. E. G." In short, General Y is clearly meant to be Edward Geary Lansdale.[53]

Having starred in earlier works of Cold War fiction (including by name in Sihanouk's *Shadow over Angkor*), it was perhaps fitting that Edward Lansdale should also appear, right at the Cold War's end, in another. More than any other conspiracy theory text, *JFK* cemented in the American popular mind the notion that the Kennedy assassination was not, as the US government claimed, the crime of a sociopathic loner, but rather the work of the government itself. As such, it helped pave the way for a post–Cold War era in which many ordinary Americans came to view institutions of the "deep state" such as the CIA as enemies of the people rather than their defender—just one of the many boomerang legacies of covert empire inherited by America in the twenty-first century.

The Global War on Terror

I n March 2018, Republican president Donald Trump announced his
intention to nominate Gina Haspel as director of the Central Intelligence Agency.

For a president known for his contentious national security appoint-
ments and unprecedentedly turbulent relationship with the intelligence
community, the nomination seemed at first a surprisingly uncontro-
versial one. The sixty-one-year-old Haspel was a respected career CIA
officer who had joined the Agency in 1985 and worked her way up
through the ranks, serving in a variety of posts overseas and leadership
roles at home, including deputy director of the clandestine service. In
an organization many still regarded as elitist, she was also a refresh-
ingly unshowy personality from a relatively humble background, a
"girl out of Kentucky who liked Johnny Cash," as one former colleague
described her. True, she had attended high school in England—but as

an Air Force brat rather than a boarder at a posh public school. Instead of Harvard and Yale, her degrees were from the University of Louisville and Northeastern University. Most significantly, she was, as her supporters were quick to point out, the first woman tapped to lead the CIA. Quite apart from the obvious merit of her nomination in terms of gender equality and workforce diversity, this was potentially a good thing for an agency whose past blunders could partly be blamed on the masculine behavioral codes of its historically male-dominated leadership cadre, the "imperial brotherhood."[1]

However, there was one big strike against Haspel's nomination. In 2002, she had served as chief of a secret CIA prison or "black site" in Thailand where suspected terrorists had been subjected to enhanced interrogation techniques (EITs). These included, in addition to sleep deprivation and forced stress positions, a practice known as "waterboarding": strapping prisoners to a board, covering their faces with cloth, and pouring water on them so that they experienced the sensation of drowning. Not only that, in 2005, a year after the publication of photographs depicting prisoner abuse at Abu Ghraib, a US military prison in Iraq, Haspel had participated in the destruction of dozens of videotape recordings of interrogations at Thailand and other locations.

Evidently, none of this much concerned Donald Trump, who during his 2016 presidential campaign had spoken of the need to "bring back waterboarding . . . and a hell of a lot worse." But it did concern others. A former officer of the American Civil Liberties Union described Haspel as "quite literally a war criminal." Women human rights campaigners objected to officials in the Trump administration and CIA portraying Haspel's nomination as a victory for feminism, pointing out that neither Trump nor the Agency had exactly been friends of women's rights in the past. Most worryingly for Haspel's prospects, several

CIA director nominee Gina Haspel in 2018, taking the oath during her contentious confirmation hearing before the Senate Select Committee on Intelligence.
Mandel Ngan/AFP, Getty Images

influential senators declared themselves opposed to her confirmation. These included not only Democrats such as Dianne Feinstein, who had chaired a lengthy and controversial Senate Intelligence Committee inquiry into EITs (during which the CIA had spied on Senate staffers), but some Republicans as well. Among the latter was former presidential candidate John McCain, himself a victim of hostile interrogation during the Vietnam War. "It's all torture," McCain told former CIA director Porter J. Goss.[2]

Gina Haspel did face some intense questioning about her role in the EIT program during her Senate confirmation hearing, most notably from future vice president Kamala Harris. At one point during the proceedings, a protester yelled, "Waterboarding is torture! Bloody Gina!" But, in the end, senators accepted Haspel's assurances that, with her as its director, the CIA would not revive enhanced interrogations no matter how much pressure it might come under from the Trump administration to do so. On May 17, 2018, Haspel was confirmed by the full Senate in a mostly party-line vote, 54-45. The nomination flap was over.[3]

Still, the episode had reminded the US public of a chapter in the CIA's history the Agency itself would probably rather it forget: the early years of the Global War on Terror (GWOT), the name given to the international campaign against Islamist terrorists carried out by the United States in the wake of al-Qaeda's attacks on the American homeland on September 11, 2001.

The GWOT had an ambiguous impact on the CIA. On the one hand, it helped restore a clear sense of mission to an agency that had been adrift since the end of the Cold War, placing it, once again, at the cutting edge of American power in the world. Using operational authorities of the sort it had been denied since the intelligence reforms of the 1970s, such as license to use "lethal force," CIA operatives, in just a little over two months, pursued al-Qaeda to its hiding place in Afghanistan and helped overthrow the Taliban government that had given it sanctuary. Roughly a decade later, the Agency also succeeded in hunting down al-Qaeda's leader, the Saudi Osama bin Laden, in a hideout in Pakistan, where he had fled from Afghanistan. Meanwhile, other leading Islamist terrorists died in "targeted killings" by unmanned aerial vehicles or "drones" in a program again entrusted to the CIA.

But the GWOT era also witnessed some of the darkest days in the CIA's existence. Looming over the period were two catastrophic intelligence errors: the Agency's failure to predict the 9/11 attacks, and its subsequent mistaken claim that the Iraqi leader Saddam Hussein possessed weapons of mass destruction (WMD), the principal justification for the United States' invasion of Iraq in 2003. While officials in the administration of President George W. Bush were arguably just as much, if not more, to blame for both these blunders, it was the CIA that carried the can. Following the publication of devastating reports about 9/11 and the WMD debacle in 2004, Congress passed the Intelligence Reform and Terrorism Prevention Act, effectively demoting the director of the CIA by creating the Office of Director of National Intelligence to oversee the entire intelligence community. Consequently, when Gina Haspel received her nomination in 2018, it was to serve not as Director of Central Intelligence, an office that no longer existed, but rather merely as director of the CIA, just one of a rapidly growing number of US intelligence agencies (eighteen at current count). This is to say nothing of the scandal that also erupted around the CIA's use of EITs, which became public in 2005, despite Haspel's efforts to conceal it.[4]

All this—the story of the CIA's conduct of the Global War on Terror and its domestic reverberations—is probably familiar to anyone who has followed the news headlines in the past few decades. Less obvious is the way in which, like the Cold War that preceded it, the GWOT echoed the imperial past—an influence so persistent that not even Gina Haspel, whose nomination had appeared to signal a break from the tradition of the imperial brotherhood, could elude it.

The point of this Epilogue, therefore, is less to provide a detailed account of the CIA's history since 2001 than to flesh out the continuities and correspondences between the War on Terror and prior imperial history. This means considering the domestic, boomerang effects of the GWOT, of which Gina Haspel's nomination controversy was merely one of the more obvious. First, though, it is necessary to identify the ways in which the GWOT itself replicated certain elements of earlier, colonial "small wars." Adopting such an approach does not, of course, explain every aspect of the War on Terror, but it does place several key phases of the conflict in a new, revealing light: its origins, the reasons the CIA failed to predict the al-Qaeda attacks, and the tactics employed by the United States in its conduct of the GWOT in Afghanistan and Iraq, both already centuries-old imperial battlegrounds. None of this is intended to excuse the murderous atrocities of 9/11; the aim is rather to improve understanding of their causes in hopes of helping prevent anything like them from occurring again.

"Why do they hate us?" George Bush asked rhetorically in a State of the Union address nine days after 9/11. The most popular explanation of the roots of the al-Qaeda attacks on America at the time and since has been that they were produced by a "clash of civilizations": the lashing out of a medieval, theocratic way of life against a modern, democratic one. While there may be some elements of truth to this thesis, it fails to take account of several factors, including a long tradition of admiration for US modernity within Arab and Muslim societies—and, for that matter, a reciprocal tendency toward "Arabism" among some Americans, including CIA officers such as Kim Roosevelt.[5]

A better explanation of anti-American feeling in the Middle East would focus on a more immediate set of causes: post–World War II US interventions in the region that its inhabitants perceived—with, as we have seen, some justification—as basically continuing the colonial policies of older imperial powers. Viewed against this background, 9/11 looks less like the product of an inexorable civilizational conflict than a case of imperial blowback, albeit a particularly terrible and tragic one. Historically, terror attacks on imperial metropoles have been one of the asymmetrical tactics favored by militant anti-colonial movements, obvious examples being the bombing campaigns carried out by the

Irish Republican Army on the British mainland and by the Algerian National Liberation Front in Paris and its suburbs during the Algerian War. Although more important as a factor in 9/11, religious motivation also played a role in earlier instances of nationalist terrorism, again, for example, in Ireland. Of course, not every aspect of the al-Qaeda attacks is reducible to the neocolonial dimensions of US–Middle Eastern relations—their scale, for example, was unprecedented in the history of anti-colonial terrorism—but the imperial past offers at least as good an explanation of their origins as theories about a clash of civilizations.[6]

There is also another, narrower sense in which 9/11 might be viewed as blowback from US interventionism in the Muslim world: the partial origins of al-Qaeda in the 1980s jihadist insurgency against the Soviet occupation of Afghanistan, a cause heavily aided by covert support from the CIA. This is not to say, as some conspiracy theorists have argued, that the Agency created Osama bin Laden: thanks to the considerable wealth of his family, the Saudi terrorist had his own sources of support independent of the CIA, and there is no credible evidence of the Agency funding or training him, despite conspiracist claims to the contrary. Nevertheless, by supplying the mujahideen, the United States was indirectly contributing to the radicalization of young Arabs like bin Laden who traveled to Afghanistan in the 1980s to join in the war against the Soviets. Moreover, the anarchic conditions that prevailed in the country after the mujahideen's victory undoubtedly enabled the rise of the Taliban and the establishment of an Afghan refuge by al-Qaeda. If, in retrospect, the United States' backing of jihadists to fight the Soviet Union looks unwise, it could perhaps be said in Americans' defense that earlier Western powers had adopted much the same tactic, especially the British, who since the late 1800s had tried several times to create a pan-Islamic, pro-British movement in the arc of Muslim societies undergirding the Russian Empire's southern flank, making the CIA's Afghan operations of the 1980s yet another echo of the Great Game.[7]

A set of similar points could be made about the surprise nature of 9/11. To be sure, there was a host of reasons for the CIA's failure to provide an actionable warning of the attacks specific to their immediate time and place: a lack of communication between the Agency and the FBI in the run-up to September 2001 (the result in part of 1970s intelligence reforms designed to prevent further Agency encroachments on the domestic sphere); a round of post–Cold War budget and job cuts in the 1990s that deprived Langley of crucial area experience and expertise at just the moment al-Qaeda was starting to target the United States; and, arguably, the Agency's traditional preference for technological forms of intelligence collection—satellite imagery, for example—and scientific, Kentian methods of analysis, neither of which equipped it particularly well to meet the intelligence challenges posed by a group of terrorists who lived in caves and, in the case of Osama bin Laden, expressed their intentions in poetry.

But viewed through a wider historical lens, 9/11 also looks like a classic imperial intelligence failure. The agents of Western powers had long faced difficulties penetrating non-Western societies so that they could collect intelligence about them. The British in India, for example, were painfully aware that they were, as one scholar puts it, "extraordinarily visible, culturally ignorant, and linguistically maladroit." This was an important reason for the enduring Western fantasy—seen in Kipling, Lawrence, and others—of the white man who could pass as a "native" (a notion, by the way, that received an echo during the GWOT in the form of media celebration of the CIA team operating in Afghanistan in the immediate aftermath of 9/11, of which more in a moment).

Although factors peculiar to the specific context of the late 1990s and early 2000s obviously contributed to the 9/11 failure, it was above all issues of a kind that had always bedeviled imperial intelligence—the practical difficulties of conducting espionage in the colonial, or here postcolonial, world—that hamstrung the CIA in its attempts to penetrate al-Qaeda. At the time of the attacks, the Agency contained few Muslims or Arabic-speakers. No officers spoke Pashto, the main language of the Taliban. As mentioned earlier, most lived in suburban northern Virginia. These were not people likely to pass in an Afghan cave.[8]

Leaving behind the causes of the 9/11 attacks and the CIA's failure to avert them, the actual US conduct of the resulting GWOT also contained strong traces of the imperial past. The most apparent of these were discernible in Jawbreaker, the tiny CIA unit that bravely led the charge against the Taliban in the fall of 2001. Navigating the mountainous Afghan terrain on horseback alongside tribesmen from the Northern Alliance, Jawbreaker conjured up earlier battles in the Great Game that took place in precisely the same landscape and were subsequently fictionalized by Rudyard Kipling, or T. E. Lawrence's heroic rides across the Arabian desert with bands of Bedouin. Meanwhile, back in Washington, perhaps partly in reaction to the shock of the 9/11 attacks, the CIA men charged with planning the campaign against the Taliban exhibited the sort of masculine bravado that had also been displayed by earlier imperial adventurers. At one crucial planning meeting, J. Cofer Black, the gung-ho head of CIA counterterrorism, reportedly impressed George Bush by assuring him that the terrorists would soon have "flies walking across their eyeballs."[9]

The US-supported regime that replaced the Taliban, led by exiled tribal elder Hamid Karzai, was likewise a rather typical colonial affair. As historian Alfred McCoy pointed out, Karzai was in several respects a sort of Afghan version of an earlier American client leader in the Global South, Vietnam's Ngo Dinh Diem. Both men depended for their survival on backing from America and therefore lacked legitimacy in the eyes of many of those they were trying to govern; both proved surprisingly determined to pursue their own notions of what was best for their respective nations and came to suspect US conspiracies to overthrow them; and both eventually fell from power as their regimes crumbled in the face of provincial insurgencies. Stepping back further into the imperial past, another historical parallel suggests itself, this one between the Karzai government and that of the nineteenth-century Afghan king Shah Shuja Durrani. Installed on his throne by Britain in 1839, Shah Shuja was assassinated three years later when the British withdrew from Kabul (the retreat that turned into a ghastly rout). Writing in 2013, historian William Dalrymple noted the eerie resemblance of the US occupation of Afghanistan to the First Anglo-Afghan War: "The same tribal rivalries exist and the same battles are being fought in the same places under the guise of new flags, new ideologies, and new political puppeteers." Karzai was even descended from the leaders of the same tribe as Shah Shuja.[10]

The occupation that followed the United States' invasion of Iraq was similarly haunted by ghosts of the imperial past. With America's image tarnished by Abu Ghraib, and Iraqi attacks on US forces escalating into a full-blown insurgency, military strategists such as General David Petraeus cast around for counterinsurgency doctrine to guide the American response. They found it in old imperial texts such as *Small Wars*, an 1896 work by British major general Charles Callwell that originally bore the subtitle *A Tactical Textbook for Imperial Soldiers*. T. E. Lawrence, too, enjoyed a revival: the original, 1922 version of his *Seven Pillars* was reissued in 2005, and quotations from his writings furnished the titles of influential new works on counterinsurgency such as the 2006 paper "Twenty-Eight Articles" by Australian COIN theorist David Kilcullen, an obvious homage to Lawrence's 1917 pamphlet "Twenty-Seven Articles." Edward Lansdale's friend David Galula, who had adapted nineteenth-century French theories of colonial pacification for the Algerian War, became required reading at the US Army's Command and General Staff College. When in 2007 General Petraeus (later director of the CIA) led a "surge" of US occupation forces, he was explicitly operationalizing such doctrines. Like Hubert Lyautey in North Africa, Petraeus helped redeem the US cause by achieving a semblance of victory in Iraq, all while building up a personal legend in friendly domestic media as a heroic warrior-intellectual.[11]

It was not just US counterinsurgency tactics on the ground in the Middle East that evoked previous empires; so too did the American presence in the skies above the region. US media coverage of the CIA's drone campaign celebrated the technological prowess of the new military hardware. A headline of the day, "Attack of the Drones," played on a *Star Wars* movie title to convey the weapon's ultra-modern, even futuristic, character. It was left to a historian, Stanford's Priya Satia, to point out that, actually, a Western power using covert aerial warfare in the Middle East was not new. During the 1920s, Britain had deployed the Royal Air Force (RAF) over the just-invented state of Iraq and India's northwestern frontier with Afghanistan. For the British, airpower seemed the answer to the need to surveil and control its vast post–World War I mandate in the Middle East without having to occupy it militarily. RAF pilots could monitor the region's notoriously inhospitable landscape from on high and drop bombs on insurgents below—a fearsome prospect that, it was assumed, would also cow the wider population into obedience. Although US drones were far more precise in their targeting of terror suspects, their near-constant presence above the "AfPak" tribal areas, emitting a noise that inhabitants likened to the sound of a wasp, had a similarly intimidating effect. Moreover, American drone strikes were not as surgical as their boosters suggested. An undisclosed number caused "collateral damage," the official euphemism for the death of innocent bystanders. One attack in north Waziristan blew up dozens of tribal leaders meeting to resolve a dispute over local mining rights. Like the British years before, Americans now discovered that while undeclared air wars might kill some insurgents, they created others. US State Department officials blamed the drones for an upsurge in recruitment by the Pakistani Taliban.[12]

The CIA Rendition, Detention, and Interrogation Program (RDI), in which Gina Haspel participated, had an impact similar to CIA drone strikes. After details of it began to emerge in public, it too served unintentionally as a recruitment tool for Islamist terror groups. Military detention centers had much the same effect, reminiscent of the old imperial pattern of colonial prisons producing future anti-colonial leaders. When the Islamic State emerged as a successor to al-Qaeda in Iraq, conquering swaths of territory in 2014, the Baghdad government calculated that seventeen of its top twenty-five leaders had previously been detained by the US Army. For other imperial precedents, observers had to look no further than the "dirty" colonial wars of the post–World War II era. The French had resorted to torture in Algeria, as had the British in Malaya, Kenya, and Northern Ireland. One of the enhanced interrogation techniques employed by the CIA, waterboarding, was reminiscent of a practice from the more distant imperial past: the "water cure" that US troops had used against Filipino prisoners a hundred years earlier. The location of the most notorious of all the American detention camps, Guantánamo Bay or "Gitmo," in Cuba, dated back to the aftermath of the Spanish-American War—a relic of the United States' brief foray into New Imperialism. There was also a trans-imperial dimension to RDI: in 2018, UK parliamentary committees confirmed that British intelligence personnel had contributed to the program.[13]

Given all these continuities from the imperial past, it was perhaps little wonder that many Middle Easterners saw the GWOT as just the latest in a long series of colonial wars in the region—or that, as in similar moments in prior imperial history, the war should have boomeranged back to the US metropole.

In the mid-1970s, when journalists and congressional inquisitors revealed the CIA's excesses and abuses from the first decades of the Cold War, the Agency's founding generation faced a collective hour of reckoning. In the GWOT era, in contrast, Agency officers who participated in the RDI program and subsequent attempts to cover up their use of enhanced interrogation techniques experienced few if any consequences (although, as we will see, one was prosecuted for exposing EITs). Gina Haspel was even confirmed as director of the CIA.

The reason for this contrast in the fates of two different CIA generations lies in the domestic boomerang effects of the GWOT. The main one of these was a massive expansion of the US national security state. Determined to prevent further terrorist attacks on their watch, successive post-9/11 administrations plowed staggeringly huge sums of federal dollars into the sprawling intelligence-industrial complex. Some estimates of George Bush's total expenditure on the intelligence community pegged it at almost $500 billion. The spending continued, to the tune of $80 billion a year, under President Barack Obama who, in a revealing moment, clearly forgot the name of one of his government's many intelligence organizations, his voice trailing off as he tried to pronounce "National Geospatial-Intelligence Agency." Private contractors, too, profited from the bonanza, taking over a host of functions that would previously have been performed by the state, from electronic data analysis to providing base security for CIA stations overseas. The Agency itself, despite having lost its institutional primacy in the intelligence community to the Office of the Director of National Intelligence, saw its funding surge massively, especially under Obama, who prized its efficiency as, in the words of one national security reporter, a terrorist "killing machine." "The CIA gets what it wants," Obama told his nominee as director in 2009, former congressman and White House chief of staff Leon J. Panetta. Although felt across the United States, most of this growth took place in the nation's covert capital, among the malls and drive-thrus of suburban northern Virginia. Journalists commented on the surreal juxtaposition of CIA officers remotely ordering drone strikes on terrorists in AfPak, then stepping out of the office into the bright Virginia day.[14]

As earlier, it was impossible to hide all this covert apparatus entirely from the American public, but this did not stop the government from trying. In 2017 alone, the United States spent $18.4 billion on measures intended to preserve official secrecy. As Columbia historian Matthew Connelly puts it, if there was a Department of Secrets in America, its budget would be fifty times greater than that of the Department of the Treasury. Much of this expenditure was due to overclassification, the tendency of officials to designate even the most mundane document secret to avoid possibly embarrassing public scrutiny. Despite occasional presidential attempts to tackle the problem, overclassification had increased steadily throughout the Cold War, then skyrocketed in the GWOT. According to Matthew Connelly, there are now 28 million cubic feet of government files locked up in various repositories around the nation, the equivalent of twenty-six Washington Monuments—and this is to say nothing of the even greater volume of classified electronic data. No doubt a Cold War secrecy maven such as James Angleton would have been gladdened by the existence of this vast edifice—except that it has not proved very good at protecting secrets. The combination of excessive classification and new electronic technologies created the conditions for massive unauthorized data dumps such as those waged by WikiLeaks since its 2006 founding by Australian computer programmer Julian Assange. At the same time, the enforced ignorance of the American public bred the suspicion that the government was shielding even more sinister secrets than it actually was.[15]

But the most insidious domestic consequence of the national security state's GWOT-era expansion was in the realm of surveillance. In October 2001, as part of his administration's revival of secret executive powers canceled during the 1970s, George Bush effectively resurrected the practice of warrantless domestic wiretapping by signing into law the USA PATRIOT Act. As revealed by computer intelligence expert and whistleblower Edward Snowden in 2013, the main government entity to take advantage of the expanded surveillance powers permitted under the new regime was the National Security Agency. But the CIA was involved as well, empowered as it was by Congress in 2002 to access US financial records and eavesdrop on electronic communications routed through American territory. In a move reminiscent of the Angleton era, the Agency also cooperated with local law enforcement agencies such as the New York Police Department in the surveillance of Muslim citizens, until an inspector general's inquiry ended the arrangement in 2012. Some such steps were necessary, of course, to ward off further possible terror attacks, but the GWOT's combination of societal intelligence coverage with the selection of a particular group for more aggressive measures smacked of a foreign counterinsurgency campaign, only without the insurgency.[16]

In a further boomerang effect, biometric identification techniques such as fingerprinting and iris scans that had first been employed by occupation forces in Iraq and Afghanistan looped back to the United States for use by homeland security agencies. The new electronic surveillance regime was in part the product of a trans-imperial collaboration, with the UK equivalent of the National Security Agency, the Government Communications Headquarters (GCHQ), tapping fiber-optic cables that passed through Britain and sharing the intelligence it gleaned with the United States. (The fact that so much of the cabling that carried international telecommunications crossed the territory of the Anglosphere powers that made up the Five Eyes intelligence alliance—the United States, United Kingdom, Canada, Australia, and New Zealand—gave them a huge advantage in the transformed information environment of the twenty-first century.) As recently as 2022, two Democrats on the Senate Intelligence Committee called for the release of details of a still-classified CIA program involving the bulk collection of data from warrantless electronic surveillance.[17]

If surveillance was largely invisible to the US public, the same could hardly be said of the GWOT's impact on American urban policing. Under Program 1033, the Department of Defense transferred tons of surplus military equipment—ranging from body armor to armored personnel carriers—to state and local agencies. The most conspicuous use of this military-grade matériel came in response to racial unrest such as the 2014 disturbances in Ferguson, Missouri, when SWAT teams resembling military units in a foreign war fired rubber bullets and canisters of CS gas at predominantly Black crowds protesting the recent police shooting of Michael Brown. However, the diffusion of Defense Department inventory was not limited to such locales. Thanks to Program 1033, police in Keene, New Hampshire, a city with a population of 23,000, were able to purchase a BearCat, an eight-ton armored personnel carrier. Again, the CIA was not the main player in these developments, but commentators noted the echoes of the 1960s and the domestic boomeranging of Office of Public Safety foreign operations, as well as the earlier repatriation of counterinsurgent techniques invented during the occupation of the Philippines.[18]

Although less glaring, the two GWOT programs in which the CIA did take the lead role—Rendition, Detention, and Interrogation and targeted killings—also had their domestic dimensions. Richard Zuley, a Chicago homicide detective and Navy reservist assigned to the Guantánamo Bay detention camp, appears to have employed similarly brutal interrogation techniques on both US suspects and foreign detainees. Other military interrogators who used EITs at sites such as Abu Ghraib displayed symptoms of post-traumatic stress disorder after their return home, including drug dependency, panic attacks, and domestic violence. But the most significant home-front reverberation of the CIA's RDI program was the involvement in it of the same profession that had earlier conducted Agency-funded "mind-control" experiments: psychologists. It was two retired US Air Force psychologists working under CIA contract, James Mitchell and Bruce Jessen, who invented EITs, reverse-engineering a Korean War–era Air Force training program, SERE, designed to help captured US pilots withstand communist "brainwashing." Mitchell and Jessen personally used the techniques for the first time on detainees being held at the black site in Thailand commanded by Gina Haspel. Far from condemning the involvement of psychologists in such practices, the American Psychological Association revised its ethics rules in 2002 to permit their continuation, a decision affirmed by an APA-organized task force in 2005. It was not until 2015 that the APA renounced EITs and apologized for its earlier actions, following another internal inquiry and an investigation by reporter James Risen.[19]

Drone operations leading to targeted killings had a variety of boomerang effects. A few US citizens died in overseas strikes, among them Anwar Nasser al-Awlaki, a firebrand Islamist cleric born in New Mexico who had gone on to become a senior al-Qaeda operative linked to attacks on US targets, and his sixteen-year-old, Denver-born son Abdulrahman, both blown up in Yemen in 2011 in separate incidents. (Although Anwar al-Awlaki was arguably more deserving of this fate than Abdulrahman, whom all sources identify as an innocent bystander, civil liberties advocates pointed out that both killings were in effect extrajudicial executions that deprived the targets of the constitutional right of due process.) Meanwhile, domestic law enforcement agencies began operating surveillance drones in the skies above the United States, at first along the nation's southern border with Mexico, then in states such as North Dakota, where in 2015 legislators permitted their weaponization with tear gas, rubber bullets, and tasers. Some sources reported a growing incidence of PTSD among overseas drone operators based in the United States similar to that detected among interrogators who had employed EITs. Two immigrants from the AfPak region—the Afghan American Najibullah Zazi and the Pakistan-born Faisal Shahzad—plotted terror attacks against targets in New York City because, so they claimed later, of drone strikes on their countries of origin.[20]

Why, then, did none of this provoke the sort of anti-CIA backlash that had occurred in the 1970s? An obvious reason was the mood of the US public in the wake of the atrocious 9/11 attacks: a mixture of grief, panic, and desire for revenge. The CIA itself, despite its reputation for scientific objectivity, experienced the same emotions. Henry Crumpton, then a deputy in the Agency's Counterterrorist Center, later recalled working during the fall of 2001 "in a barely bounded rage," consumed as he was by "a burning need for retribution rooted in a sense of shameful violation." If anything, such feelings intensified as the war on al-Qaeda and the hunt for Osama bin Laden wore on, fueled in 2009 by a jihadi attack on a US base in Afghanistan that killed six CIA officers, among them a twenty-year Agency veteran and mother of three, Jennifer L. Matthews. When, eventually, in 2010, CIA analysts located bin Laden's whereabouts in the Pakistani city of Abbottabad, and the following year Navy SEALs killed him in an operation formally run by the Agency, the mood at Langley changed to one of jubilation. The US public joined in the rejoicing, as crowds outside the White House chanted "CIA! CIA!" With the well-liked and politically savvy Leon Panetta still director, and opinion polls suggesting widespread approval of both its analytical and operational performance, the Agency had restored its position as *primus inter pares* in the US intelligence community.[21]

But this redemption was not an entirely spontaneous process. It was also the outcome of a publicity campaign like the one carried out by David Atlee Phillips after 1975, the Year of Intelligence, only on a much bigger scale. In this instance, the role played earlier by Phillips was performed by Jose A. Rodriguez Jr., a grizzled former chief of the CIA's Counterterrorist Center (and mentor of Gina Haspel) who had retired in 2008. Taking advantage of the celebration surrounding bin Laden's death, Rodriguez set out to rehabilitate the reputation of the Agency's enhanced interrogation regime, calling it "the most effective and carefully managed program I was involved with in my thirty-one years at the CIA." In particular, he claimed that EITs were crucial in the tracking down of Osama bin Laden, telling *Time* magazine that they produced "lead information" about an al-Qaeda courier that guided the Agency to the terrorist's lair in Abbottabad. Some disputed this assertion, arguing that torture never yields good intelligence, and that it was other sources—for example, an alert Pakistani agent following the courier—that enabled bin Laden's detection. Rodriguez's claims, though, won widespread credence, repeated as they were by intelligence leaders, reporters, and, most influentially, the 2012 movie *Zero Dark Thirty*.[22]

Hollywood's participation in the EIT influence campaign should not come as a surprise. The CIA had occasionally collaborated with the motion picture industry on specific productions during the Cold War—*The Quiet American*, for example. During the 1990s, it had taken the relationship a step further, appointing Chase Brandon, a veteran of the clandestine service with preexisting links to the movie world (he was a cousin of actor Tommy Lee Jones), to the role of entertainment liaison officer. Hollywood was keen to avail itself of the expertise and locations the CIA had to offer, and Brandon was invited to consult on numerous TV and movie productions, ensuring the insertion of positive material about the Agency in some and the removal of negative depictions from others. He also hosted actors such as Patrick Stewart and Ben Affleck on tours of Langley, the latter as he prepared for the role of intelligence officer Jack Ryan in a 2002 adaptation of the Tom Clancy novel *The Sum of All Fears*. Affleck's well-received 2012 movie about a CIA operation to rescue US embassy workers after the 1979 Iranian Revolution, *Argo*, was in part a product of this earlier groundwork. ("We will do the agency proud, I promise you," Affleck had assured an

Agency official.) Meanwhile, several TV shows made in the decade after 9/11 depicted scenes of US agents torturing terrorist captives and, in the process, acquiring vital intelligence. A repeated story line in Fox's hugely popular *24*—its hero, Jack Bauer, using torture to learn the location of a ticking time bomb—became a real-world justification for enhanced interrogation, invoked repeatedly in election campaigns, legal arguments, and confirmation hearings. Here was another example, if any were needed, of spy fiction's power to shape reality.[23]

Zero Dark Thirty made an argument similar to *24*'s, but in more sophisticated form. Directed by Kathryn Bigelow and written by Mark Boal, the same team behind the Oscar-winning 2008 *The Hurt Locker*, the 2012 movie presented itself as a reportorial account of the CIA's manhunt for Osama bin Laden, beginning with scenes of enhanced interrogation, including waterboarding, and concluding with the 2011 SEAL raid in Pakistan. Its hero, an Agency officer played by Jessica Chastain, is at first distressed by the brutality of the EITs she witnesses but comes to accept their necessity as the information they revealed about bin Laden's courier is shown to be the key to his discovery—essentially, the same claim made by Jose Rodriguez. As columnist Frank Bruni summed up the movie's narrative in the *New York Times*, "No waterboarding, no Bin Laden."[24]

Zero Dark Thirty was an immediate commercial and critical success, generating Oscar buzz like *The Hurt Locker*. Shortly after its release, however, details about its production emerged that discomfited some audience members. Declassified emails revealed that Bigelow and Boal had met numerous times with CIA officials involved in the hunt for bin Laden, including the counterterrorist officer Alfreda F. Bikowsky, on whom the Chastain character was reportedly based. (The choice of a female lead was significant, not least as the movie also prominently featured another woman character clearly based on Jennifer Matthews, the CIA officer killed in the 2009 attack in Afghanistan; positive publicity concerning the CIA during the GWOT often emphasized the contributions and sacrifice of women officers, in a sort of fictional rehearsal for Gina Haspel's 2018 nomination as director.) To show their gratitude for this extraordinary access, the moviemakers had showered their intelligence contacts with intimate gifts and restaurant meals. Critics wondered if they had gone too far. Bigelow and Boal were suffering from "access drift," one claimed; another accused them of "embedded filmmaking." Politicians echoed these concerns. Dianne Feinstein, who as leader of the Senate investigation of the RDI program had already concluded that EITs did not work, reportedly walked out of a special showing of the movie after just fifteen minutes.[25]

The pushback against *Zero Dark Thirty* shows that, even in the wake of the bin Laden takedown, criticism of the CIA had not died out entirely. Indeed, some of the voices raised against the Agency during the GWOT were reminiscent of the anti-imperial movement of earlier decades. There was, for example, a CIA whistleblower, John Kiriakou, not as outspoken as his predecessor Philip Agee, nor as famous as his contemporary Edward Snowden, but important nonetheless as a former Agency insider moved to denounce enhanced interrogation. The CIA's retaliatory response also harked back to the 1970s. In 2013, Kiriakou was convicted under the 1982 Intelligence Identities Protection Act and sentenced to thirty months in prison, making him the only Agency officer to serve time in connection with the RDI program. As earlier, a CIA publicity offensive went hand in hand with a push for greater secrecy. Complaints about the heavy-handedness of the Publications Review Board from retired intelligence officers trying to publish their memoirs grew so numerous as to become a small literary genre of their own.[26]

Increasingly, however, it was another narrative genre, less authoritative but more popular than whistleblower testimony, that became the dominant mode of criticism of the CIA. Conspiracy theory flourished in post-9/11 America. Some narratives concerned familiar themes such as the Kennedy assassination, driven by supposed new revelations in government documents released in the wake of Oliver Stone's *JFK* and a reported deathbed confession by Howard Hunt that implicated Cord Meyer. A best-selling 2016 book by veteran leftist David Talbot placed Allen Dulles at the center of a corporate and government plot to kill not only John Kennedy but his brother Bobby as well.[27]

But some GWOT-era CIA conspiracy theories were new: the US government either had advance knowledge of the 9/11 attacks and still let them happen or carried them out itself, with the CIA responsible for the controlled demolition of the World Trade Center; the killing of Osama bin Laden was staged, the terrorist's actual death years earlier having been concealed to prolong the GWOT; above all, the CIA was part of the "deep state," a cabal of unelected officials seeking to undermine and possibly overthrow the people's elected representatives, including the US president himself, Donald Trump.[28]

The concept of the "deep state," borrowed from scholarship about the role of Turkey's military in Turkish political life, was basically a retooling of the "silent coup" thesis propagated by associates of Richard Nixon in the wake of Watergate, and now taken up by supporters of Donald Trump in retaliation against the CIA and FBI for their part in uncovering evidence of Soviet interference in the 2016 presidential election. But the concept's extraordinary popularity—according to the findings of a 2018 Monmouth University poll, 74 percent of Americans believed that "a group of unelected government and military officials" was "manipulating or directing" national politics—transcended its immediate political context. Essentially, the deep state theory was merely the latest expression of a long-standing and deep-seated tendency in modern American political culture: a rational fear of the threat to American liberty posed by a greatly expanded national security establishment mixed with a touch of paranoia, the latter a product of both a national cultural predisposition—Hofstadter's "paranoid style"—and more recent exposure to imperial conspiracism.[29]

The irony was that, against the backdrop of the Trump presidency, the rise of a conservative, populist conspiracy theory about the CIA actually aided the Agency's cause in the eyes of liberals who had previously been critical of it. John Brennan, for example, the outgoing director of the CIA, became something of a darling of the liberal news media thanks to his readiness to defend the Agency against Donald Trump's attacks. Here, then, was another reason for the apparent impunity of officers involved in the RDI program such as Gina Haspel: the reemergence of the Agency's early Cold War public image as the "good CIA."[30]

Gina Haspel stepped down as director of the CIA in January 2021, just before a new Democratic administration that included as vice president one of her most insistent inquisitors during her confirmation hearings, Kamala Harris, entered office. Her spell as DCIA had been predictably challenging. She had worked hard to avoid antagonizing President Trump, rarely leaving Langley and never giving interviews. Indeed, her profile was so low that some intelligence community colleagues feared she was failing to tell Trump news he did not want to hear and to defend the CIA against his attacks. Still, not even this performance was enough to placate the thin-skinned president, who was rumored to have considered firing her on numerous occasions. By November 2020, with

Trump refusing to accept the results of a presidential election and dismissing other officials on an almost daily basis, Haspel had had enough. "We are on the way to a right-wing coup," she told the chair of the Joint Chiefs of Staff. "He is acting out like a six-year-old with a tantrum." It is easy to imagine her breathing a sigh of relief as she left the director's office and, following a path trodden by several other retired US intelligence leaders, accepted a lucrative position with a law firm advising clients on national security matters.[31]

Gina Haspel could look back over a meritorious career of national service that included major contributions to diversifying the leadership of the CIA (in addition to her own achievement in becoming director, she appointed women to several deputy roles during her tenure). However, it seems likely that, outside Washington intelligence circles, she will be remembered principally for two other aspects of her career: her ordeal serving as an intelligence community leader under Donald Trump, and her earlier involvement in the Agency's GWOT interrogation program. In June 2022, the *New York Times* reported that, during hearings before a military tribunal in Guantánamo Bay, the EIT psychologist James Mitchell testified that Haspel had personally observed the torture of a Saudi prisoner, including his waterboarding.[32]

As the example of Kermit Roosevelt and others shows, Haspel was not the first CIA officer to see her personal reputation tarnished by the Agency's past; nor, sadly, is she likely to be the last. The current indications are that, with the GWOT still not entirely over, the United States is entering a new Cold War, with the CIA again on the front line.

CONCLUSION

During her Senate confirmation hearings, Gina Haspel reflected on the reasons she had become an intelligence officer in the first place. The main one, she reckoned, was the call to national service she had felt ever since her Air Force brat upbringing, when she had followed her father on postings all over the globe. On joining the CIA, she quickly realized she also had a particular knack for espionage tradecraft, for "brush passes, dead drops, [and] meetings in dusty back alleys of third world capitals," as she put it. "It was the beginning of an adventure I had only dreamed of," she recalled fondly.[1]

Haspel's remarks about her choice of career could equally well have applied to the founding cohort of CIA officers described in this book—they too were answering calls to both service and adventure—except in their case there was an additional motive: a strong sense of international idealism inherited from earlier generations of Americans who had lived overseas, Protestant missionaries in particular. Before joining the Agency, Middle East expert Kermit "Kim" Roosevelt wrote and lectured about the need for a US alliance with the young nationalist leaders of the decolonizing Arab world. Edward Lansdale, the United States' most influential secret agent in

Southeast Asia, deplored the imperial legacy of European interventions in the region, calling for a US-Asian relationship based instead on fraternal love. Cord Meyer lacked Lansdale's sunny optimism but devoted several years of his pre-CIA career to campaigning vigorously for the utopian cause of world federalism.

In each of these cases, however, the men concerned were unable to translate their ideals into action. In fact, the opposite happened. Kim Roosevelt found himself carrying out covert operations to preserve pro-Western monarchies in the Middle East. Ed Lansdale ended up working (unsuccessfully) to stabilize a repressive US client regime in Vietnam and reverse a nationalist revolution in Cuba. Cord Meyer became a prominent figure in the demonology of the anti-imperial left, not just in the United States but, ironically enough, in the old imperial center of London as well.

A similar dynamic occurred in the realm of intelligence analysis. The discipline's most important American theorist, Sherman Kent, rejected European powers' emphasis on cultural understanding and intuition in favor of scientific values but was unable to turn his vision of a predictive science into practice. Among the "legendary" CIA founding fathers described here, only the counterintelligence chief James Angleton appears to have sought consciously to continue the legacy of European imperial intelligence, and he eventually descended into incapacitating paranoia.

The reason for the inability of these CIA legends to transcend the imperial past lay partly in historical forces beyond their control. Despite its own origins in an anti-colonial insurgency, the United States assumed an imperial role in the world after World War II, competing with the Soviet Union and communist China for primacy in those regions where European colonialism was receding. Several factors obliged US officials to hide this fact—the anti-colonial logic of decolonization, the potentially cataclysmic consequences of an overt superpower confrontation, and the persistence of anti-imperialism within the United States itself—meaning that, thanks to its covert powers, the CIA became, somewhat against its own will, the vanguard of American interventionism in the postcolonial world. Hence individual Agency officers constantly found themselves, regardless of their personal beliefs, using colonial-era scripts to perform the intelligence-gathering and covert action missions with which they were charged.

While the role of imperial agent conflicted with these individuals' anti-colonialism, in other ways it came all too easily. The likes of Kim Roosevelt, Cord Meyer, and James Angleton had grown up within quasi-imperial institutions consuming fictions of imperial romance, including stories about secret imperial agents. Their upbringing and education had prepared them to act the part. Edward Lansdale was not of the "imperial brotherhood," but even he delighted in the opportunities for frontier adventure, masculine intimacy, and sexual license afforded by the global Cold War.

In other words, the imperialism came not only from without, from the grand, impersonal forces of history, but from human, intimate places within.

At the beginning of this book, I announced my intention of comparing, contrasting, and connecting the history of the CIA with that of the imperial European intelligence services. What has this three-legged approach revealed?

Viewed from a comparative perspective, US and European imperial intelligence—British especially but French as well—appear fundamentally similar, despite exceptionalist American claims to the contrary. Both engaged in covert struggles for influence with Russian/Soviet power in the colonial, then postcolonial, world (the Great Game), while at the same time trying to contain and curb local anti-colonial, nationalist movements. Both struggled to collect reliable intelligence on non-Western societies and were therefore prone to intelligence failures. Both employed population-centric counterinsurgency to defend friendly regimes against nationalist uprisings and Russian meddling while working to overthrow undesirable governments by a variety of means, including covertly instigated coups. Finally, in keeping with the concept of the imperial boomerang, both left deep imprints on their host societies, some intentional (domestic surveillance and influence operations) and others unintentional (boomeranging population flows and conspiracism).

To be sure, there were also some contrasts between US and European spy services. American intelligence officers placed a greater premium on science and technology than their European counterparts, while the peculiar circumstances of the United States' post–World War II moment in the imperial sun—decolonization and superpower nuclear rivalry—necessitated a greater American reliance on covert as opposed to overt action. This was why the CIA-engineered coup became the signature US Cold War foreign intervention, in contrast with Lord Palmerston's overtly menacing gunboats. At the same time, the greater democratic accountability of US intelligence and relative strength of American anti-imperialism made the CIA more vulnerable to domestic media and parliamentary scrutiny than its European counterparts. This helps explain the Agency's characteristic combination of hypersecrecy on the one hand and preoccupation with its public image on the other. In sum, if the CIA was not exceptional, it was at least distinctive.

Still, for all these contrasts, it is the similarities—and the connections—that are most striking. CIA officers trying to gather intelligence in the Global South were unable to break away from the legacy of previous Western spies; they inherited agents, attitudes, and even housing from them. It did not help that, despite decolonization, the European imperial powers were working hard to maintain de facto control of their former colonies, often via their intelligence services. This meant US intelligence officers, whatever their personal scruples, had to undertake joint operations with European colleagues—the British in Iran, for example, and the French in Vietnam. Meanwhile, Americans trying to defeat nationalist and communist insurgencies in the developing world inevitably turned for guidance to imperial experts, living as well as dead. Counterinsurgency theorists David Galula and Robert Thompson connected the colonial and postcolonial eras as they traveled between "small wars" in Africa and Asia advising both European and US forces. This is to say nothing of the formal and informal intelligence collaborations of the era: the 1946 UKUSA agreement, for example, which later expanded into the Five Eyes alliance, and James Angleton's meetings of counterintelligence officials from the same English-speaking nations, CAZAB.

In summary, the CIA possessed several distinctive traits reflecting its national heritage and the specific international setting in which it came into existence—but it had even more in common with the European intelligence agencies of the previous imperial age.

At the time of writing, the United States appears to be winding down the Global War on Terror. In August 2021, it withdrew from Afghanistan in chaotic circumstances reminiscent of the 1975 American evacuation of Saigon or, further back in time but more analogous geographically, of the British retreat from Kabul in 1842. Meanwhile, there are signs at home of an emerging consensus around the principle of restraint in foreign affairs, with "America First" conservatives joining anti-imperial progressives in an across-the-spectrum backlash against American globalism.

But the consensus is fragile at best. The military, industrial, and intelligence interests that benefited from the GWOT and, before it, the Cold War have not gone away, and the Washington foreign policy "blob" remains deeply invested in the United States maintaining its global footing. Attention is now shifting from the asymmetrical threats posed by "rogue states" and stateless terrorists to a revival of peer or "near-peer" competition. In a move correctly predicted by the CIA, the revanchist Russian president Vladimir Putin, having apparently forgotten the lessons of the earlier Soviet misadventure in Afghanistan, launched a bloody invasion of Ukraine in February 2022. Tension with China, arguably a more serious challenger to US global primacy than Russia has ever been, is mounting in a manner reminiscent of the early Cold War. Non-aligned nations in the Global South, stronger economically and more assertive politically than during the era of decolonization, are watching the maneuvering of the great powers with the same combination of anxiety, skepticism, and opportunism as before.

For those contemplating the use of the CIA as an instrument of covert action in this new international environment—say, in the Southeast Asian nations surrounding China—the history of the Agency presented here suggests a few lessons. First, covert regime-change operations fail more often than they succeed and, even when successful, have unforeseen consequences. To cite the most obvious example: the

1953 restoration of Iran's shah created widespread anti-American feeling in that country that surged in the 1979 revolution and has bedeviled US-Iranian relations ever since. This is to say nothing of the civil wars, economic turmoil, and democratic backsliding that enveloped other nations in the Global South where US-backed regime change took place during the Cold War and GWOT. Similarly, covert efforts to reinforce or coup-proof client states often have the opposite of their intended effect, undermining the legitimacy of the governments in question and necessitating a resort to ever more repressive forms of counterinsurgency, a pattern seen most conspicuously in Ngo Dinh Diem's South Vietnam. Where US observers perceive regime change and counterinsurgency as "democracy promotion" and "nation-building," those at the receiving end in the Global South see them instead as acts of Western imperialism. (There is also evidence to suggest that American covert action has a similar effect on the nation's near-peer rivals, thereby contributing to the current downward spiral of great power relations. Among Vladimir Putin's justifications for the Russian invasion of Ukraine is his claim that the United States had carried out a "coup" in Kyiv via the CIA-descended National Endowment for Democracy, which had spent $14 million on Ukrainian democracy projects in the lead-up to the ousting of President Viktor Yanukovych in 2014.)[2]

Second, the consequences of covert overseas interventions do not necessarily stay overseas. In the US case, some of the boomerang effects are obvious: retaliatory acts of terror that, while different in their points of origin and scale, invite comparison with earlier terrorist attacks upon other imperial metropoles. (In this connection, it is worth mentioning that some commentators have interpreted Russian cyber meddling in the 2016 US presidential election as in part blowback from previous US election-influence operations overseas, including intrusions in Ukraine.) Other impacts are more subtle—for example, the domestication of neocolonial surveillance and counterinsurgency tactics, and the rise of a vast, secretive intelligence-industrial complex. It is a bitter irony that, all too often, one US generation's sincere effort to protect national security has ended up threatening the rights and freedoms of the next. The anti-imperialists were right: imperial adventures abroad imperil liberty at home.[3]

This is not to deny the legitimacy and value of the CIA's other main function, indeed, its founding purpose: the analysis of foreign intelligence. This mission was already a difficult one, with its own practical and perceptual pitfalls, some self-inflicted, such as the rather simplistic scientism that has affected the Agency's analytical approach since the days of Sherman Kent. By distracting attention and draining resources from intelligence, the cult of covert action that sprang up around the CIA during the early years of the Cold War only made it all the more challenging. A similar effect occurred during the GWOT, as successive administrations charged the Agency with a basically military task, the pursuit and killing of terrorists. The convergence of two events in 2011 symbolized the militarization of the CIA and its adverse impact on the Agency's intelligence mission: the appointment of General David Petraeus as director coinciding with the spread of the Arab Spring protests in the Middle East—a development CIA analysts had failed to predict. In short, it is high time that the Agency reprioritized its original mission as an intelligence agency. Then, perhaps, it can properly reckon with security threats facing not just the United States but the whole world today: global inequality, population movements, pandemics, and climate change.

How likely these lessons are to be heeded by the nation's foreign policy establishment is far from obvious. On the one hand, there are welcome indications that the CIA is pivoting away from counterterrorism, with the creation in 2021 of two new Agency mission centers, one devoted to China and the other to emerging technologies, the climate, and global health. At the same time, however, there are equally clear signs that, despite all the recent pressures for greater restraint, Washington remains basically wedded to the globalist vision of US power in the world that has guided its foreign policy since the end of World War II, including its frequent resort to the covert action capabilities of the CIA. The rise of talk across the American political spectrum about a possible war with China in the South China Sea is perhaps the clearest of these signs. China might represent a formidable challenge to US national security in the realm of espionage (the proper business of the CIA) but this does not mean that the United States should risk a third world war over the future of Taiwan.[4]

As long as America continues to behave like an empire while denying it is one, it will carry on reaching for covert action as an instrument of its foreign relations, with the same baleful foreign and domestic consequences as during the Cold War and War on Terror.

Put another way, the imperial history of the CIA is likely not over yet.

ACKNOWLEDGMENTS

Writing a book is essentially a solitary experience, especially during a pandemic. In this case, however, so many people contributed in one way or another that at times it felt more like a group project. Early conversations with Emily Rosenberg, Salim Yaqub, and Inderjeet Parmar helped bring the subject matter into focus. As I researched, others kindly provided information, insight, or both: Richard Aldrich, Sarah-Jane Corke, Rory Cormac, Chris Endy, Merve Fejzula, Molly Geidel, Simon Hall, Patrick Iber, Ali İğmen, Andy Jenks, Stephen Kinzer, Sean Malloy, Kaeten Mistry, Christopher Moran, Timothy Naftali, Jonathan Nashel, Amy Offner, Kathryn Olmsted, Kenneth Osgood, Susan Perlman, Tony Shaw, Carlos Nunes Silva, Mark Stout, William Tyrer, and Myriam Yakoubi. Several colleagues performed the ultimate scholarly favor: they read either portions or the whole of the manuscript. My heartfelt thanks go to Rhodri Jeffreys-Jones (who had already done this for me several times before), Eileen Luhr, Chris Moran, Kathy Olmsted, and Jay Sexton. Simon Willmetts was a source of intellectual stimulation throughout the project and a superbly close reading of the manuscript at its end. With their lively and sometimes amused interest, students in my senior and graduate seminars at California State University, Long Beach, helped me conceive and test new approaches and arguments. Also at CSULB, my department chair, David Shafer, was hugely accommodating and enabling; President Jane Close Conoley went out of her way to support my research personally; and staff throughout the university offered unfailingly cheerful and efficient assistance, particularly Susan Tsuji, Terie Bostic, and Nazareth Lijiam. I am also grateful to the university for the fall 2022 sabbatical during which much of the book was written and the assigned time and travel awards I have received from the College of Liberal Arts. Two other institutions funded my research along the way: the Gilder Lehrman Institute of American History, with a grant that allowed me to visit archives on the East Coast, and the National Endowment for the Humanities, with a fellowship that, while awarded for another project, gave me some much-needed time to think through issues of empire and intimacy. I am forever in the debt of some outstandingly collegial scholars who wrote letters to accompany these and other grant applications: Susan Carruthers, Ken Osgood, Inderjeet Parmar, and Emily Rosenberg. Staff at archives in the United States and London helped me locate documents and images, while the tireless librarians of CSULB processed a veritable mountain of interlibrary loan book and article requests. Dear family friends in Long Beach provided vital childcare, comradeship, and hospitality, especially Amy, Neal, Lewis, and Jackson; and Akiko, Henry, and Nathaniel. Steve and Anne put me up during research trips to London and New York, as did my sister-in-law Carol and her lovely family in Palo Alto. Other Wilford and Cleary siblings and their families also aided in innumerable ways, sometimes without knowing it. In the United Kingdom, Sally Holloway of Felicity Bryan Associates graciously took over my representation after the terribly sad passing of Felicity herself. Like so many other authors, I count myself deeply fortunate merely to have known Felicity, a truly delightful person as well as a professional legend. In the United States, George Lucas of Inkwell Management helped me lick the book proposal into shape with his usual mix of meticulousness and good humor. At Basic Books, Lara Heimert and Brandon Proia, ably assisted by Roger Labrie, Kristen Kim, Melissa Veronesi, and Sue Warga, have done a fantastic job shepherding the book to publication (thank you so much, Lara, for your continuing confidence in my work). The main reason, though, that this book exists in any form is the extraordinary patience, competence, and kindness of my wife, colleague, and collaborator, Patricia Cleary; in her, I am truly blessed. And, as for our son Jonathan, I wish to record my deepest gratitude for his putting up with my work during the last five years when, like any sensible person, I should have been playing two-square and working on RCs.

NOTES

Introduction

1. For two particularly stimulating accounts of European imperial intelligence, see Martin Thomas, *Empires of Intelligence: Security Services and Colonial Disorder After 1914* (Berkeley: University of California Press, 2008), and Priya Satia, *Spies in Arabia: The Great War and the Cultural Foundations of Britain's Covert Empire in the Middle East* (Oxford: Oxford University Press, 2008).

2. The now-classic account of the Cold War as essentially an imperial contest in the Global South is Odd Arne Westad, *The Global Cold War: Third World Interventions and the Making of Our Times* (Cambridge: Cambridge University Press, 2005).

3. Daniel Immerwahr, *How to Hide an Empire: A History of the Greater United States* (New York: Farrar, Straus and Giroux, 2019). As the endnotes that follow make clear, this book is indebted to the efforts of numerous scholars working to expand the boundaries of both the history of American foreign relations and intelligence history. For important surveys of scholarship in these fields, see, respectively, Paul A. Kramer, "Power and Connection: Imperial Histories of the United States in the World," *American Historical Review* 116, no. 5 (2011): 1348–1391; Simon Willmetts, "The Cultural Turn in Intelligence Studies," *Intelligence and National Security* 34, no. 6 (2019): 800–817.

4. For recent works centering the Global South's experience of Cold War–era US interventionism, see Vijay Prashad, *Washington Bullets: A History of the CIA, Coups, and Assassinations* (New York: Monthly Review Press, 2020); Vincent Bevins, *The Jakarta Method: Washington's Anticommunist Crusade and the Mass Murder Program That Shaped Our World* (New York: PublicAffairs, 2020); and Paul Thomas Chamberlin, *The Cold War's Killing Fields: Rethinking the Long Peace* (New York: HarperCollins, 2018).

Prologue

1. See Katharine Bjork, *Prairie Imperialists: The Indian Country Origins of American Empire* (Philadelphia: University of Pennsylvania Press, 2019).

2. Quoted in David Gilmour, *The Long Recessional: The Imperial Life of Rudyard Kipling* (New York: Farrar, Straus and Giroux, 2002), 28; ibid., 123.

3. See C. A. Bayly, *Empire and Information: Intelligence Gathering and Social Communication in India, 1780–1870* (Cambridge: Cambridge University Press, 1996). For a recent history of the Raj emphasizing British anxiety, see Jon Wilson, *India Conquered: Britain's Raj and the Chaos of Empire* (London: Simon & Schuster, 2016).

4. See Peter Hopkirk, *The Great Game: On Secret Service in High Asia* (London: John Murray, 1990).

5. Rudyard Kipling, *Kim: Authoritative Text, Backgrounds, Criticism*, ed. Zohreh T. Sullivan (New York: W. W. Norton, 2002), 101. See A. Michael Matin, "*Kim*, Invasion-Scare Literature, and the Russian Threat to British India," in ibid., 358–374.

6. See Christopher Moran and Robert Johnson, "In the Service of Empire: Imperialism and the British Spy Thriller, 1901–1914," *Studies in Intelligence* 54, no. 2 (2010): 1–22.

7. See Christopher Benfey, *If: The Untold Story of Kipling's American Years* (New York: Penguin, 2019).

8. Gilmour, *Long Recessional*, 128.

9. Christian Gury, *Lyautey-Charlus* (Paris: Klimé, 1998). See also Barnett Singer, "Lyautey: An Interpretation of the Man and French Imperialism," *Journal of Contemporary History* 26, no. 1 (1991): 131–157.

10. Quoted in Berny Sèbe, *Heroic Imperialists in Africa: The Promotion of British and French Colonial Heroes, 1870–1939* (Manchester: Manchester University Press, 2013), 165; Edward Berenson, *Heroes of Empire: Five Charismatic Men and the Conquest of Africa* (Berkeley: University of California Press, 2011), 237. See also Michael P. M. Finch, *A Progressive Occupation? The Gallieni-Lyautey Method and Colonial Pacification in Tonkin and Madagascar, 1885–1900* (Oxford: Oxford University Press, 2013).

11. Berenson, *Heroes of Empire*, 236.

12. Quoted in ibid., 230; Daniel Rivet, quoted in ibid., 261.

13. Quoted in Edward Berenson, "Making a Colonial Culture? Empire and the French Public, 1880–1940," *French Politics, Culture, and Society* 22, no. 2 (2004): 146; quoted in Berenson, *Heroes of Empire*, 268.

14. There are literally hundreds of books about Lawrence. The most authoritative biography remains Jeremy Wilson, *Lawrence of Arabia: The Authorized Biography of T. E. Lawrence* (New York: Atheneum, 1990).

15. See, for example, Christopher Andrew, *The Secret World: A History of Intelligence* (New Haven, CT: Yale University Press, 2018), 508. Recent works based on new archaeological evidence have supported Lawrence's claims about his wartime actions. See, for example, Neil Faulkner, *Lawrence of Arabia's War: The Arabs, the British, and the Remaking of the Middle East in World War I* (New Haven, CT: Yale University Press, 2016).

16. See Priya Satia, *Spies in Arabia: The Great War and the Cultural Foundations of Britain's Covert Empire in the Middle East* (Oxford: Oxford University Press, 2008).

17. Quoted in ibid., 176.

18. Wilson, *Lawrence of Arabia*, 706.

19. See Edward W. Said, *Orientalism* (New York: Vintage Books, 1979), 240–245; Wilson, *Lawrence of Arabia*, 834.

20. Quoted in Satia, *Spies in Arabia*, 301 (and see also 321); Wilson, *Lawrence of Arabia*, 858.

21. See Christopher Capozzola, *Bound by War: How the United States and the Philippines Built America's First Pacific Century* (New York: Basic Books, 2020).

22. Thomas R. Metcalf, "From One Empire to Another: The Influence of the British Raj on American Colonialism in the Philippines," *Ab Imperio* 3/2012: 25–41.

23. Harold H. Elarth quoted in Jeremy Kuzmarov, *Modernizing Repression: Police Training and Nation-Building in the American Century* (Amherst: University of Massachusetts Press, 2012), 24.

24. See Marc B. Powe, "A Sketch of a Man and His Times," in *The Final Memoranda: Major General Ralph H. Van Deman, USA Ret., 1865–1952, Father of U.S. Military Intelligence*, ed. Ralph E. Weber (Wilmington, DE: Scholarly Resources, 1988), ix–xxii; Kathryn Olmsted, "British and U.S. Anticommunism Between the World Wars," *Journal of Contemporary History* 53, no. 1 (2018): 89–108; Adam Hochschild, "How a Young Army Officer Built America's Empire of Paranoia from 85,000 Index Cards," *Mother Jones*, Jan.–Feb. 2018, www.motherjones.com/politics/2018/01/how-a-young-army-officer-built-americas -empire-of-paranoia-with-torture-surveillance-and-85000-index-cards/.

25. Quoted in Olmsted, "British and U.S. Anticommunism," 97. The classic work on the "imperial boomerang" effects of US colonialism is the monumental study by Alfred W. McCoy, *Policing America's Empire: The United States, the Philippines, and the Rise of the Surveillance State* (Madison: University of Wisconsin Press, 2010).

26. Alfred W. McCoy, *In the Shadows of the American Century: The Rise and Decline of U.S. Global Power* (Chicago: Haymarket, 2017), 117.

Chapter 1

1. Quoted in Jack Davis, "Sherman Kent and the Profession of Intelligence Analysis," *The Sherman Kent Center for Intelligence Analysis Occasional Papers* 1, no. 5 (2002): 8, https://apps.dtic.mil/sti/pdfs/ADA526587.pdf.

2. Quoted in Milo Jones and Philippe Silberzahn, *Constructing Cassandra: Reframing Intelligence Failure at the CIA, 1947–2001* (Stanford, CA: Stanford University Press, 2013), 18, 58.

3. Sherman Kent, *Strategic Intelligence for American World Policy* (Princeton, NJ: Princeton University Press, 1949). For more on Kent's life and career, see Sherman Kent, *Reminiscences of a Varied Life: An Autobiography by Sherman Kent*, assisted by Sally Newell Thacher (San Rafael, CA: The Printing Factory, 1991); J. Peter Scoblic, "Beacon and Warning: Sherman Kent, Scientific Hubris, and the CIA's Office of National Estimates," *Texas National Security Review* 1, no. 4 (2018): 99–117.

4. Donald P. Steury, "Introduction," in *Sherman Kent and the Board of National Estimates*, ed. Donald P. Steury (Washington, DC: Central Intelligence Agency, 1994), www .webharvest.gov/peth04/20041020220904/http://www.cia.gov/csi/books/shermankent /intro.html; Harold P. Ford, "A Tribute to Sherman Kent," in ibid.

5. Robert Callum, "The Case for Cultural Diversity in the Intelligence Community," *International Journal of Intelligence and CounterIntelligence* 14, no. 1 (2001): 25–48; Jackie Benn Porter, "Typists and Trailblazers: Defining the Roles of Women in the Early Years of the CIA," in *From Typist to Trailblazer: The Evolving View of Women in the CIA Workforce*

(Washington, DC: Central Intelligence Agency, 2013), 6–15. For the few women officers, see Nathalia Holt, *Wise Gals: The Spies Who Built the CIA and Changed the Future of Espionage* (New York: G. P. Putnam's Sons, 2022); Liza Mundy, *The Sisterhood: The Secret History of Women at the CIA* (New York: Crown, 2023).

6. Robin Winks, *Cloak and Gown: Scholars in the Secret War, 1939–1961*, 2nd ed. (New Haven, CT: Yale University Press, 1996), 55, 35. The flow of traffic from the Ivy League to US intelligence also occurred in the opposite direction. Sherman Kent's papers at Yale reveal something of an OSS old boys' network operating in the early Cold War history profession, with Kent recommending wartime comrades for tenure-track positions at Ivy League schools. See, for example, John E. Sawyer to Sherman Kent, Jan. 26, 1948, box 15, folder 329, Sherman Kent Papers, Sterling Memorial Library, Yale University, New Haven, CT. After Kent contacted the OSS veteran and economic historian Sawyer about possible academic positions opening up at Yale, Sawyer responded, "When you first called, I didn't know whether you were talking of a govt't job or a teaching job."

7. Quoted in Walter Isaacson and Evan Thomas, *The Wise Men: Six Friends and the World They Made: Acheson, Bohlen, Harriman, Kennan, Lovett, McCloy* (New York: Simon & Schuster, 1986), 30; quoted in Robert D. Dean, *Imperial Brotherhood: Gender and the Making of Cold War Foreign Policy* (Amherst: University of Massachusetts Press, 2001), 19. The latter work is an especially insightful description of this milieu.

8. Rufus Phillips, *Why Vietnam Matters: An Eyewitness Account of Lessons Not Learned* (Annapolis, MD: Naval Institute Press, 2008), 8; quoted in Carole McGranahan, "Love and Empire: The CIA, Tibet, and Covert Humanitarianism," in *Ethnographies of U.S. Empire*, ed. Carole McGranahan and John F. Collins (Durham, NC: Duke University Press, 2018), 342; William Colby and Peter Forbath, *Honorable Men: My Life in the CIA* (New York: Simon & Schuster, 1978), 37; Duane R. Clarridge, *A Spy for All Seasons: My Life in the CIA* (New York: Scribner, 1997), 13.

9. Another British spy in the United States during World War I, the baronet businessman Sir William Wiseman, protected British imperial interests by working to suppress Irish and Indian nationalists operating there. See Rhodri Jeffreys-Jones, *In Spies We Trust: The Story of Western Intelligence* (Oxford: Oxford University Press, 2013), chaps. 2–3; Keith Jeffery, *The Secret History of MI6* (New York: Penguin, 2010), 109–120. For more on the Room, see Joseph E. Persico, *Roosevelt's Secret War: FDR and World War II Espionage* (New York: Random House, 2001), 10–13.

10. Rhodri Jeffreys-Jones, "The Role of British Intelligence in the Mythologies Underpinning the OSS and early CIA," *Intelligence and National Security* 15, no. 2 (2000): 5–19; Jeffery, *Secret History*, 438–453.

11. Kent, *Reminiscences of a Varied Life*, 249.

12. Robert Wargas, "Why Catholics Thrive in the CIA," *Catholic Herald*, May 5, 2016, https://catholicherald.co.uk/issues/may-6th-2016/why-catholics-thrive-in-the-cia/; Clarridge, *Spy for All Seasons*, 115; Orin D. Parker, "Interesting Times . . . and Places . . . and People. Comments on My Life Experiences," unpublished memoir in author's possession.

13. William Eddy, "The Moors Draw Their Knives in Tangier," unpublished memoir, 1957, 17.1, William Alfred Eddy Papers, Seeley G. Mudd Manuscript Library, Princeton University, Princeton, NJ. On the missionaries, see David A. Hollinger, *Protestants Abroad: How Missionaries Tried to Change the World but Changed America* (Princeton, NJ: Prince-

ton University Press, 2017); Matthew Avery Sutton, *Double Crossed: The Missionaries Who Spied for the United States During the Second World War* (New York: Basic Books, 2019).

14. Quoted in Rhodri Jeffreys-Jones, "The Socio-Educational Composition of the CIA Elite: A Statistical Note," *Journal of American Studies* 19, no. 3 (1985): 424; Dean, *Imperial Brotherhood*. For another fine depiction of the Dulles-era CIA, see Evan Thomas, *The Very Best Men: Four Who Dared: The Early Years of the CIA* (New York: Simon & Schuster, 1995). Norman Mailer's CIA novel *Harlot's Ghost* (New York: Random House, 1991) uses fiction to portray the same environment.

15. See Odd Arne Westad's masterful account of these processes, *The Global Cold War: Third World Interventions and the Making of Our Times* (Cambridge: Cambridge University Press, 2005). For an excellent synthesis of more recent scholarship, see Jessica M. Chapman, *Remaking the World: Decolonization and the Cold War* (Lexington: University Press of Kentucky, 2023).

16. OPC figure in Richard H. Immerman, *The Hidden Hand: A Brief History of the CIA* (Somerset, NJ: John Wiley & Sons, 2014), 43.

17. Wm. Roger Louis and Ronald Robinson, "The Imperialism of Decolonization," *Journal of Imperial and Commonwealth History* 22, no. 3 (1994): 462–511; Graham Greene, *The Quiet American* (New York: Penguin USA, 2004). For the Philby episode, see James Hanning, *Love and Deception: Philby in Beirut* (London: Corsair, 2021). The "imperialism of decolonization" effect also occurred in the realm of technological intelligence, with the Americans using British signals bases in places such as Cyprus. See Calder Walton, *Empire of Secrets: British Intelligence, the Cold War, and the Twilight of Empire* (London: William Collins, 2013), 155.

18. Clarridge, *Spy for All Seasons*, 86–88; Robert Baer, *See No Evil: The True Story of a Ground Soldier in the CIA's War on Terrorism* (New York: Crown Publishers, 2002), 47; Larry Devlin, *Chief of Station, Congo: A Memoir, 1960–67* (New York: PublicAffairs, 2007), x.

19. Lorraine Copeland, emails to author, Nov. 25, 2010; Nov. 23, 2010.

20. Ann Laura Stoler, "Tense and Tender Ties: The Politics of Comparison in North American History and (Post) Colonial Studies," *Journal of American History* 88, no. 3 (2001): 829–865; Karen L. Chiao and Mariellen B. O'Brien, eds., *Spies' Wives: Stories of CIA Families Abroad* (Berkeley, CA: Creative Arts Book Company, 2001). On CIA wives providing operational support to their husbands, see Mundy, *Sisterhood*, chap. 7.

21. Clarridge, *Spy for All Seasons*, 82; David Atlee Phillips, *The Night Watch* (New York: Atheneum, 1977), 65.

22. *The Man Nobody Knew*, dir. Carl Colby (First Run Features, 2011).

23. Baer, *See No Evil*, 36; Frank Snepp, *Decent Interval* (New York: Random House, 1977), 4; John Stockwell, *In Search of Enemies: A CIA Story* (New York: W. W. Norton, 1978), 128.

24. Greene, *Quiet American*. See Ann Laura Stoler, "Carnal Knowledge and Imperial Power: Race and the Intimate in Colonial Rule," in *The New Imperial Histories Reader*, ed. Stephen Howe (London: Routledge, 2010), 177–194.

25. Baer, *See No Evil*, 81.

26. See Loch Johnson, "Evaluating 'Humint': The Role of Foreign Agents in U.S. Security," *Comparative Strategy* 29, no. 4 (2010): 312–313; Victor Marchetti and John D. Marks, *The CIA and the Cult of Intelligence* (New York: Alfred A. Knopf, 1980), 255–269.

27. See Randy Burkett, "An Alternative Framework for Agent Recruitment: From MICE to RASCLS," *Studies in Intelligence* 57, no. 1 (2013): 7–17; Henry A. Crumpton, *The Art of Intelligence: Lessons from a Life in the CIA's Clandestine Service* (New York: Penguin, 2012), 43–58.

28. Percentages in Crumpton, *Art of Intelligence*, 34; Stockwell, *In Search of Enemies*, 104. Quotations in Devlin, *Chief of Station*, 29; Clarridge, *Spy for All Seasons*, 80. Novelist Norman Mailer noticed CIA men's habit of likening agent recruitment to sex. In his Agency epic *Harlot's Ghost*, a senior officer briefing junior colleagues about agent acquisition describes the process as "disinterested seduction." Mailer, *Harlot's Ghost*, 374.

29. Crumpton, *Art of Intelligence*, 42, 51; Philip Agee, *Inside the Company: CIA Diary* (New York: Bantam Books, 1976), 269, 142, 163; "James Noland Obituary," Aug. 28, 2009, *Durango Herald*, www.legacy.com/us/obituaries/durangoheraldnamejames-noland-obituary?id=44676411.

30. Agee, *Inside the Company*, 87; Crumpton, *Art of Intelligence*, 60; Gil Kindelan, "The Humanity of Espionage," Catholic University of America Intelligence Studies Colloquium, Feb. 28, 2019, https://ihe.catholic.edu/event/espionage/; Snepp, *Decent Interval*. It later emerged that Snepp had also been forced to leave behind his Vietnamese lover and their child, both of whom subsequently died. See Frank Snepp, *Irreparable Harm: A Firsthand Account of How One Agent Took on the CIA in an Epic Battle Over Secrecy and Free Speech* (New York: Random House, 1999).

31. Eddy, "Our Communist Allies," unpublished memoir, 1957, 17.1, Eddy Papers; Colby, *Man Nobody Knew*.

32. John Bennett, Catholic University Colloquium.

33. For an outstanding recent work emphasizing agents' agency, see Susan McCall Perlman, *Contesting France: Intelligence and US Foreign Policy in the Early Cold War* (Cambridge: Cambridge University Press, 2023).

34. Sherman Kent, "A Crucial Estimate Relived," *Studies in Intelligence* 8, no. 2 (1964), www.cia.gov/resources/csi/studies-in-intelligence/1992-2/a-crucial-estimate-relived/; Kent, *Reminiscences of a Varied Life*, 277.

35. Two notable exceptions are Jones and Silberzahn, *Constructing Cassandra*; and Patrick A. Kelley, *Imperial Secrets: Remapping the Mind of Empire* (Washington, DC: Center for Strategic Intelligence Research, National Defense Intelligence College, 2008).

36. See Westad, *Global Cold War*.

37. James N. Eichelberger, "Cairo Station Views Pertinent to OMEGA Planning," May 2, 1956, 55, Omega Vol. 4, Lot 61D417, Department of State Lot Files, Record Group 59, National Archives and Records Administration (NARA), College Park, MD. On the Sino-Soviet Studies Group, see Calder Walton, *Spies: The Epic Intelligence War Between East and West* (New York: Simon & Schuster, 2023), 357–358.

38. M. R. Gubbins, quoted in Kelley, *Imperial Secrets*, 114.

39. See John Ferris, "The British Empire vs. the Hidden Hand: British Intelligence and Strategy and 'The CUP-Jew-German-Bolshevik Combination,' 1918–1924," in *The British Way in Warfare: Power and the International System*, ed. Greg Kennedy and Keith Neilson (Farnham, UK: Routledge, 2010), 325–346.

40. See Mark Bradley, "Slouching Toward Bethlehem: Culture, Diplomacy, and the Origins of the Cold War in Vietnam," in *Cold War Constructions: The Political Culture of United States Imperialism, 1945–1966*, ed. Christian G. Appy (Amherst: University of Massachusetts Press, 2000), 11–34; Dina Rezk, *The Arab World and Western Intelligence: Analysing the Middle East, 1956–81* (Edinburgh: Edinburgh University Press, 2017), chap. 1; Oliver Kearns, *The Covert Colour Line: The Racialised Politics of Western State Intelligence* (London: Pluto Press, 2023).

41. See Hugh Wilford, *America's Great Game: The CIA's Secret Arabists and the Shaping of the Modern Middle East* (New York: Basic Books, 2013); Perlman, *Contesting France.*

42. Quoted in Scoblic, "Beacon and Warning," 113; Steury, "Introduction."

43. Kent, *Reminiscences of a Varied Life*, 291, 293.

Chapter 2

1. Kermit Roosevelt, "Memorandum of CIA Representative," attached to Walter Bedell Smith to Dwight D. Eisenhower, no date [late Aug./early Sep. 1953], box 32, folder Iran, 1953 through 1959 (8), International Series, Dwight D. Eisenhower Papers as President of the United States, 1952–61 (Ann Whitman File), Dwight D. Eisenhower Library, Abilene, KS; quoted in Kermit Roosevelt, *Countercoup: The Struggle for the Control of Iran* (New York: McGraw-Hill, 1979), 207.

2. Quoted in Roosevelt, *Countercoup*, 199. On the Iran coup, see Stephen Kinzer, *All the Shah's Men: An American Coup and the Roots of Middle East Terror*, 2nd ed. (Hoboken, NJ: Wiley & Sons, 2008); Ali Rahnema, *Behind the 1953 Coup in Iran: Thugs, Turncoats, Soldiers, and Spooks* (Cambridge: Cambridge University Press, 2015); Mark J. Gasiorowski and Malcolm Byrne, eds., *Mohammad Mosaddeq and the 1953 Coup in Iran* (Syracuse, NY: Syracuse University Press, 2004); Ervand Abrahamian, *Oil Crisis in Iran: From Nationalism to Coup d'Etat* (Cambridge: Cambridge University Press, 2021); David S. Painter and Gregory Brew, *The Struggle for Iran: Oil, Autocracy, and the Cold War, 1951–1954* (Chapel Hill: University of North Carolina Press, 2022).

3. Roosevelt, *Countercoup*, 209. On the Guatemala coup, see Richard H. Immerman, *The CIA in Guatemala: The Foreign Policy of Intervention* (Austin: University of Texas Press, 1982); Piero Gleijeses, *Shattered Hope: The Guatemalan Revolution and the United States, 1944–1954* (Princeton, NJ: Princeton University Press, 1991); Nick Cullather, *Secret History: The CIA's Classified Account of Its Operations in Guatemala, 1952–1954* (Stanford, CA: Stanford University Press, 1999).

4. Donald N. Wilber, "Overthrow of Premier Mossadeq of Iran, November 1952–August 1953," CIA Historical Paper No. 208, Mar. 1954, 81.

5. Quoted in Robin Winks, *Cloak and Gown: Scholars in the Secret War, 1939–1961*, 2nd ed. (New Haven, CT: Yale University Press, 1996), 451.

6. See Sarah-Jane Corke, *U.S. Covert Operations and Cold War Strategy: Truman, Secret Warfare, and the CIA* (London: Routledge, 2008).

7. On early CIA efforts to stabilize postwar Western Europe, see Sallie Pisani, *The CIA and the Marshall Plan* (Lawrence: University Press of Kansas, 1991). On rollback, see Peter Grose, *Operation Rollback: America's Secret War Behind the Iron Curtain* (Boston: Houghton Mifflin, 2000). On Japan, see Brad Williams, "U.S. Covert Action in Cold War Japan: The Politics of Cultivating Conservative Elites and Its Consequences," *Journal of Contemporary Asia* 50, no. 4 (2020): 593–617.

8. Merle Miller, *Plain Speaking: An Oral Biography of Harry S. Truman* (New York: G. P. Putnam's Sons, 1973), 391.

9. Stephen Kinzer, *The Brothers: John Foster Dulles, Allen Dulles, and Their Secret World War* (New York: Times Books, 2013).

10. Noel Maurer, *The Empire Trap: The Rise and Fall of U.S. Intervention to Protect American Property Overseas, 1893–2013* (Princeton, NJ: Princeton University Press, 2013).

11. José Manuel Fortuny quoted in Gleijeses, *Shattered Hope*, 366.

12. For a fine recent discussion of US motives in Iran, see Gregory Brew, "The Collapse Narrative: The United States, Mohammed Mossadegh, and the Coup Decision of 1953," *Texas National Security Review* 2, no. 4 (2019): 38–59.

13. Quoted in Julian Go, *Patterns of Empire: The British and American Empires, 1688 to the Present* (Cambridge: Cambridge University Press, 2011), 114.

14. On the factors deterring overt US interventions, see Michael Poznansky, *In the Shadow of International Law: Secrecy and Regime Change in the Postwar World* (New York: Oxford University Press, 2020).

15. See William Dalrymple, *The Anarchy: The Relentless Rise of the East India Company* (London: Bloomsbury, 2019); William Dalrymple, *Return of a King: The Battle for Afghanistan* (London: Bloomsbury, 2014).

16. See Abdel Razzaq Takriti, "Colonial Coups and the War on Popular Sovereignty," *American Historical Review* 124, no. 3 (2019): 878–909; Robert Aldrich, "When Did Decolonization End? France and the Ending of Empire," in *Endless Empire: Spain's Retreat, Europe's Eclipse, America's Decline*, ed. Alfred W. McCoy, Josep M. Fradera, and Stephen Jacobson (Madison: University of Wisconsin Press, 2012), 216–229.

17. Kermit Roosevelt, *Arabs, Oil, and History: The Story of the Middle East* (Port Washington, NY: Kennikat Press, 1967), 271. For more detail, see Hugh Wilford, *America's Great Game: The CIA's Secret Arabists and the Shaping of the Modern Middle East* (New York: Basic Books, 2013), chap. 7.

18. Kermit Roosevelt, *A Sentimental Safari* (New York: Alfred A. Knopf, 1963), xiii.

19. Ibid., vii–viii; Kermit Roosevelt, *War in the Garden of Eden* (New York: Scribner's Sons, 1919), 201–204.

20. Andrew Friedman, *Covert Capital: Landscapes of Denial and the Making of U.S. Empire in the Suburbs of Northern Virginia* (Berkeley: University of California Press, 2013), 40–41; Kermit "Kim" Roosevelt Jr., "The Lure of the East," *The American Boy—Youth's Companion* 58 (May 1931): 58.

21. Quoted in Roosevelt, *Countercoup*, 110.

22. See Wilford, *America's Great Game*, chaps. 9–11.

23. Roosevelt, *Countercoup*, 2, 77, 85–86.

24. *Foreign Relations of the United States, 1952–1954, Iran, 1951–1954*, ed. James C. Van Hook (Washington, DC: US Government Printing Office, 2017) (hereafter *FRUS, Iran*). On the divide between CIA operatives and analysts over Iran, see CIA History Staff, "Zendebad, Shah!: The Central Intelligence Agency and the Fall of Iranian Prime Minister Mohammad Mosaddeq, August 1953," by Scott A. Koch, June 1998, Appendix E. For recent research using Soviet sources, see Vladislav M. Zubok, "Stalin, Soviet Intelligence, and the Struggle for Iran, 1945–53," *Diplomatic History* 44, no. 1 (2020): 22–46.

25. *FRUS, Iran*, Documents 7, 25.

26. See Mark Gasiorowski, "The CIA's TPBEDAMN and Stay-Behind Operations in Iran," July 11, 2017, *Sources and Methods* (blog), Wilson Center, www.wilsoncenter.org /blog-post/the-cias-tpbedamn-and-stay-behind-operations-iran.

27. *FRUS, Iran*, Document 48; Mark Gasiorowski, "The US Stay-Behind Operation in Iran, 1948–1953," *Intelligence and National Security* 34, no. 2 (2019): 170.

28. *FRUS, Iran*, Document 122.

29. C. M. Woodhouse, *Something Ventured* (London: Granta, 1982), 117.

30. Ibid., 120; Polly Roosevelt to Belle Roosevelt, May 24, 1954, 143; Roosevelt, Mary Gaddis (Polly), undated, 1950–1959, Kermit Roosevelt and Belle Roosevelt Papers, Library of Congress, Washington, DC; Roosevelt, *Countercoup*, 115.

31. Roosevelt, *Countercoup*, 138, 140, 78, 172.

32. Quoted in Painter and Brew, *Struggle for Iran*, 168.

33. *FRUS, Iran*, Document 273.

34. Quoted in Bethany Allen-Ebrahimian, "64 Years Later, the CIA Finally Released Details of the Coup in Iran," *Business Insider*, June 25, 2017, www.businessinsider.com /cia-releases-details-of-iranian-coup-2017-6; CIA History Staff, "Zendebad, Shah!," 79.

35. Anonymous CIA officer quoted in Mark J. Gasiorowski, "The 1953 Coup d'Etat Against Mosaddeq," in *Mohammad Mosaddeq*, ed. Gasiorowski and Byrne, 231.

36. Roosevelt, *Arabs, Oil, and History*, 7.

37. Quoted in Calder Walton, *Empire of Secrets: British Intelligence, the Cold War, and the Twilight of Empire* (London: William Collins, 2013), 298.

38. See Matthew Jones, "Anglo-American Relations After Suez, the Rise and Decline of the Working Group Experiment, and the French Challenge to NATO, 1957–59," *Diplomacy and Statecraft* 14, no. 1 (2003): 49–79.

39. On British support for US covert operations, see Rory Cormac, *Disrupt and Deny: Spies, Special Forces, and the Secret Pursuit of British Foreign Policy* (Oxford: Oxford University Press, 2018). Britain was even active in the Western Hemisphere through the Information Research Department (IRD), a secret anti-communist propaganda unit in the Foreign Office. IRD's targets in Latin America included Jacobo Árbenz's government in Guatemala. See Aaron Coy Moulton, "'We Are Meddling': Anti-Colonialism and the British Cold War Against the Guatemalan Revolution, 1944–1954," *International History Review* 44, no. 5 (2022): 1108–1126.

40. Wilford, *America's Great Game*, chap. 18; Kenneth Conboy and James Morrison, *Feet to the Fire: CIA Covert Operations in Indonesia, 1957–1958* (Annapolis, MD: Naval Institute Press, 1999); Emmanuel Gerard and Bruce Kuklick, *Death in the Congo: Murdering Patrice Lumumba* (Cambridge, MA: Harvard University Press, 2015).

41. Don Bohning, *The Castro Obsession: U.S. Covert Operations Against Cuba, 1959–1965* (Washington, DC: Potomac Books, 2005); Howard Jones, *The Bay of Pigs* (Oxford: Oxford University Press, 2008).

42. Quoted in Cormac, *Disrupt and Deny*, 150.

43. Evan Thomas, *The Very Best Men: Four Who Dared: The Early Years of the CIA* (New York: Simon & Schuster, 1995), 119. See Zachary Karabell, *Architects of Intervention: The United States, the Third World, and the Cold War, 1946–1962* (Baton Rouge: Louisiana State University Press, 1999).

44. See Darioush Bayandor, *Iran and the CIA: The Fall of Mosaddeq Revisited* (New York: Palgrave Macmillan, 2010); Ray Takeyh and Steven Simon, *The Pragmatic Superpower: Winning the Cold War in the Middle East* (New York: W. W. Norton, 2016), 53–89; Ray Takeyh, "What Really Happened in Iran: The CIA, the Ouster of Mosaddeq, and the Restoration of the Shah," *Foreign Affairs* 93, no. 4 (2014): 2–14.

45. For an example of a CIA colleague criticizing Roosevelt, see Donald N. Wilber, *Adventures in the Middle East: Excursions and Incursions* (Princeton, NJ: Darwin, 1986), 9, 189. On the ayatollahs, see Malcolm Byrne and Mark Gasiorowski, eds., "New Findings on

Clerical Involvement in the 1953 Coup in Iran," National Security Archive Briefing Book #619, Mar. 7, 2018, https://nsarchive.gwu.edu/briefing-book/iran/2018-03-07/new-findings -clerical-involvement-1953-coup-iran. For a recent account emphasizing the British contribution, see Michael Smith, *The Real Special Relationship: The True Story of How MI6 and the CIA Work Together* (New York: Arcade, 2023), chap. 9.

46. For critiques of Iran coup revisionism, see Fakhreddin Azimi, "The Overthrow of the Government of Mosaddeq Reconsidered," *Iranian Studies* 45, no. 5 (2012): 693–712; Greg Brew, "Misreading the 1953 Coup," Lobe Log, https://lobelog.com/misreading -the-1953-coup/comment-page-2/#comments.

47. Kennedy quoted in Kinzer, *Brothers*, 303. See Christopher Moran, "Ian Fleming and the Public Profile of the CIA," *Journal of Cold War Studies* 15, no. 1 (2013): 119–146.

48. Quoted in Walton, *Empire of Secrets*, 161. See Stephen G. Rabe, *The Killing Zone: The United States Wages Cold War in Latin America* (New York: Oxford University Press, 2011); Michael Grow, *U.S. Presidents and Latin American Interventions: Pursuing Regime Change in the Cold War* (Lawrence: University Press of Kansas, 2008).

49. Quoted in Richard H. Immerman, *The Hidden Hand: A Brief History of the CIA* (Somerset, NJ: John Wiley & Sons, 2014), 89. As in the case of Iran, some recent scholarship has deemphasized the Agency's contribution to Allende's overthrow in favor of the Chilean military and neighboring Latin American governments. See, for example, Kristian Gustafson, *Hostile Intent: U.S. Covert Operations in Chile, 1964–1974* (Washington, DC: Potomac Books, 2007); Tanya Harmer, *Allende's Chile and the Inter-American Cold War* (Chapel Hill: University of North Carolina Press, 2011).

50. Quoted in Immerman, *Hidden Hand*, 126. On the Contra operation, see Malcolm Byrne, *Iran-Contra: Reagan's Scandal and the Unchecked Abuse of Presidential Power* (Lawrence: University Press of Kansas, 2014). On mercenaries, see Kyle Burke, *Revolutionaries for the Right: Anticommunist Internationalism and Paramilitary Warfare in the Cold War* (Chapel Hill: University of North Carolina Press, 2018); Andrew Thomson, *Outsourced Empire: How Militias, Mercenaries, and Contractors Support U.S. Statecraft* (London: Pluto Press, 2018); and Klaas Voß, "Plausibly Deniable: Mercenaries in U.S. Covert Interventions During the Cold War, 1964–1987," *Cold War History* 16, no. 1 (2016): 37–60.

51. Lindsay A. O'Rourke, *Covert Regime Change: America's Secret Cold War* (Ithaca, NY: Cornell University Press, 2018), 73.

52. See Michael J. Sullivan III, *American Adventurism Abroad: 30 Invasions, Interventions, and Regime Changes Since World War II* (Westport, CT: Praeger, 2004).

53. Quoted in Voß, "Plausibly Deniable," 51.

54. Dinkar Sonwalkar quoted in Paul Michael McGarr, "'Quiet Americans in India': The CIA and the Politics of Intelligence in Cold War South Asia," *Diplomatic History* 38, no. 5 (2014): 1046.

55. Quoted in CIA History Staff, "Zendebad, Shah!," 79; R. Harris Smith, notes on interview with Kermit Roosevelt, 10, R. Harris Smith Collection, Hoover Institution, Stanford University, Palo Alto, CA.

56. Jonathan Roosevelt, telephone interview by author, Feb. 20, 2010.

57. See Hugh Wilford, "'Essentially a Work of Fiction': Kermit 'Kim' Roosevelt, Imperial Romance, and the Iran Coup of 1953," *Diplomatic History* 40, no. 5 (2016): 943–944.

58. Richard W. Cottam, review of *Countercoup: The Struggle for the Control of Iran*, by Kermit Roosevelt, *Iranian Studies* 14, nos. 3–4 (1981): 269; Thomas Powers, "A Book Held Hostage," *The Nation*, Apr. 12, 1980, 438, 437; Roosevelt, *Countercoup*, ix.

Chapter 3

1. William J. Lederer and Eugene Burdick, *The Ugly American* (New York: W. W. Norton, 1999); Edward Lansdale, *In the Midst of Wars* (New York: Harper and Row, 1972); Cecil B. Currey, *Edward Lansdale: The Unquiet American* (Boston: Houghton Mifflin, 1988); Max Boot, *The Road Not Taken: Edward Lansdale and the American Tragedy in Vietnam* (New York: Liveright, 2018). See also the important study of the Lansdale legend by cultural historian Jonathan Nashel, *Edward Lansdale's Cold War* (Amherst: University of Massachusetts Press, 2005).

2. There is an extensive literature on counterinsurgency, much of it of the "how-to" variety, by military historians, political scientists, and other members of the "irregular warfare" community. For a brilliant critical history of the doctrine, see Douglas Porch, *Counterinsurgency: Exposing the Myths of the New Way of War* (New York: Cambridge University Press, 2013).

3. Edward Lansdale, interview by Ted Gittinger, June 5, 1981, Lyndon Baines Johnson Library Oral History Project, box 79, Edward Geary Lansdale Papers, Hoover Institution, Stanford University, Palo Alto, CA.

4. Quoted in Nashel, *Edward Lansdale's Cold War*, 108; Norman Mailer, *Harlot's Ghost* (New York: Random House, 1991), 1023.

5. See Colleen Woods, *Freedom Incorporated: Anticommunism and Philippine Independence in the Age of Decolonization* (Ithaca, NY: Cornell University Press, 2020).

6. Edward Lansdale, Diary, Dec. 26, 1946, 72, folder Diaries 1946–48, Lansdale Papers.

7. Quoted in Boot, *Road Not Taken*, 64.

8. Edward Lansdale, "Civic Action," speech, Special Warfare Center, Fort Bragg, Feb. 24, 1961, 74, Lansdale Papers. There is an extensive US Army literature on Magsaysay and Lansdale's campaign against the Huks. Most acute is Andrew J. Birtle, *U.S. Army Counterinsurgency and Contingency Operations Doctrine, 1942–1976* (Washington, DC: US Army Center of Military History, 2006), 55–66.

9. Quoted in Michael Graziano, *Errand into the Wilderness of Mirrors: Religion and the History of the CIA* (Chicago: University of Chicago Press, 2021), 136. See Daniel Immerwahr, *Thinking Small: The United States and the Lure of Community Development* (Cambridge, MA: Harvard University Press, 2015); Christina Klein, *Cold War Orientalism: Asia in the Middlebrow Imagination, 1945–61* (Berkeley: University of California Press, 2003).

10. Christopher Capozzola, *Bound by War: How the United States and the Philippines Built America's First Pacific Century* (New York: Basic Books, 2020), 241; C. T. R. Bohannan, "Unconventional Operations," speech, Special Warfare Center, Fort Bragg, June 15, 1961, 79, Lansdale Papers; quoted in Capozzola, *Bound by War*, 241; Daniel Immerwahr, *How to Hide an Empire: A History of the Greater United States* (New York: Farrar, Straus and Giroux, 2019), 104; quoted in Eva-Lotta E. Hedman, "Late Imperial Romance: Magsaysay, Lansdale, and the Philippine-American 'Special Relationship,'" *Intelligence and National Security* 14, no. 4 (1999): 192.

11. Bohannan, "Unconventional Operations"; quoted in Brian D'Haeseleer, *The Salvadoran Crucible: The Failure of U.S. Counterinsurgency in El Salvador, 1979–1992* (Lawrence: University Press of Kansas, 2017), 24; quoted in Daniel Immerwahr, "The Ugly American: Peeling the Onion of an Iconic Cold War Text," *Journal of American–East Asian Relations* 26, no. 1 (2019): 15; see also Jacqueline L. Hazelton, *Bullets Not Ballots: Success in Counterinsurgency Warfare* (Ithaca, NY: Cornell University Press, 2021), 69–73.

12. See Hedman, "Late Imperial Romance"; Molly Geidel, *Peace Corps Fantasies: How Development Shaped the Global Sixties* (Minneapolis: University of Minnesota Press, 2015).

13. Edward Lansdale, "Introductory Comments on the Campaign," speech, Fort Bragg, June 15, 1961, 74, Lansdale Papers. See Nick Cullather, "America's Boy? Ramon Magsaysay and the Illusion of Influence," *Pacific Historical Review* 62, no. 3 (1993): 305–338.

14. Boot, *Road Not Taken*, chap. 10; "Geoffrey S. Villiers" to Director, KUBARK, "The Philippines Election, 1953," Nov. 20, 1953, 98.5, Lansdale Papers.

15. "Villiers," "Philippines Election, 1953."

16. See Kathryn C. Statler, *Replacing France: The Origins of American Intervention in Vietnam* (Lexington: University Press of Kentucky, 2007).

17. See Seth Jacobs, *America's Miracle Man in Vietnam: Ngo Dinh Diem, Religion, Race, and U.S. Intervention in Southeast Asia, 1950–1957* (Durham, NC: Duke University Press, 2004); Edward Miller, *Misalliance: Ngo Dinh Diem, the United States, and the Fate of South Vietnam* (Cambridge, MA: Harvard University Press, 2013).

18. Quoted in Lansdale, interview. For more on SMM operations, see Lansdale's own report, "Lansdale Team's Report on Covert Saigon Mission in '54 and '55," in Neil Sheehan et al., *The Pentagon Papers as Published by* The New York Times (New York: Quadrangle Books, 1971), 54–67.

19. Nashel, *Edward Lansdale's Cold War*, 56.

20. Quoted in Thomas L. Ahern Jr., *CIA and the House of Ngo: Covert Action in South Vietnam, 1954–1963* (Washington, DC: Center for the Study of Intelligence, 2000), 46–47.

21. Quoted in Nashel, *Edward Lansdale's Cold War*, 111; Boot, *Road Not Taken*, 294; Ahern, *CIA and House of Ngo*, 26; Andrew Friedman, *Covert Capital: Landscapes of Denial and the Making of U.S. Empire in the Suburbs of Northern Virginia* (Berkeley: University of California Press, 2013), 144.

22. Quoted in Nashel, *Edward Lansdale's Cold War*, 53; Boot, *Road Not Taken*, 277–280; quoted in Ahern, *CIA and House of Ngo*, 30; quoted in Friedman, *Covert Capital*, 145.

23. Quoted in Nashel, *Edward Lansdale's Cold War*, 61; quoted in Simeon Man, *Soldiering Through Empire: Race and the Making of the Decolonizing Pacific* (Berkeley: University of California Press, 2018), 60; Edward Lansdale, report on Operation Brotherhood, no date, 35, Operation Brotherhood, Lansdale Papers.

24. See Man, *Soldiering Through Empire*, 66–73; Woods, *Freedom Incorporated*, chap. 5.

25. See Jeremy Kuzmarov, *Modernizing Repression: Police Training and Nation-Building in the American Century* (Amherst: University of Massachusetts Press, 2012); Stuart Schrader, *Badges Without Borders: How Global Counterinsurgency Transformed American Policing* (Berkeley: University of California Press, 2019).

26. See William Rosenau, *U.S. Internal Security Assistance to South Vietnam: Insurgency, Subversion, and Public Order* (London: Routledge, 2005).

27. As with Kermit Roosevelt's role in the 1953 Iran coup, historians disagree about exactly how much credit Lansdale deserves for Diem's survival. For a recent account emphasizing Diem's own contribution, see Miller, *Misalliance*, chap. 3.

28. Lansdale, *In the Midst of Wars*, 214. On the problems of the MSU program, see Jessica Breiteneicher Elkind, *Aid Under Fire: Nation Building and the Vietnam War* (Lexington: University Press of Kentucky, 2016), chap. 4.

29. Quoted in Elkind, *Aid Under Fire*, 21.

30. Quoted in Thomas A. Bass, *The Spy Who Loved Us: The Vietnam War and Pham Xuan An's Dangerous Game* (New York: PublicAffairs, 2009), 1. See Jean-Marc LePage and Elie Tenenbaum, "The 'Unquiet' Allies: French and American Intelligence Relations During the First Indochina War, 1950–54," *Studies in Intelligence* 55, no. 3 (2011): 25–37.

31. Anon., "Réalités Cambodiennes," Jan. 6, 1961, 47, Personal, Lansdale Papers; Arthur M. Schlesinger Jr., *A Thousand Days: John F. Kennedy in the White House* (New York: Houghton Mifflin, 2002), 538; quoted in Miller, *Misalliance*, 256; quoted in Bass, *Spy Who Loved Us*, 94; Friedman, *Covert Capital*, 139; quoted in Christopher Benfey, *If: The Untold Story of Kipling's American Years* (New York: Penguin, 2019), 208. Madame Nhu spearheaded an effort by the Diem regime to wipe out the South Vietnamese sex industry. See Amanda Boczar, *An American Brothel: Sex and Diplomacy During the Vietnam War* (Ithaca, NY: Cornell University Press, 2022), 35–46.

32. See Lien-Hang T. Nguyen, *Hanoi's War: An International History of the War for Peace in Vietnam* (Chapel Hill: University of North Carolina Press, 2012).

33. See the correspondence in 38, Galula, David, Lansdale Papers; Edward Lansdale to Charles Cabell, Oct. 23, 1963, 37, Cabell, General C. P., Lansdale Papers. See also Boot, *Road Not Taken*, chap. 21.

34. See Wen-Qing Ngoei, *Arc of Containment: Britain, the United States, and Anticommunism in Southeast Asia* (Ithaca, NY: Cornell University Press, 2019), chap. 3.

35. David French, "Nasty Not Nice: British Counterinsurgency Doctrine and Practice, 1945–1967," *Small Wars and Insurgencies* 23, nos. 4–5 (2012): 744–761; Calder Walton, *Empire of Secrets: British Intelligence, the Cold War, and the Twilight of Empire* (London: William Collins, 2013), 208.

36. Miller, *Misalliance*, 232–234.

37. Rufus Phillips to James S. Killen, "Vietnam," July 9, 1964, 48, Phillips, Rufus, Lansdale Papers.

38. See Michael E. Latham, "Redirecting the Revolution? The USA and the Failure of Nation-Building in South Vietnam," *Third World Quarterly* 27, no. 1 (2006): 27–41; Hannah Gurman, "Vietnam—Uprooting the Revolution: Counterinsurgency in Vietnam," in *Hearts and Minds: A People's History of Counterinsurgency*, ed. Hannah Gurman (New York: New Press, 2013), 77–103.

39. Quoted in Boot, *Road Not Taken*, 412. On the coup against Diem, see Ahern, *CIA and House of Ngo*, chap. 12, and Miller, *Misalliance*, chap. 9.

40. Quoted in Nashel, *Edward Lansdale's Cold War*, 210.

41. Ngoei, *Arc of Containment*; Tim Weiner, *Legacy of Ashes: The History of the CIA* (New York: Doubleday, 2007), chap. 12; Man, *Soldiering Through Empire*, 6. The military coup that deposed Sukarno was accompanied by an anti-communist massacre that, according to some estimates, killed as many as 1 million Indonesians. See Vincent Bevins, *The*

Jakarta Method: Washington's Anticommunist Crusade and the Mass Murder Program That Shaped Our World (New York: PublicAffairs, 2020).

42. Douglas Little, "Mission Impossible: The CIA and the Cult of Covert Action in the Middle East," *Diplomatic History* 28, no. 5 (2004): 663–701; Andrew Cockburn and Leslie Cockburn, *Dangerous Liaison: The Inside Story of the U.S.-Israeli Covert Relationship* (New York: HarperCollins, 1991).

43. David Robarge, "CIA's Covert Operations in the Congo, 1960–1968: Insights from Newly Declassified Documents," *Studies in Intelligence* 58, no. 3 (2014): 1–9; Adam Taylor, "The CIA's Mysterious Role in the Arrest of Nelson Mandela," *Washington Post*, May 16, 2016, www.washingtonpost.com/news/worldviews/wp/2016/05/16/the-cias-mysterious -role-in-the-arrest-of-nelson-mandela/.

44. Greg Grandin, *Empire's Workshop: Latin America, the United States, and the Rise of the New Imperialism* (New York: Henry Holt, 2006); D'Haeseleer, *Salvadoran Crucible*.

45. Jefferson Morley, *Our Man in Mexico: Winston Scott and the Hidden History of the CIA* (Lawrence: University Press of Kansas, 2008); Jack O'Connell, *King's Counsel: A Memoir of War, Espionage, and Diplomacy in the Middle East* (New York: W. W. Norton, 2011); Larry Devlin, *Chief of Station, Congo: Fighting the Cold War in a Hot Zone* (New York: PublicAffairs, 2007); Sobukwe Odinga, "'The Privileged Friendship': Reassessing the Central Intelligence Agency Operation at Zaire's Kamina Airbase," *Diplomacy and Statecraft* 29, no. 4 (2018): 692–715.

46. D'Haeseleer, *Salvadoran Crucible*. See also Thomas C. Field, *From Development to Dictatorship: Bolivia and the Alliance for Progress in the Kennedy Era* (Ithaca, NY: Cornell University Press, 2014).

47. Schrader, *Badges Without Borders*.

48. Ibid., 155–156. See also Alfred W. McCoy, *A Question of Torture: CIA Interrogation, from the Cold War to the War on Terror* (New York: Metropolitan Books, 2006); Alfred W. McCoy, *Torture and Impunity: The U.S. Doctrine of Coercive Interrogation* (Madison: University of Wisconsin Press, 2012).

49. Klaas Voß, "Plausibly Deniable: Mercenaries in U.S. Covert Interventions During the Cold War, 1964–1987," *Cold War History* 16, no. 1 (2016): 49. See Kyle Burke, *Revolutionaries for the Right: Anticommunist Internationalism and Paramilitary Warfare in the Cold War* (Chapel Hill: University of North Carolina Press, 2018).

50. Edward Lansdale, "Some Thoughts About Central America," typescript, May 10, 1983, 80, Lansdale Papers; quoted in Boot, *Road Not Taken*, 589–590.

51. Immerwahr, *How to Hide an Empire*, 105, 107.

52. A. J. Langguth, "America's History of Torture," *Los Angeles Times*, May 3, 2009, www.latimes.com/archives/la-xpm-2009-may-03-oe-langguth3-story.html.

Chapter 4

1. Quoted in Christopher J. Coyne and Abigail R. Hall, *Tyranny Comes Home: The Domestic Fate of U.S. Militarism* (Stanford, CA: Stanford University Press, 2018), 8; quoted in Thomas Bender, "The American Way of Empire," *World Policy Journal* 23, no. 1 (2006): 49; quoted in Frank Ninkovich, "Anti-Imperialism in U.S. Foreign Relations," in *Vietnam and the American Political Tradition: The Politics of Dissent*, ed. Randall B. Woods (Cambridge: Cambridge University Press, 2003), 21–22. See Ian Tyrrell and Jay Sexton, eds.,

Empire's Twin: U.S. Anti-Imperialism from the Founding Era to the Age of Terrorism (Ithaca, NY: Cornell University Press, 2015).

2. See Connor Woodman, "The Imperial Boomerang: How Colonial Methods of Repression Migrate Back to the Metropolis," *Verso Blog*, June 9, 2020, www.versobooks .com/blogs/4383-the-imperial-boomerang-how-colonial-methods-of-repression-migrate -back-to-the-metropolis. The concept of the imperial boomerang is principally associated with the French historian Michel Foucault, German American political theorist Hannah Arendt, and Martinican poet Aimé Césaire. Although similar in meaning to the CIA-coined term "blowback," it refers in particular to the European importation of colonial techniques of surveillance and counterinsurgency, which is why I generally prefer it here in this, a comparative study of European and US imperial intelligence. For a landmark text on blowback, see Chalmers Johnson, *Blowback: The Costs and Consequences of American Empire* (New York: Henry Holt, 2000).

3. Tom Mangold, *Cold Warrior: James Jesus Angleton: The CIA's Master Spy Hunter* (New York: Simon & Schuster, 1991); Robin Winks, *Cloak and Gown: Scholars in the Secret War, 1939–1961*, 2nd ed. (New Haven, CT: Yale University Press, 1996), chap. 6; Michael Holzman, *James Jesus Angleton, the CIA, and the Craft of Counterintelligence* (Amherst: University of Massachusetts Press, 2008); Jefferson Morley, *The Ghost: The Secret Life of CIA Spymaster James Jesus Angleton* (New York: St. Martin's Press, 2017); Bruce Hoffman and Christian Ostermann, eds., *Moles, Defectors, and Deceptions: James Angleton and His Influence on U.S. Counterintelligence* (Washington, DC: Woodrow Wilson International Center for Scholars, 2014).

4. Quoted in Mangold, *Cold Warrior*, 34; Winks, *Cloak and Gown*, 333; "James Jesus Angleton," box 17, folder 7, Richard M. Helms Papers, Part 1, Georgetown University Library Booth Family Center for Special Collections, Washington, DC.

5. Kim Philby, *My Silent War* (New York: Grove Press, 1968), 92. See Winks, *Cloak and Gown*, chap. 5; Ben Macintyre, *A Spy Among Friends: Kim Philby and the Great Betrayal* (New York: Crown Publishers, 2014); Michael Holzman, *Kim and Jim: Philby and Angleton: Friends and Enemies in the Cold War* (London: Weidenfeld & Nicolson, 2021). Winks also explores Angleton's friendships with various French intelligence leaders. See Winks, *Cloak and Gown*, 376–377.

6. Robarge in Hoffman and Ostermann, *Moles, Defectors, and Deceptions*, 93. See also David Robarge, "Moles, Defectors, and Deceptions: James Angleton and CIA Counterintelligence," *Journal of Intelligence History* 3, no. 2 (2003): 28–29.

7. On imperial British intelligence, see Calder Walton, *Empire of Secrets: British Intelligence, the Cold War, and the Twilight of Empire* (London: William Collins, 2013).

8. Philby, *My Silent War*, 98–99. On imperial paranoia see, among others, Patrick A. Kelley, *Imperial Secrets: Remapping the Mind of Empire* (Washington, DC: National Defense Intelligence College, 2008).

9. Alistair Black and Rodney Brunt, "MI5, 1909–1945: An Information Management Perspective," *Journal of Information Science* 26, no. 3 (2000): 185–197; quoted in Holzman, *James Jesus Angleton*, 48–49; Mangold, *Cold Warrior*, 64.

10. *Report to the President by the Commission on CIA Activities Within the United States, 1975* (Rockefeller Commission) (Washington, DC: US Government Printing Office, 1975), chap. 9; Senate Select Committee to Study Governmental Operations with Respect to Intelligence Activities, 1975–76 (Church Committee), *Final Report, S. Rep. No. 94-755*

(1976), Book III, Supplementary Detailed Staff Reports on Intelligence Activities and the Rights of Americans (Washington, DC: US Government Printing Office, 1976), 561–624.

11. Church Committee, *Final Report*, 572. On British mail-opening, see Walton, *Empire of Secrets*, 18.

12. James Angleton, interview by Harrison E. Salisbury, May 27, 1979, 156, "General CIA," Harrison E. Salisbury Papers, Rare Book and Manuscript Library, Columbia University Libraries, New York.

13. On Angleton and the New Criticism, see John Kimsey, "'The Ends of a State': James Angleton, Counterintelligence, and the New Criticism," *The Space Between: Literature and Culture 1914–1945* 13 (2017), https://scalar.usc.edu/works/the-space -between-literature-and-culture-1914-1945/vol13_2017_kimsey.

14. John Hart, "The Monster Plot: Counterintelligence in the Case of Yuriy Ivanovich Nosenko" (1976), 178, www.archives.gov/files/research/jfk/releases/104-10534-10205 .pdf; Mark Riebling, *Wedge: The Secret War Between the FBI and CIA* (New York: Alfred A. Knopf, 1994), 133–134.

15. Peter Wright with Paul Greengrass, *Spycatcher: The Candid Autobiography of a Senior Intelligence Officer* (New York: Viking Penguin, 1987), 174, 308.

16. Cleveland C. Cram, draft review of Edward Jay Epstein, *Deception: The Invisible War Between the KGB and CIA*, no date, copy in possession of William Tyrer. I am very grateful to Mr. Tyrer for allowing me to see this and copies of other documents from the Cram Papers held by the Georgetown University Booth Family Center for Special Collections. This collection is currently closed to researchers "pending review by the CIA."

17. Cram, draft review. The classic account of the "mole hunt" is David Wise, *Molehunt: The Secret Search for Traitors That Shattered the CIA* (New York: Random House, 1992).

18. Wright, *Spycatcher*, 307.

19. See Christopher Moran, *Classified: Secrecy and the State in Modern Britain* (Cambridge: Cambridge University Press, 2013).

20. See Van Gosse, *Where the Boys Are: Cuba, Cold War America and the Making of the American Left* (London: Verso, 1993); Cynthia A. Young, *Soul Power: Culture, Radicalism, and the Making of a U.S. Third World Left* (Durham, NC: Duke University Press, 2006).

21. C. Wright Mills, *Listen, Yankee!: The Revolution in Cuba* (New York: Ballantine Books, 1960), 156–157; FPCC, "Cuba: A Declaration of Conscience by Afro-Americans: Advertisement in the *New York Post*," Apr. 25, 1961, quoted in Van Gosse, *The Movements of the New Left, 1950–1975: A Brief History with Documents* (Boston: Bedford/St. Martin's, 2005), 55–56; Robert E. Light and Carl Marzani, *Cuba Versus CIA* (New York: Marzani & Munsell, 1961). I am grateful to Simon Willmetts for first drawing my attention to the anti-colonial origins of 1960s anti-CIA protest.

22. David Wise and Thomas B. Ross, *The Invisible Government* (New York: Random House, 1964); Kwame Nkrumah, *Neo-Colonialism: The Last Stage of Imperialism* (New York: International Publishers, 1966).

23. Young, *Soul Power*, 3. See Peter Richardson, *A Bomb in Every Issue: How the Short, Unruly Life of* Ramparts *Magazine Changed America* (New York: New Press, 2009).

24. Quoted in Bill Simpich, "Fair Play for Cuba and the Cuban Revolution," *Counterpunch*, July 24, 2009, www.counterpunch.org/2009/07/24fair-play-for-cuba-and-the-cuban -revolution/.

25. Quoted in Angus Mackenzie, *Secrets: The CIA's War at Home* (Berkeley: University of California Press, 1997), 19; "Biographical Sketch," no date, 1.2, Richard Ober Papers, Hoover Institution, Stanford University, Palo Alto, CA.

26. Quoted in Joshua Bloom and Waldo E. Martin Jr., *Black Against Empire: The History and Politics of the Black Panther Party* (Berkeley: University of California Press, 2016), 103. For Merrimac and Resistance, see John Prados, *The Family Jewels: The CIA, Secrecy, and Presidential Power*, updated ed. (Austin: University of Texas Press, 2014), chap 3.

27. Quoted in Church Committee, *Final Report*, 691; Matthew Sweet, *Operation Chaos: The Vietnam Deserters Who Fought the CIA* (New York: Henry Holt, 2018), 91.

28. Oleg Kalugin, *Spymaster: My Thirty-Two Years in Intelligence and Espionage Against the West* (New York: Basic Books, 2009), 45. See Calder Walton, "Spying on Americans: U.S. Intelligence, Race Protests, and Dissident Movements, an Applied History Analysis," *Journal of Applied History* 3, nos. 1–2 (2021): 47–71.

29. Teishan A. Latner, *Cuban Revolution in America: Havana and the Making of a United States Left, 1968–1992* (Chapel Hill: University of North Carolina Press, 2018), 28; Judy Tzu-Chun Wu, *Radicals on the Road: Internationalism, Orientalism, and Feminism During the Vietnam Era* (Ithaca, NY: Cornell University Press, 2013), 108; Sean L. Malloy, *Out of Oakland: Black Panther Party Internationalism During the Cold War* (Ithaca, NY: Cornell University Press, 2017); "RYBAT/MHCHAOS/Transmittal of Contact Report," July 11, 1969, document number 104-10063-10250, CIA Documents: Operation CHAOS, Internet Archive, https://archive.org/details/CIA-Operation-CHAOS/104-10063-10250/.

30. Rockefeller Commission, *Report*, 138.

31. Quoted in Mackenzie, *Secrets*, 34; quoted in Dale M. Brumfield, *Independent Press in D.C. and Virginia: An Underground History* (Charleston, SC: History Press, 2015), 66.

32. Church Committee, *Final Report*, 688; Tom Charles Huston to DDCI, June 20, 1969, 16.9, Ober Papers; quoted in Church Committee, *Final Report*, 700.

33. See, for example, DDP Staff Meeting, Sep. 10, 1969, 17.1, Ober Papers; Frank J. Rafalko, *MH/CHAOS: The CIA's Campaign Against the Radical New Left and the Black Panthers* (Annapolis, MD: Naval Institute Press, 2011), 31; quoted in Church Committee, *Final Report*, 710.

34. "MHCHAOS INDOCTRINATION," no date, 17.2, Ober Papers; Rafalko, *MH/CHAOS*, 58–59, 29, 41; Mackenzie, *Secrets*, 28.

35. Mackenzie, *Secrets*, 36; Brumfield, *Independent Press*, 65; Wu, *Radicals on the Road*, 182; document number 104-10063-10250, Internet Archive; Sweet, *Operation Chaos*.

36. Arthur M. Schlesinger Jr., *The Imperial Presidency* (Boston: Houghton Mifflin, 1973).

37. Riebling, *Wedge*, 260. There were faint echoes here of the discomfort felt by British gentlemen spies around the turn of the twentieth century when expanding government departments began hiring clerical staff from the "lower" orders. Historians have suggested that class-based anxiety about the loyalty of this new breed of civil servant contributed to the creation of Britain's oppressive official secrecy regime. See David Vincent, *The Culture of Secrecy: Britain, 1832–1998* (Oxford: Oxford University Press, 1998).

38. Victor Marchetti, *The Rope-Dancer* (New York: Grosset & Dunlap, 1971).

39. Kaeten Mistry, "The Rise and Fall of Anti-Imperial Whistleblowing in the Long 1970s," in *Whistleblowing Nation: The History of National Security Disclosures and the Cult of State Secrecy*, ed. Kaeten Mistry and Hannah Gurman (New York: Columbia University

Press, 2020), 123–152; quoted in Christopher Moran, *Company Confessions: Secrets, Memoirs, and the CIA* (New York: Thomas Dunne Books, 2015), 114; Jonathan Stevenson, *A Drop of Treason: Philip Agee and His Exposure of the CIA* (Chicago: University of Chicago Press, 2021).

40. Victor Marchetti and John D. Marks, *The CIA and the Cult of Intelligence* (New York: Alfred A. Knopf, 1980). See Moran, *Company Confessions*, chap. 3; Mackenzie, *Secrets*, chap. 3; Prados, *Family Jewels*, chap. 8.

41. Rockefeller Commission, *Report*, 130; Rafalko, *MH/CHAOS*, 60; William V. Broe, Inspector General, to Executive Director-Comptroller [Colby], "MHCHAOS," Nov. 9, 1972, 17.4–5, Ober Papers; quoted in Rafalko, *MH/CHAOS*, 217.

42. Quoted in Wise, *Molehunt*, 41.

43. Quoted in Rockefeller Commission, *Report*, 147.

44. Quoted in John Prados, *The Ghosts of Langley: Into the CIA's Heart of Darkness* (New York: New Press, 2017), 272; Rafalko, *MH/CHAOS*, 13. Most HTLINGUAL records were destroyed later, in 1990.

45. Harold P. Ford, *William E. Colby as Director of Central Intelligence, 1973–1976* (Washington, DC: History Staff, Center for the Study of Intelligence, 1993), 88–89.

46. On the Hersh story, see Kathryn S. Olmsted, *Challenging the Secret Government: The Post-Watergate Investigations of the CIA and FBI* (Chapel Hill: University of North Carolina Press, 1996), chap. 2.

47. Quoted in Holzman, *James Jesus Angleton*, 295–296.

48. Philip Agee, *Inside the Company: CIA Diary* (New York: Bantam Books, 1976).

49. Quoted in Rhodri Jeffreys-Jones, *Cloak and Dollar: A History of American Secret Intelligence*, 2nd ed. (New Haven, CT: Yale University Press, 2003), 207; quoted in Olmsted, *Challenging Secret Government*, 142; Morley, *The Ghost*, 253; Church Committee, *Final Report*, 72.

50. Mangold, *Cold Warrior*, 306; Hart, "Monster Plot," 180.

51. Ober, "Appeal of Proposed Separation," no date, 1.9, Ober Papers; Ober, untitled document, no date, 1.10, Ober Papers.

52. James Angleton to Cord Meyer, Apr. 28, 1975, 2.5, Cord Meyer Jr. Papers, Library of Congress, Washington, DC.

53. Tom Griffin, *State-Private Networks and Intelligence Theory: From Cold War Liberalism to Neoconservatism* (London: Routledge, 2022), 117; James Angleton, interview by Harrison E. Salisbury, Dec. 8, 1978, 156, General CIA, Salisbury Papers.

54. Report by the Former Chief of the Counterintelligence Staff, Central Intelligence Agency (Angleton) to the Commission on CIA Activities Within the United States, Washington, no date, *Foreign Relations of the United States, 1969–1976*, Vol. 38, Part 2, *Organization and Management of Foreign Policy; Public Diplomacy, 1973–1976*, Document 41, https://history.state.gov/historicaldocuments/frus1969-76v38p2/d41; Church Committee, *Final Report*, 75. There is evidence suggesting that Angleton was temporarily rehired by the CIA during the Year of Intelligence for purposes unknown. See Emma North-Best, "The Mystery of Disgraced CIA Spymaster James Angleton's 'Retirement,'" *MuckRock*, Oct. 19, 2017, www.muckrock.com/news/archives/2017/oct/19/angleton-return/. In a January 1975 letter to Cord Meyer, Angleton mentioned that he would "stay on to help on the transition." James Angleton to Cord Meyer, Jan. 26, 1975, 2.5, Meyer Papers.

55. Quoted in Griffin, *State-Private Networks*, 100; Emma North-Best, "James Angleton and the Author of Report That 'Debunked' His Work Agreed on One Thing," *MuckRock*, Oct. 20, 2017, www.muckrock.com/news/archives/2017/oct/20/angleton-monster-plot/. Hard-line intelligence and counterintelligence officials in Britain had a similar set of experiences in the 1970s. Displaced from government employment in agencies such as the Foreign Office's Information Research Department, they too clustered around private right-wing think tanks, chiefly in their case the Institute for the Study of Conflict. Griffin, *State-Private Networks*, is an excellent account of these developments.

56. Quoted in Moran, *Company Confessions*, 122; James Angleton to Cord Meyer, 2.7, Dec. 1, 1980, Meyer Papers; Frank Snepp, *Decent Interval* (New York: Random House, 1977).

57. See Kaeten Mistry, "A Transnational Protest Against the National Security State: Whistle-Blowing, Philip Agee, and Networks of Dissent," *Journal of American History* 106, no. 2 (2019): 362–389; Stevenson, *Drop of Treason*, 182; John Stockwell, *In Search of Enemies: A CIA Story* (New York: W. W. Norton, 1978).

58. Quoted in Mistry, "Transnational Protest," 383; Hannah Gurman, "Unfit to Print: The Press and the Contragate Whistleblowers," in *Whistleblowing Nation*, ed. Mistry and Gurman, 271–296; Greg Grandin, *Empire's Workshop: Latin America, the United States, and the Rise of the New Imperialism* (New York: Henry Holt, 2006), 138.

59. Griffin, *State-Private Networks*, 159; quoted in Emma North-Best, "Even Mandatory Retirement Couldn't Stop Spymaster James Angleton's Influence," *MuckRock*, Feb. 21, 2017, www.muckrock.com/news/archives/2017/feb/21/even-mandatory-retirement-couldnt-stop-spymaster-j/. The Angletonian revival of the 1980s was reflected in spy fiction: the best-selling novels of Tom Clancy, which represented the genre's return to Kiplingesque, imperial romance after the realist turn associated with John le Carré, constantly expressed suspicion of Soviet strategic deception. As ever, fiction influenced reality: Clancy's novels reportedly helped shape Ronald Reagan's foreign policy. See Penny Von Eschen, "Imperial Visions of the World," in *The Cambridge History of America and the World, Volume IV: 1945 to the Present*, ed. David C. Engerman et al. (Cambridge: Cambridge University Press, 2022), 315.

Chapter 5

1. Cord Meyer, *Facing Reality: From World Federalism to the CIA* (New York: Harper & Row, 1980); "A Hidden Liberal: Cord Meyer Jr.," *New York Times*, Mar. 30, 1967, 30; Cord Meyer, Personal History Statement, Mar. 27, 1951, box 5, folder 10, Cord Meyer Jr. Papers, Library of Congress, Washington, DC.

2. Cord Meyer Jr., "A Serviceman Looks at the Peace," *Atlantic Monthly* 176, no. 3 (Sep. 1945): 1–6; "Young Men Who Care," *Glamour*, July 1947, 27; Merle Miller quoted in Miller, "One Man's Journey—From a One-World Crusade to the 'Department of Dirty Tricks,'" *New York Times*, Jan. 7, 1973, 9. On world federalism, see Fritz Bartel, "Surviving the Years of Grace: The Atomic Bomb and the Specter of World Government, 1945–1950," *Diplomatic History* 39, no. 2 (2015): 275–302.

3. Meyer, *Facing Reality*, 50; Myron C. Fagan, *Reds Behind World Federalism*, Aug. 1949, 7.5, Meyer Papers. On the AVC, see Ángel Alcalde, "War Veterans, International Politics, and the Early Cold War, 1945–50," *Cold War History* 18, no. 4 (2018): 409–427.

4. Meyer, "Serviceman Looks at Peace," 6; Cord Meyer, Journal, Nov. 12, 1945, 5.4, Meyer Papers.

5. Meyer, Journal, Jan. 3, 1950; May 24, 1951; Meyer, *Facing Reality*, 64–65.

6. Quoted in Yale Class of 1943, 25th Reunion Book, 1.10, Meyer Papers.

7. See Christopher Moran, *Company Confessions: Secrets, Memoirs, and the CIA* (New York: Thomas Dunne Books, 2015), 57–73; Simon Willmetts, *In Secrecy's Shadow: The OSS and CIA in Hollywood Cinema, 1941–1979* (Edinburgh: Edinburgh University Press, 2016), chap. 2.

8. Moran, *Company Confessions*, 73–88; Willmetts, *In Secrecy's Shadow*, 159–163; quoted in David Shamus McCarthy, *Selling the CIA: Public Relations and the Culture of Secrecy* (Lawrence: University of Kansas Press, 2018), 18; quoted in Kathryn J. McGarr, *City of Newsmen: Public Lies and Professional Secrets in Cold War Washington* (Chicago: University of Chicago Press, 2022), 199. On the CIA's episodic relationship with Hollywood, see Willmetts, *In Secrecy's Shadow*.

9. Robert Amory, interview by Harrison Salisbury, July 19, 1979, 156, "General CIA," Harrison E. Salisbury Papers, Rare Book and Manuscript Library, Columbia University Libraries, New York; quoted in Carl Bernstein, "The CIA and the Media," *Rolling Stone*, Oct. 20, 1977, 57; Harrison E. Salisbury, *Without Fear or Favor: The New York Times and Its Times* (New York: Times Books, 1980), 497; Amory interview.

10. Gregg Herken, *The Georgetown Set* (New York: Alfred A. Knopf, 2014), 166; quoted in Senior Staff Meeting minutes, May 1, 1955, CIA Records Search Tool (CREST).

11. Quoted in Herken, *Georgetown Set*, 228. For journalists' skepticism about news management, see McGarr, *City of Newsmen*.

12. Quoted in Evan Thomas, *The Very Best Men: Four Who Dared: The Early Years of the CIA* (New York: Simon & Schuster, 1995), 63. For an excellent history of CIA relations with the press, see David P. Hadley, *The Rising Clamor: The American Press, the Central Intelligence Agency, and the Cold War* (Lexington: University Press of Kentucky, 2019). On the Continental Press, see Steven T. Usdin, *Bureau of Spies: The Secret Connections Between Espionage and Journalism in Washington* (Amherst, NY: Prometheus Books, 2018), chap. 15.

13. Quoted in Hadley, *Rising Clamor*, 48; quoted in Herken, *Georgetown Set*, 178; Hadley, *Rising Clamor*, 52.

14. James B. Reston to Robert E. Garst, Aug. 10, 1956, James B. Reston Papers, University of Illinois Archives, https://digital.library.illinois.edu/items/aa433ce0-6478-0134-1dda-0050569601ca-e; Salisbury, *Without Fear or Favor*, 479; Deputies Meeting minutes, Apr. 16, 1953, CREST; Richard Bissell, interview by Harrison Salisbury, May 11, 1979, 156, "General CIA," Salisbury Papers.

15. Quoted in Richard H. Immerman, *The CIA in Guatemala: The Foreign Policy of Intervention* (Austin: University of Texas Press, 1982), 181; quoted in Hadley, *Rising Clamor*, 61.

16. See Rory Cormac, "British 'Black' Productions: Forgeries, Front Groups, and Propaganda, 1951–1977," *Journal of Cold War Studies* 24, no. 3 (2022): 4-42; Jamie Doward, "Sex, Ska and Malcolm X: MI6's Covert 1960s Mission to Woo West Indians," *The Guardian*, Jan. 26, 2019, www.theguardian.com/world/2019/jan/26/west-indiansflamingo-magazine-m6-anti-communist-mission.

17. Alcalde, "War Veterans," 417–425; Gilbert Harrison, *Parts of a Past* (New York: iUniverse, 2009), chap. 8.

18. Hugh Wilford, *The Mighty Wurlitzer: How the CIA Played America* (Cambridge, MA: Harvard University Press, 2008); Karen M. Paget, *Patriotic Betrayal: The Inside Story of the CIA's Secret Campaign to Enroll American Students in the Crusade Against Communism*

(New Haven, CT: Yale University Press, 2015); Anthony Carew, *American Labour's Cold War Abroad: From Deep Freeze to Detente, 1945–1970* (Edmonton, AB: Athabasca University Press, 2018); Patrick Iber, *Neither Peace nor Freedom: The Cultural Cold War in Latin America* (Cambridge, MA: Harvard University Press, 2015).

19. Thomas W. Braden, "I'm Glad the CIA Is 'Immoral,'" *Saturday Evening Post*, May 20, 1967, 10.

20. Meyer, *Facing Reality*, chap. 4; Wayne G. Jackson, *Allen Welsh Dulles as Director of Central Intelligence, 26 February 1953–29 November 1961, Volume I: Allen Dulles, the Man* (Washington, DC: Historical Staff, Central Intelligence Agency, 1973), 60; Cord Meyer, "A Question of Innocence," 6.5, Meyer Papers.

21. Quoted in Adekeye Adebajo, "Wole Soyinka vs Caroline Davis—The CIA Controversy," *Johannesburg Review of Books*, May 2, 2022, https://johannesburgreviewofbooks.com/2022/05/02/wole-soyinka-vs-caroline-davis-the-cia-controversy-by-adekeye-adebajo/. The works that offended Soyinka are Caroline Davis, *African Literature and the CIA: Networks of Authorship and Publishing* (Cambridge: Cambridge University Press, 2021), and Juliana Spahr, *Du Bois's Telegram: Literary Resistance and State Containment* (Cambridge, MA: Harvard University Press, 2018).

22. William Eddy to Cornelius Van H. Engert, Dec. 29, 1950, uncataloged box, Postwar Correspondence and MSS, folder 1950–51, Cornelius Van H. Engert Papers, Special Collections, Georgetown University Library, Washington, DC; "American Friends of the Middle East: Second Meeting of the Charter Members," Dec. 12, 1951, 2.13, Dorothy Thompson Papers, Special Collections Research Center, Syracuse University Library, Syracuse, NY.

23. Michael Warner, *Hearts and Minds: Three Case Studies of the CIA's Covert Support of American Anti-Communist Groups in the Cold War, 1949–1967* (Washington, DC: Center for the Study of Intelligence, 1999), 140; Elmer Berger to George Levison, Dec. 20, 1951, 75.1, American Council for Judaism Papers, Wisconsin Historical Society, Madison, WI. See Hugh Wilford, "American Friends of the Middle East: The CIA, U.S. Citizens, and the Battle for American Public Opinion in the Arab-Israeli Conflict, 1947–1967," *Journal of American Studies* 51, no. 1 (2017): 93–116.

24. "Egypt: The Revolutionary," *Time*, Sep. 26, 1955, 25–28; Gamal Abdel Nasser, *Egypt's Liberation: The Philosophy of the Revolution* (Washington, DC: Public Affairs Press, 1955); State to Damascus, "AFME Views on Arab-Israel Problem," Jan. 11, 1956, 684A.86/1-1156, RG 59, NARA.

25. Quoted in Justin Simundson, "Propaganda Images and Manufacturing Consent in 'Free' Vietnam, 1950–1963," PhD diss., Texas Tech University, 2017, 202. On AFV, see Joseph G. Morgan, *The Vietnam Lobby: The American Friends of Vietnam, 1955–1975* (Chapel Hill: University of North Carolina Press, 1997); Eric Thomas Chester, *Covert Network: Progressives, the International Rescue Committee, and the CIA* (New York: M. E. Sharpe, 1995), chap. 13.

26. Simundson, "Propaganda Images," 201; quoted in Morgan, *Vietnam Lobby*, 154.

27. Thomas L. Ahern Jr., *CIA and the House of Ngo: Covert Action in South Vietnam, 1954–1963* (Washington, DC: Center for the Study of Intelligence, 2000), 75.

28. James T. Fisher, *Dr. America: The Lives of Thomas A. Dooley, 1927–1961* (Amherst: University of Massachusetts Press, 1997); quoted in Edward F. Palm, *An American Pie: Lansdale, Lederer, Dooley, and Modern Memory* (Las Vegas, NV: CreateSpace Publishing, 2013), 20, 22.

29. Jonathan Nashel, *Edward Lansdale's Cold War* (Amherst: University of Massachusetts Press, 2005), 54–55.

30. Quoted in Simundson, "Propaganda Images," 271; Edward Lansdale to Ngo Dinh Diem, Oct. 28, 39.1052, Edward Geary Lansdale Papers, Hoover Institution, Stanford University, Palo Alto, CA; Wilford, *Mighty Wurlitzer*, 178. See also Nashel, *Edward Lansdale's Cold War*, 163–173; Willmetts, *In Secrecy's Shadow*, 142–159. Willmetts stresses the proactive role of Mankiewicz in changing the story for the screen but acknowledges Lansdale's contribution to the production and promotion of the movie.

31. See Hugh Wilford, "The American Society of African Culture: The CIA and Transnational Networks of African Diaspora Intellectuals in the Cold War," in *Transnational Anti-Communism and the Cold War: Agents, Activities, and Networks*, ed. Luc van Dongen, Stéphanie Roulin, and Giles Scott-Smith (New York: Palgrave Macmillan, 2014), 23–34.

32. Mary Helen Washington, *The Other Blacklist: The African American Literary and Cultural Left of the 1950s* (New York: Columbia University Press, 2014), 260–264.

33. Quoted in Lonneke Geerlings, "Performances in the Theatre of the Cold War: The American Society of African Culture and the 1961 Lagos Festival," *Journal of Transatlantic Studies* 16, no. 1 (2018): 15.

34. Quoted in "Hidden Liberal."

35. Quoted in Morgan, *Vietnam Lobby*, 155; Robert Scheer and Warren Hinckle, "The Vietnam Lobby," *Ramparts*, July 1965, 16–24.

36. Quoted in Salisbury, *Without Fear or Favor*, 159. On Szulc, see Richard J. Aldrich, "American Journalism and the Landscape of Secrecy: Tad Szulc, the CIA, and Cuba," *History* 100, no. 2 (2015): 189–209; on Brewer, see Salisbury, *Without Fear or Favor*, 503–508; on MOCKINGBIRD, see Usdin, *Bureau of Spies*, chap. 16.

37. David Robarge, *John McCone as Director of Central Intelligence, 1961–1965* (Washington, DC: Center for the Study of Intelligence, 2005), 385; Herken, *Georgetown Set*, 306–310; Emma North-Best, "Memo Offers a Look into the CIA's Private Press Pool," *MuckRock*, Feb. 15, 2017, www.muckrock.com/news/archives/2017/feb/15/memo-offers-look-cias-private-press-pool/; Simon Willmetts, "The Burgeoning Fissures of Dissent: Allen Dulles and the Selling of the CIA in the Aftermath of the Bay of Pigs," *History* 100, no. 2 (2015): 167–188.

38. P. Braestrup to Tom Wicker, Oct. 10, 1965, 159, "CIA Series," Salisbury Papers; Salisbury, *Without Fear or Favor*, 519.

39. Sol Stern, "A Short Account of International Student Politics with Particular Reference to the NSA, CIA, Etc.," *Ramparts*, Mar. 1967, 29–38. See Paget, *Patriotic Betrayal*, chap. 23; Robarge, *John McCone*, 306–309.

40. Quoted in Wilford, *Mighty Wurlitzer*, 241; quoted in Rhodri Jeffreys-Jones, *The CIA and American Democracy*, 3rd ed. (New Haven, CT: Yale University Press, 1989), 162.

41. Michael Warner, "Sophisticated Spies: CIA's Links to Liberal Anti-Communists, 1949–67," *International Journal of Intelligence and Counterintelligence* 9, no. 4 (1996): 426.

42. Meyer, *Facing Reality*, 90; Citation, Distinguished Intelligence Medal, no date, 6.10, Meyer Papers; quoted in Miller, "One Man's Journey," 70.

43. Meyer, *Facing Reality*, 168–172, 221.

44. On Meyer's family troubles, see, for example, Mark and Quentin Meyer to Cord Meyer, May 18, 1971, 2.1, Meyer Papers; quoted in Meyer, *Facing Reality*, 280.

45. Quoted in McCarthy, *Selling the CIA*, 22. For more on Colby's role, see M. Todd Bennett, *Neither Confirm nor Deny: How the Glomar Mission Shielded the CIA from Transparency* (New York: Columbia University Press, 2023), esp. chaps. 8–9.

46. "From Phillips for All Personnel," May 1975, 1, General Correspondence, 1929–85, David Atlee Phillips Papers, Library of Congress, Washington, DC; David Atlee Phillips, *The Night Watch* (New York: Atheneum, 1977), 271. See also Moran, *Company Confessions*, 148–160; McCarthy, *Selling the CIA*, chap. 1.

47. Biographical Profile, Fall 1982, I:1.1, Ray S. Cline Papers, Library of Congress, Washington, DC; quoted in McCarthy, *Selling the CIA*, 25; Cord Meyer to Ray Cline, July 17, 1974, I:1.7, Cline Papers.

48. McCarthy, *Selling the CIA*, 39. See ibid., chap. 2; and Moran, *Company Confessions*, 160–178.

49. Julian S. Bach Jr. to Cord Meyer, Apr. 6, 1967, 1.9, Meyer Papers; Meyer, *Facing Reality*, xi–xii; Erwin A. Glikes to Cord Meyer, June 6, 1977, 2.7, Meyer Papers.

50. Quoted in Burton Hersh, *The Old Boys: The American Elite and the Origins of the CIA* (St. Petersburg, FL: Tree Farm Books, 2002), 333; Meyer, *Facing Reality*, 166; see, for example, Godfrey Hodgson, "Cord Meyer: Superspook," in *Dirty Work: The CIA in Western Europe*, ed. Philip Agee and Louis Wolf (Secaucus, NJ: L. Stuart, 1978), 61.

51. Thomas Powers, "The Young Man Who Grew Old," *New York Times*, Oct. 26, 1980, A.11, 34.

52. Quoted in Moran, *Company Confessions*, 177.

53. Quoted in Robert Parry, *Lost History: Contras, Cocaine, the Press and "Project Truth"* (Arlington, VA: Media Consortium, 1999), 49. My account of Raymond's campaign is indebted to Robert Parry's pathbreaking research.

54. Greg Grandin, *Empire's Workshop: Latin America, the United States, and the Rise of the New Imperialism* (New York: Henry Holt, 2006), 126.

55. Otto Reich quoted in Document 1, "Public Diplomacy and Covert Propaganda: The Declassified Record of Ambassador Otto Juan Reich," ed. Thomas Blanton, National Security Archive Briefing Book #40, Mar. 2, 2001, https://nsarchive2.gwu.edu/NSAEBB/NSAEBB40/; Grandin, *Empire's Workshop*, 124.

56. Quoted in Document 3, Blanton, "Public Diplomacy and Covert Propaganda"; "Talking Points on Public Diplomacy," Apr. 1, 1986, RAC box 4, folder CENTAM Meetings (4/01/1986–4/07/1986), Walter Raymond Jr. Papers, Ronald Reagan Presidential Library, Simi Valley, CA. For more on the S/LPD, see Robert Parry and Peter Kornbluh, "Iran-Contra's Untold Story," *Foreign Policy* 72 (Autumn 1988): 3–30.

57. Quoted in Parry and Kornbluh, "Iran-Contra's Untold Story," 19–20.

Chapter 6

1. A sign by the front door of 54 Broadway read "Minimax Fire Extinguisher Company." Luke Jones, "The Time When Spy Agencies Officially Didn't Exist," BBC News, Nov. 8, 2014, www.bbc.com/news/magazine-29938135.

2. Trevor Paglen, *Blank Spots on the Map: The Dark Geography of the Pentagon's Secret World* (New York: Penguin, 2009), 170.

3. Andrew Friedman, *Covert Capital: Landscapes of Denial and the Making of U.S. Empire in the Suburbs of Northern Virginia* (Berkeley: University of California Press, 2013). My analysis here is indebted to Friedman's outstanding scholarship.

4. Quoted in Deborah Shnookal, *Operation Pedro Pan and the Exodus of Cuba's Children* (Gainesville: University Press of Florida, 2020), 187.

5. Don Bohning, *The Castro Obsession: U.S. Covert Operations Against Cuba, 1959–1965* (Washington, DC: Potomac Books, 2005), 1; quoted in ibid., 130; quoted in ibid., 134. See also Steven Hach, *Cold War in South Florida: Historic Resource Study* (ed. Jennifer Dickey), National Park Service Southeast Regional Office, US Department of the Interior, Oct. 2004.

6. T. D. Allman, *Finding Florida: The True History of the Sunshine State* (New York: Atlantic Monthly Press, 2013), 346–348.

7. On Cuban émigré terrorism, see Hideaki Kami, *Diplomacy Meets Migration: U.S. Relations with Cuba During the Cold War* (Cambridge: Cambridge University Press, 2018), chap. 2.

8. Friedman, *Covert Capital*, chap. 4.

9. Ibid., chap. 5, 271.

10. Greg Miller, "CIA Looks to Los Angeles for Would-Be Iranian Spies," *Los Angeles Times*, Jan. 15, 2002, www.latimes.com/archives/la-xpm-2002-jan-15-mn-22685-story.html; Phuong Tran Nguyen, *Becoming Refugee American: The Politics of Rescue in Little Saigon* (Urbana: University of Illinois Press, 2017); Viet Thanh Nguyen, *The Sympathizer* (New York: Grove Press, 2015).

11. See Steven Dudley, *MS-13: The Making of America's Most Notorious Gang* (New York: Hanover Square Press, 2020).

12. See Kyle Burke, *Revolutionaries for the Right: Anticommunist Internationalism and Paramilitary Warfare in the Cold War* (Chapel Hill: University of North Carolina Press, 2018).

13. Quoted in Ian Sanjay Patel, *We're Here Because You Were There: Immigration and the End of Empire* (London: Verso, 2021), 1.

14. Edward Lansdale, "The Challenge of Subversive Insurgency," speech, Michigan State University, Feb. 29, 1964, 74, Edward Geary Lansdale Papers, Hoover Institution, Stanford University, Palo Alto, CA.

15. Quoted in Eric Scigliano, "The University That Launched a CIA Front Operation in Vietnam," *Politico*, Mar. 25, 2018, www.politico.com/magazine/story/2018/03/25/vietnam-war-secret-msu-michigan-state-217705/. See Nils Gilman, "The Cold War as Intellectual Force Field," *Modern Intellectual History* 13, no. 2 (2016): 507–523.

16. Bruce Cumings, "Boundary Displacement: Area Studies and International Studies During and After the Cold War," *Bulletin of Concerned Asian Scholars* 29, no. 1 (1997): 6–26; David C. Engerman, *Know Your Enemy: The Rise and Fall of America's Soviet Experts* (Oxford: Oxford University Press, 2009).

17. Osamah F. Khalil, *America's Dream Palace: Middle East Expertise and the Rise of the National Security State* (Cambridge, MA: Harvard University Press, 2016).

18. Quoted in Michael C. Desch, *Cult of the Irrelevant: The Waning Influence of Social Science on National Security* (Princeton, NJ: Princeton University Press, 2019), 92.

19. David H. Price, *Cold War Anthropology: The CIA, the Pentagon, and the Growth of Dual Use Anthropology* (Durham, NC: Duke University Press, 2016), 94; quoted in ibid., 95; see also Benjamin Breen, *Tripping on Utopia: Margaret Mead, the Cold War, and the Troubled Birth of Psychedelic Science* (New York: Grand Central Publishing, 2024).

20. See Robin Winks, *Cloak and Gown: Scholars in the Secret War, 1939–1961*, 2nd ed. (New Haven, CT: Yale University Press, 1996), 495–498; Eric Bennett, *Workshops of*

Empire: Stegner, Engle, and American Creative Writing During the Cold War (Iowa City: University of Iowa Press, 2015).

21. There are several studies of this subject. John D. Marks blazed the trail with *The Search for the "Manchurian Candidate": The CIA and Mind Control* (New York: Times Books, 1979). More recently, two outstanding works have placed the CIA's psychology experiments within the longer history of American torture: Alfred W. McCoy, *Torture and Impunity: The U.S. Doctrine of Coercive Interrogation* (Madison: University of Wisconsin Press, 2012), and W. Fitzhugh Brundage, *Civilizing Torture: An American Tradition* (Cambridge, MA: Harvard University Press, 2018). For an account emphasizing the mutually reinforcing relationship between Cold War fantasies about "brainwashing" and Agency mind-control research, see Timothy Melley, *Covert Sphere: Secrecy, Fiction, and the National Security State* (Ithaca, NY: Cornell University Press, 2012), chap. 1.

22. Sidney Gottlieb would later supply the native African poisons intended for use in the assassination plot against Patrice Lumumba. For an excellent biography of Gottlieb, see Stephen Kinzer, *Poisoner in Chief: Sidney Gottlieb and the CIA Search for Mind Control* (New York: Henry Holt, 2019).

23. Michael Otterman, *American Torture: From the Cold War to Abu Ghraib and Beyond* (London: Pluto Press, 2007), 24.

24. Kinzer, *Poisoner in Chief*, chaps. 7–8.

25. Quoted in ibid., 117.

26. Ibid., chap. 11; Breen, *Tripping on Utopia*, chap. 18.

27. McCoy, *Torture and Impunity*, chaps. 3–4.

28. Quoted in William Rosenau, "'Our Ghettos, Too, Need a Lansdale': American Counter-Insurgency Abroad and at Home in the Vietnam Era," in *The New Counter-Insurgency Era in Critical Perspective*, ed. C. W. Gventer et al. (London: Palgrave Macmillan, 2014), 113, 111; quoted in Stuart Schrader, *Badges Without Borders: How Global Counterinsurgency Transformed American Policing* (Berkeley: University of California Press, 2019), 116, 117; Schrader, *Badges Without Borders*, 221; F. P. Bishop, Inspector, [], Memorandum for the Record, "Interview with [], Office of Security," May 31, 1973, 649, "Family Jewels," www.cia.gov/readingroom/docs/DOC_0001451843.pdf. See also Julian Go, *Policing Empires: Militarization, Race, and the Imperial Boomerang in Britain and the US* (New York: Oxford University Press, 2024), chap. 5.

29. Daniel Golden, *Spy Schools: How the CIA, FBI, and Foreign Intelligence Secretly Exploit America's Universities* (New York: Henry Holt, 2017), 169.

30. Quoted in Joseph G. Morgan, *Wesley Fishel and Vietnam: A Great and Tragic American Experiment* (Lanham, MD: Lexington Books, 2021), 144, 146.

31. Wilbur Crane Eveland, *Ropes of Sand: America's Failure in the Middle East* (New York: W. W. Norton, 1980), 246; Jonathan Nashel, *Edward Lansdale's Cold War* (Amherst: University of Massachusetts Press, 2005), 195.

32. Richard Hofstadter, *The Paranoid Style in American Politics and Other Essays* (New York: Alfred A. Knopf, 1965).

33. The argument here is influenced by two important works: Kathryn S. Olmsted, *Real Enemies: Conspiracy Theories and American Democracy, World War I to 9/11*, 10th Anniversary Edition (New York: Oxford University Press, 2019); Melley, *Covert Sphere*.

34. Deborah Davis, *Katharine the Great: Katharine Graham and* The Washington Post (New York: Harcourt Brace Jovanovich, 1979).

35. Quoted in Eve Pell, "Killing 'Katharine the Great,'" *The Nation*, Nov. 12, 1983, 464.

36. On the draft resisters and LaRouche, see Matthew Sweet, *Operation Chaos: The Vietnam Deserters Who Fought the CIA* (New York: Henry Holt, 2018); on Manson, see Tom O'Neill, *Chaos: Charles Manson, the CIA, and the Secret History of the Sixties* (New York: Little, Brown, 2019). In 2017, the CIA added further fuel to such speculation when it declassified records relating to Project Star Gate, a research program investigating the intelligence applications of extrasensory perception undertaken at a Bay Area CIA laboratory during the 1970s. See Annie Jacobsen, *Phenomena: The Secret History of the U.S. Government's Investigations into Extrasensory Perception and Psychokinesis* (New York: Little, Brown, 2017).

37. Quoted in Olmsted, *Real Enemies*, 189, 188. For more on the Contra-run drug network, see Alfred W. McCoy, *In the Shadows of the American Century: The Rise and Decline of U.S. Global Power* (Chicago: Haymarket, 2017), 86–91. One poll found that 12 percent of African Americans also believed that the CIA created the human immunodeficiency virus (HIV) to wipe out Blacks and homosexuals. Lindsay A. O'Rourke, *Covert Regime Change: America's Secret Cold War* (Ithaca, NY: Cornell University Press, 2018), 227.

38. Quoted in Peter Knight, *The Kennedy Assassination* (Edinburgh: Edinburgh University Press, 2007), 43. For a recent discussion of the commission's failure to investigate the Cuban possibility, see James H. Johnston, *Murder, Inc.: The CIA Under John F. Kennedy* (Lincoln, NE: Potomac Books, 2019).

39. Quoted in Knight, *Kennedy Assassination*, 65; quoted in Susan Williams, *White Malice: The CIA and the Covert Recolonization of Africa* (New York: PublicAffairs, 2021), 487; quoted in Olmsted, *Real Enemies*, 137.

40. Quoted in Olmsted, *Real Enemies*, 137. On Lane, see David Talbot, *The Devil's Chessboard: Allen Dulles, the CIA, and the Rise of America's Secret Government* (New York: HarperCollins, 2016), 594–595.

41. Quoted in Olmsted, *Real Enemies*, 141. See Alecia P. Long, *Cruising for Conspirators: How a New Orleans DA Prosecuted the Kennedy Assassination as a Sex Crime* (Chapel Hill: University of North Carolina Press, 2021).

42. Clay Shaw, it later emerged, had earlier had some contact with the Agency, but probably none of it related to the assassination. See Rex Bradford, "The CIA and the JFK Assassination," Mary Ferrell Foundation, May 2019, www.maryferrell.org/pages/The_CIA _and_the_JFK_Assassination.html.

43. David Atlee Phillips, "The Man Nobody Bothered to Call," *Columbia Journalism Review* 25, no. 5 (1987): 31.

44. David Atlee Phillips, "A Statement," May 20, 1980, 1, Kennedy, John F., Assassination, Articles, Phillips Papers.

45. Phillips, "Man Nobody Bothered to Call."

46. Bill Gertz, "Ex-CIA Agent Thinks Libel Award Will End Accusations in JFK Death," *Washington Times*, Nov. 4, 1986, 5A; Joseph Goulden to David Atlee Phillips, Sep. 16, 1981, 5, Correspondence with Joseph Goulden, 1981, Phillips Papers; quoted in Knight, *Kennedy Assassination*, 93.

47. Bernie Ward and Granville Toogood, "Former Vice President of *Washington Post* Reveals JFK 2 Year White House Romance," *National Enquirer*, Mar. 2, 1976, 4; Timothy Leary, *Flashbacks* (London: Heinemann, 1983), 129, 194; Benjamin C. Bradlee, *A Good Life: Newspapering and Other Adventures* (New York: Simon & Schuster, 1995), 265–271.

48.   Peter Janney, *Mary's Mosaic: The CIA Conspiracy to Murder John F. Kennedy, Mary Pinchot Meyer, and Their Vision for World Peace*, 3rd ed. (New York: Skyhorse Publishing, 2016). See Nina Burleigh, "The Mysterious Murder of Mary Pinchot Meyer—Revisited," *Daily Beast*, Apr. 2, 2012 (updated Jul. 13, 2017), www.thedailybeast.com /the-mysterious-murder-of-mary-pinchot-meyerrevisited.

49.   Quoted in Mark Shanahan, "JFK Love Letter to His Alleged Mistress Sells for Big Money," *Boston Globe*, June 24, 2016, www.bostonglobe.com/lifestyle/names/2016/06/24 /jfk-love-letter-sells-for-big-money/eEXTw3JN7Qi9CIDhGdtwtM/story.html.

50.   Quoted in Jefferson Morley, *The Ghost: The Secret Life of CIA Spymaster James Jesus Angleton* (New York: St. Martin's Press, 2017), 168; quoted in C. David Heymann, *The Georgetown Ladies' Social Club: Power, Passion, and Politics in the Nation's Capital* (New York: Atria Books, 2003), 168.

51.   Morley, *The Ghost*, 265.

52.   For a riposte to Morley, see Thomas Powers, "The Monster Plot," *London Review of Books* 40, no. 9 (May 10, 2018), www.lrb.co.uk/the-paper/v40/n09/thomas-powers /the-monster-plot.

53.   See Nashel, *Edward Lansdale's Cold War*, 201–203; Max Boot, *The Road Not Taken: Edward Lansdale and the American Tragedy in Vietnam* (New York: Liveright, 2018), 420–423. For a thorough rebuttal of the Prouty JFK-Lansdale thesis, see Michel Jacques Gagné, *Thinking Critically About the Kennedy Assassination: Debunking the Myths and Conspiracy Theories* (London: Routledge, 2022), 251–253.

Epilogue

1.   Quoted in Chris Whipple, *The Spymasters: How the CIA Directors Shape History and the Future* (New York: Scribner, 2020), 195.

2.   Quoted in ibid., 302; quoted in John Prados, "The Misleading Rationales for Gina Haspel's Nomination as CIA Director," History News Network, May 13, 2018, https:// historynewsnetwork.org/article/169013.

3.   Quoted in Whipple, *Spymasters*, 303.

4.   For an excellent narrative of the post-9/11 history of the CIA, see Rhodri Jeffreys-Jones, *A Question of Standing: The History of the CIA* (Oxford: Oxford University Press, 2022).

5.   Quoted in "Transcript of President Bush's Address: September 20, 2001," CNN Politics, www.cnn.com/specials/politics/bush-transcript-september-2001. The "clash of civilizations" thesis was originally expounded by Harvard political scientist Samuel P. Huntington. See his *The Clash of Civilizations and the Remaking of World Order* (New York: Simon & Schuster, 1996).

6.   See Ussama Makdisi, "'Anti-Americanism' in the Arab World: An Interpretation of a Brief History," *Journal of American History* 89, no. 2 (2002): 538–557.

7.   See Lawrence Wright, *The Looming Tower: Al-Qaeda's Road to 9/11* (New York: Alfred A. Knopf, 2006). On British backing of Islamic fundamentalists, see Robert Dreyfuss, *Devil's Game: How the United States Helped Islamic Fundamentalism* (New York: Metropolitan Books/Henry Holt, 2005), chaps. 1–2. MI6 also ran operations supplying anti-Soviet Afghan rebels during the 1980s. See Michael Smith, *The Real Special Relationship: The True Story of How MI6 and the CIA Work Together* (New York: Arcade, 2023), 424–427.

8. Patrick Williams, "*Kim* and Orientalism," in Rudyard Kipling, *Kim: Authoritative Text, Backgrounds, Criticism*, ed. Zohreh T. Sullivan (New York: W. W. Norton, 2002), 416. See Milo Jones and Philippe Silberzahn, *Constructing Cassandra: Reframing Intelligence Failure at the CIA, 1947–2001* (Stanford, CA: Stanford University Press, 2013), chap. 6.

9. Quoted in Peter Bergen, *The Longest War: The Enduring Conflict Between America and Al-Qaeda* (New York: Free Press, 2011), 53. As before, spy books and movies contributed to the remasculinization of the CIA. George Crile's 2003 *Charlie Wilson's War*, a best-selling account of the eponymous Texas congressman's role in the Agency's mujahideen supply operation of the 1980s, was adapted as a feature film with the same title in 2007. Celebrating the roguish imperial adventurism of its hero, both the book and movie demonstrated the circuitous relationship between spy fiction and reality. The real-life Charlie Wilson reportedly based his persona on Flashman, a fictional nineteenth-century British adventurer created by Scottish novelist George MacDonald Fraser.

10. Alfred W. McCoy, *In the Shadows of the American Century: The Rise and Decline of U.S. Global Power* (Chicago: Haymarket, 2017), 66–72; William Dalrymple, "The Ghosts of Afghanistan's Past," *New York Times*, Apr. 13, 2013, www.nytimes.com/2013/04/14/opinion /sunday/why-karzai-bites-the-hand-that-feeds-him.html.

11. Douglas Porch, *Counterinsurgency: Exposing the Myths of the New Way of War* (New York: Cambridge University Press, 2013), chap. 10; Osamah F. Khalil, *America's Dream Palace: Middle East Expertise and the Rise of the National Security State* (Cambridge, MA: Harvard University Press, 2016), 268–270.

12. Priya Satia, "Attack of the Drones," *The Nation*, Nov. 9, 2009, 14–16; Priya Satia, "How the End of World War I Brought the Beginning of Drone Warfare," *Time*, Nov. 8, 2018, https://time.com/5448125/wwi-drone-warfare-iraq/.

13. McCoy, *In the Shadows of the American Century*, 144, 154; Ian Cobain and Ewen MacAskill, "True Scale of UK Role in Torture and Rendition After 9/11 Revealed," *The Guardian*, June 28, 2018, www.theguardian.com/uk-news/2018/jun/28/uk-role-torture -kidnap-terror-suspects-after-911-revealed.

14. Quoted in Christopher J. Coyne and Abigail R. Hall, *Tyranny Comes Home: The Domestic Fate of U.S. Militarism* (Stanford, CA: Stanford University Press, 2018), 58; Mark Mazzetti, *The Way of the Knife: The CIA, a Secret Army, and a War at the Ends of the Earth* (New York: Penguin, 2013), 4; quoted in Mazzetti, *Way of the Knife*, 228; Dana Priest and William M. Arkin, *Top Secret America: The Rise of the New American Security State* (New York: Little, Brown, 2011), chap. 10. See also James Risen, *Pay Any Price: Greed, Power, and Endless War* (New York: Houghton Mifflin Harcourt, 2014).

15. Matthew Connelly, *The Declassification Engine: What History Reveals About America's Top Secrets* (New York: Pantheon, 2023), 30–31.

16. Bernard E. Harcourt, "Beyond the Counterinsurgency Paradigm of Governing," in *Reimagining the National Security State: Liberalism on the Brink*, ed. Karen J. Greenberg (Cambridge: Cambridge University Press, 2020), 141–153. On the New York program, see John Prados, *The Family Jewels: The CIA, Secrecy, and Presidential Power*, updated ed. (Austin: University of Texas Press, 2014), 61–63.

17. On biometric surveillance, see McCoy, *In the Shadows of the American Century*, 125.

18. Coyne and Hall, *Tyranny Comes Home*, 114. See Stuart Schrader, "Yes, American Police Act Like Occupying Armies. They Literally Studied Their Tactics," *The Guardian*,

June 8, 2020, www.theguardian.com/commentisfree/2020/jun/08/yes-american-police -act-like-occupying-armies-they-literally-studied-their-tactics.

19. Spencer Ackerman, "Bad Lieutenant: American Police Brutality, Exported from Chicago to Guantánamo," *The Guardian*, Feb. 18, 2015, www.theguardian.com/us-news /2015/feb/18/american-police-brutality-chicago-guantanamo; Risen, *Pay Any Price*, chap. 7; James Risen, "Outside Psychologists Shielded U.S. Torture Program, Report Finds," *New York Times*, July 10, 2015, www.nytimes.com/2015/07/11/us/psychologists-shielded -us-torture-program-report-finds.html. Meanwhile, anthropologists joined "Human Terrain Systems" teams to conduct ethnographic research in support of US occupation forces in Iraq and Afghanistan. The post-9/11 US university system generally seems to have opened campuses to the CIA and other covert government agencies in a manner reminiscent of the height of the Cold War. A recent book on the subject compared the supposedly sacred groves of academe to "a well-trampled city park." Daniel Golden, *Spy Schools: How the CIA, FBI, and Foreign Intelligence Secretly Exploit America's Universities* (New York: Henry Holt, 2017), 264. On the Human Terrain Systems, see Khalil, *America's Dream Palace*, 277–278. Interestingly, psychologists within the CIA expressed stronger objections to EITs than did the APA. In contrast, the American Anthropological Association officially condemned the Human Terrain Systems.

20. Mazzetti, *Way of the Knife*, 302–312; Coyne and Hall, *Tyranny Comes Home*, chap. 6; Madiha Tahir, "The Distributed Empire of the War on Terror," *Boston Review*, Sep. 10, 2021, www.bostonreview.net/articles/the-distributed-empire-of-the-war-on-terror/; Karen J. Greenberg, "Liberty, Security, and America's War on Terror," in *The Cambridge History of America and the World, Volume IV: 1945 to the Present*, ed. David C. Engerman et al. (Cambridge: Cambridge University Press, 2022), 700.

21. Quoted in Steve Coll, *Directorate S: The CIA and America's Secret Wars in Afghanistan and Pakistan* (New York: Penguin, 2018), 86.

22. Quoted in David Shamus McCarthy, *Selling the CIA: Public Relations and the Culture of Secrecy* (Lawrence: University Press of Kansas, 2018), 102, 110.

23. See ibid., 87–93; quoted in Tom Secker, "Documents Reveal How Ben Affleck Got into the CIA, Promising to 'Do the Agency Proud,'" RT, June 21, 2021, www.rt.com /op-ed/527187-ben-affleck-cia-agency/; Alfred W. McCoy, *Torture and Impunity: The U.S. Doctrine of Coercive Interrogation* (Madison: University of Wisconsin Press, 2012), chap. 5.

24. Quoted in McCarthy, *Selling the CIA*, 116.

25. Quoted in ibid., 118. See also Nicholas Schou, "How the CIA Hoodwinked Hollywood," *The Atlantic*, July 14, 2016, www.theatlantic.com/entertainment/archive/2016/07 /operation-tinseltown-how-the-cia-manipulates-hollywood/491138/.

26. See Jeremy Varon, "Winter Soldiers of the Dark Side: CIA Whistleblowers and National Security Dissent," in *Whistleblowing Nation: The History of National Security Disclosures and the Cult of State Secrecy*, ed. Kaeten Mistry and Hannah Gurman (New York: Columbia University Press, 2020), 153–186; Richard H. Immerman, "From the Mundane to the Absurd: The Advent and Evolution of Prepublication Review," in *Whistleblowing Nation*, ed. Mistry and Gurman, 187–212.

27. David Talbot, *The Devil's Chessboard: Allen Dulles, the CIA, and the Rise of America's Secret Government* (New York: HarperCollins, 2016). Fiction reflected the popularity of conspiracy theories about the CIA, as seen in the popularity of the Jason Bourne movies, adapted from the novels of Robert Ludlum, which offered a dark counterpoint to the romantic spy fiction of Tom Clancy.

28. Kathryn S. Olmsted, *Real Enemies: Conspiracy Theories and American Democracy, World War I to 9/11*, 10th Anniversary Edition (New York: Oxford University Press, 2019), chap. 7, Epilogue; David Rohde, *In Deep: The FBI, the CIA, and the Truth About America's "Deep State"* (New York: W. W. Norton, 2020).

29. Rohde, *In Deep*, xv.

30. Greg Barnhisel, "The Making of the 'Good CIA,'" *New Republic*, Sep. 3, 2020, https://newrepublic.com/article/159200/history-good-cia-quiet-americans-scott-anderson-book-review.

31. Whipple, *Spymasters*, 327; quoted in Bob Woodward and Robert Costa, *Peril* (New York: Simon & Schuster, 2021), 152.

32. Carol Rosenberg and Julian E. Barnes, "Gina Haspel Observed Waterboarding at C.I.A. Black Site, Psychologist Testifies," *New York Times*, June 3, 2022, www.nytimes.com/2022/06/03/us/politics/cia-gina-haspel-black-site.html.

Conclusion

1. Gina Haspel, "Statement for the Record, Senate Select Committee on Intelligence," May 9, 2018, www.intelligence.senate.gov/hearings/open-hearing-nomination-gina-haspel-be-director-central-intelligence-agency.

2. Alec Luhn, "National Endowment for Democracy Is First 'Undesirable' NGO Banned in Russia," *The Guardian*, July 28, 2015, www.theguardian.com/world/2015/jul/28/national-endowment-for-democracy-banned-russia.

3. Scott Shane, "Russia Isn't the Only One Meddling in Elections. We Do It, Too," *New York Times*, Feb. 17, 2018, www.nytimes.com/2018/02/17/sunday-review/russia-isnt-the-only-one-meddling-in-elections-we-do-it-too.html.

4. Julian E. Barnes, "C.I.A. Reorganization to Place New Focus on China," *New York Times*, Oct. 7, 2021, www.nytimes.com/2021/10/07/us/politics/cia-reorganization-china.html. For the Chinese espionage threat, see Calder Walton, *Spies: The Epic Intelligence War Between the East and the West* (New York: Simon & Schuster, 2023), chap. 18.

INDEX

Matthews, Jennifer L., 297, 300
Mau Mau uprising, 131, 135
McCain, John, 281
McCarthy, Joe, 198
McCarthyism, 201, 206, 210
McCone, John A., 60, 223
McCoy, Alfred W., 227, 259, 287
McGill University, 258
McGraw-Hill, 105
mercenaries, 249–250
Messing, F. Andy, Jr., 141
Mexico, 138
Meyer, Cord, Jr., 7, 8, 185, 197 (photo), 230
  Angleton friendship, 232
  on AVC National Planning Committee, 197
  awarded Distinguished Intelligence Medal, 226–227
  birth and early years, 195
  as chief of IO division, 211
  CIA career, 199–200, 210–211, 237
  conspiracy theories about, 239, 264, 301
  death, 233
  education, 195
  Facing Reality, 231–233
  Harvard fellowship, 199
  literary career, 194, 199–200, 233
  London posting, 227–228, 232
  marriages and family life, 195–196, 199, 220, 227–228
  on Mary's murder, 274
  military career, 195, 198–199
  New York Times exposé, 219–220, 226–227
  Peace or Anarchy, 196
  Ramparts revelations and, 225–226, 231
  resignation from CIA, 228
  social network, 210
  Virginia home, 243
  "Waves of Darkness," 195
  world government beliefs, 196, 198–199, 306
Meyer, Mary Pinchot, 195, 220, 239, 272–274
Meyer, Michael, 220
Meyer, Quentin, 195, 199
MHCHAOS. See CHAOS operation

MI5. See Security Service (UK)
MI6. See Secret Intelligence Service (UK)
MICE motivation framework, 55–56, 59
Michigan State University (MSU)
  area studies research programs, 252
  police training mission in Vietnam, 125, 127, 139, 165, 217, 254, 260
  student protests, 262
  "Winds of Change" conference, 251, 262
Middle East, 64–65. See also specific countries
Mighty Wurlitzer, 203–204, 212, 222, 223, 235, 264
Miler, Newton S., 183, 185, 187
Military Information Division of the Philippines, 29
Military Intelligence Section, 30
Millikan, Max, 252, 261
Mills, C. Wright, 162–163
mind control research programs, 256–259, 265–266
missionaries, recruitment of, 44–45, 48, 305
Mitchell, James, 295, 303
Mitrione, Dan, 140, 259
MKULTRA project, 257–259
Mobutu Sese Seko, 136, 138
Modjokuto Project, 254
Monster Plot, 159, 160, 185
Moreno, Carmen Mercedes, 150
Morley, Jefferson, 275
Mormons in the CIA, 44
Morocco, 20–21
Moro insurgency, 142
Mosaddeq, Mohammed, 70, 71, 73, 74–75, 78, 79, 82, 83–88, 90, 95–96, 104, 204
Mossad, 136
MS-13 (gang), 249
MSU. See Michigan State University
Mundt, Karl, 260
Murphy, Audie, 217

Nakano School, 72
Nasser, Gamal Abdel, 63, 65, 67, 81–82, 89–90, 103, 121, 136, 214, 221
National Endowment for Democracy, 234, 311

WASP domination in CIA, 4–5, 39–41, 44
waterboarding, 28, 115, 280, 290, 303
Watergate scandal, 174, 179, 204, 239–240, 246, 264–265
"Waves of Darkness" (Meyer), 195
weapons of mass destruction (WMD), 282, 283
Weather Underground, 261
Webb, Gary, 266
Welch, Richard S., 188, 230
whistleblowers, 27, 58, 108, 175–177, 182, 187–189, 227, 229, 230, 300–301
White, George Hunter, 258
"The White Man's Burden" (Kipling), 14, 17–18
WikiLeaks, 293
Willard, Belle Wyatt, 80
Willard, Joseph E., 80
Wilson, Harold, 160
"Winds of Change" conference, 251, 262
Winks, Robin W., 40
wiretapping, 223, 265, 293–294
Wise, David, 163–164, 223
Wisner, Frank G., 93, 202, 203, 204, 205, 212, 215, 222, 223, 227
Wolff, Harold G., 257, 258
women's experiences, 50–54
Woodhouse, Christopher, 85

Woodward, Bob, 174, 239
World Anti-Communist League, 140
world federalism, 196, 198–199
World Federation of Trade Unions, 208
World Veterans Federation, 208, 215
World War I, 1, 11, 24, 42
World War II, 1, 2, 42–44, 47, 153–155
Wright, Peter, 159–160

X, Malcolm, 267

Yale University, 35, 38, 39, 40, 150, 195
Yanukovych, Viktor, 311
Year of Intelligence, 181, 186, 187, 297
yellow press, 17
Yoh, Bernard, 251
Yom Kippur War, 178
Young Americans for Freedom, 226

Zahedi, Fazlollah, 70, 86–87, 96
Zaire, 136, 138
ZAPATA operation, 92–93, 222
Zazi, Najibullah, 296
Zenith Technical Enterprises, 244
Zero Dark Thirty (film), 298–300
Zionism, 213–214, 220–221
ZRTINDER operation, 213
Zuley, Richard, 295